D1587126

JACK LYNCH

HERO IN CRISIS

Jack Lynch
HERO IN CRISIS

Bruce Arnold

MERLIN
PUBLISHING

Published in 2001 by
Merlin Publishing
16 Upper Pembroke Street
Dublin 2
Ireland
www.merlin-publishing.com

ISBN 1-903582-06-7

British Cataloguing in Publication Data:
Arnold, Bruce, 1936–
Jack Lynch: hero in crisis
1. Lynch, Jack 2. Prime ministers – Ireland – Biography
3. Ireland – Politics and government – 1949 –
I. Title
941.7'0824'092
ISBN 1903582067

Typeset by Gough Typesetting Services, Dublin

Printed by MPG Books Limited, Cornwall.

To the English members of my family,
that they may reach a greater understanding of Ireland.

Contents

Acknowledgements

I became a journalist in 1961 on the staff of *The Irish Times* and Dublin correspondent for the *Guardian* newspaper eighteen months later. I began writing about Irish politics at that time. In the course of that work I met the Ministers in Sean Lemass's second administration, including Jack Lynch. I went on to write a political column for *Hibernia,* under Basil Clancy's editorship, and then for Nicholas Leonard, who founded *Business and Finance.* I joined the *Irish Independent* as parliamentary correspondent in 1973. I have written for that newspaper on politics since then. I owe to the newspaper, its management, its staff, and above all its editors, a debt of gratitude that goes back over many years. I am particularly grateful to Sir Anthony O'Reilly, Bartle Pitcher, Aidan Pender and Vincent Doyle.

I am indebted in particular to Dr T.K. Whitaker. He and Jack Lynch forged a bond of close personal friendship that lasted until the end of Lynch's life. It grew out of the professional association of politician and civil servant. I judge it to have been a perfect balance between two men of outstanding integrity whose professional lives were dedicated to the well-being of the State. I was privileged to have Ken Whitaker's guiding hand during the writing of this book.

Martin O'Donoghue has been a friend for a number of years and became first an adviser and then a close friend to Jack Lynch, who appointed him to Government in 1977. Martin gave me helpful advice and guidance. Eoin Ryan was called to the Bar at the same time as Jack Lynch and he and his wife Joan were friends of Jack and Máirín from the 1940s on. Closely involved in Fianna Fáil throughout his life, Eoin gave me good advice and help. I am also indebted to Paddy Lalor and to Pádraig Faulkner, close and loyal supporters of Jack Lynch, particularly during the crisis period 1969 to 1971. The former colleague, Minister and then President of Ireland, Patrick Hillery, gave me valuable insights into that same period. These and other politicians helped me greatly in understanding the very complex character of my subject. Brian Hillery, cousin to Patrick, also gave me help with the book.

Máirín Lynch supported me in writing this book and talked about her life with Jack. Her backing was an important touchstone: it unlocked other doors. I greatly valued the help and the insights of Jack Lynch's brother, Finbarr, and other members of the family. Among these were Dan Harvey, Jack's nephew, and indirectly his mother, Eva, who passed on two photographs through her son.

I owe a particular debt of gratitude to Liam Ó Tuama, author of *Jack Lynch:*

Where He Sported And Played. This work of dedicated research and unparalleled sporting knowledge, by a member of Glen Rovers and St Nick's in Cork for more than fifty years, is not only Jack Lynch's sporting life but a guide to much more in his character. The author gave me generous help. Not only did I have the use of his text in an area of knowledge where I confess to being a neophyte, he also generously supplied help with otherwise elusive illustrations. I received invaluable help from John Gibson in the Library of *The Irish Times* in finding featured photographs.

I am also grateful for the help given in respect of Jack's sporting achievements by Con Murphy, who played with him, and Billie Rackard, a noted hurling player for Wexford, who guided me initially about aspects of the game.

Among colleagues in my profession I acknowledge special help from Dick Walsh and from Michael Mills. They observed at first hand the major part of Jack Lynch's career, made accurate judgements and formed clear opinions on the critical issues. They passed these on to me, and helped in other ways. I greatly valued their help. John Horgan, Sean Lemass's biographer, gave me the benefit of his researches and certain pointers about aspects of Jack Lynch's career. As will be evident from the book, Vincent Browne did important early work on Jack Lynch, publishing Lynch's memoir in *Magill* and also publishing important material on the period of the Arms Crisis, most notably "The Peter Berry Papers" also in *Magill*.

I have been helped by many others, and the help goes back over a number of years. I first contemplated a biography of Jack Lynch towards the end of 1979, before his resignation. As an indication of how limited was the appreciation of his qualities and what he had been through, on the announcement of his resignation the publisher concerned decided not to go ahead. But the seed was there and help, advice, insights, even casual anecdotes were gathered from then on.

James Dukes, who was Jack Lynch's private secretary when he was Minister for Education, gave me valuable help on that period. Kit Ahern, who served as a nominee of Sean Lemass in the Senate, and as a Fianna Fáil deputy in the Dail under Jack Lynch, gave me valuable help.

I received help also from Seán Donlon, Charlie McCreevy, Charles Lysaght, Michael Yeats, Vera Ryan, Eric Peard, Dermot Nally, Carol Quinn, Archivist, the Boole Library UCC, and the staff of the National Archives. Others who helped include Richard Crowe, Jim Kirby, Tim Dalton, Michael Campion. Booksellers helped in finding obscure titles; in particular I would like to thank Joe Collins, John Donohoe and Cian Ó hÉigeartaigh.

I owe a special debt to my agent, Jonathan Williams. I am indebted to Selga Medenieks and Chenile Keogh of Merlin Publishing. I was greatly helped by Mary Garrioch and Jane Clancy. My thanks also to Elizabeth Senior who applied great skill and experience to the editing of the book. My wife Mavis helped me as always, both with the writing and with the analysis of the character of a man we were both privileged to know.

Prologue

Jack Lynch was a great man and a great leader. I have always admired him and writing his life is an expression of that. I believe him to have been consistently misunderstood and deliberately misrepresented, not least by his political enemies. I first met him when I was a young journalist working for the *Guardian* newspaper. He was then Minister for Industry and Commerce. As a political journalist I wrote about him as Minister for Finance, and from then on wrote of his political career as leader of Fianna Fáil and as Taoiseach. I did not belong to "The Lobby" of political correspondents and at least some of my contact with him was on a personal level, though I can claim no particular closeness. The admiration grew with the passage of time.

The greatness is hard to quantify. The character of the man is hard to embrace. Anyone writing Lynch's "Life" is faced with the need to write about the sportsman, the Corkman and the politician. Bringing these disparate elements together would never be easy; the events in which he served his country were diverse and subtle in their demands on him. Comprehending them would never be simple and Jack Lynch himself firmly believed in the principle that he should be judged by his actions and not by any explanations he might give. He chose not to explain himself. He told me this at a critical moment in his career and he turned away innumerable people seeking interviews that would explain the crowded events of his life and, above all, the periods of crisis. He kept no diary, wrote no memoirs, left no papers of significance.

In writing this biography I seemed to face many problems. Often, however, they were illusory rather than real. There seemed to be an indecisiveness in his character, a reluctance over much of what Lynch did in his political career, an ambivalence between being a lawyer and becoming a Dáil deputy. The position he adopted when Seán Lemass made known his intention of giving up the leadership of Fianna Fáil also seemed ambivalent. Perhaps most seriously of all, he was seen as having been weak and uncertain in crisis. This crisis was precipitated in the Republic of Ireland as Northern Ireland headed into increasing violence from 1968 on. Jack Lynch had to fight his first general election as party leader against a backdrop of growing internal division within his own party. His capacity to deal with disaffection within the Fianna Fáil party has been repeatedly questioned. There was schism in the country over what should be done, if anything at all, about Northern Ireland.

Then there was the apparent conspiracy to import arms illegally. This was followed by the dismissal of two senior government Ministers in May 1970. The trial and acquittal of Charles Haughey and his fellow defendants followed. Jack Lynch's leadership was challenged at this time, and debate over how he handled these matters has gone on ever since. It was a crisis of great complexity. Yet he weathered it. We had no civil strife, attitudes were changed, the law took its course. Jack Lynch cauterised the deep and lasting wounds, self-inflicted by Fianna Fáil at that time, and he held the party together. He got rid of difficult men, who would not conform; yet out of a spirit of fairness could not confront and dismiss those who went through the formality of conforming, including, of course, Haughey.

The critical views of him – and they are widely expressed and diverse in origin – are largely wrong. There was no ambivalence about going into politics. There was none about succeeding Seán Lemass. His leadership in crisis not only worked but saved the country from terrible pitfalls yawning before it. It also revealed a heroic character behind the friendly exterior. Always, he handled the essential problems with tact and courage.

Fianna Fáil was split under Jack Lynch. The split did not manifest itself in any open aggression while he was there. He was too powerful a figurehead for that, and far too clever as a politician. But the split did come later, when a significant small section of the party broke away to form another political party, the Progressive Democrats. By then the original nature and identity of the party founded by Éamon de Valera was lost. Since then it has never been recovered.

In the public view Jack Lynch, among all the leaders of government of the twentieth century in Ireland, is seen as outstandingly the best. In an opinion poll conducted at the end of 1999, thirty-five per cent of respondents said that he was the best Taoiseach ever. Seán Lemass and Éamon de Valera received eleven per cent each, while the rest, with the exception of Bertie Ahern (fourteen per cent), were in single figures.

I believe, and have always believed, that Jack Lynch's apparent passivity was a strength. It was deliberate, reasoned, considered and had a logic consistent with the man's character. Rapid reaction would have been uncharacteristic on most issues. He had a belief in letting matters run in order to fully test the extent and strength of the opposition. He did it in sport; he did it in politics. He faced a good deal of such opposition from the time he became leader of Fianna Fáil and Taoiseach in 1966. He even faced it during the process of becoming leader.

Despite the importance for him of holding the Fianna Fáil party together, it was incidental to his personal sense of public service in holding the country together and giving to it what he described, in another context, as "the best that's in me". This was his purpose in public life. He sought to bind the country together and give it a new vision of itself. In respect of Northern Ireland, which predominated politically during much of his period in power, he sought to teach the Republic the overriding political principle of consent, and to persuade people to apply this to the North.

In some of the things he did he was criticised strongly. Yet one of his most outspoken critics, Conor Cruise O'Brien, writing in the early 1970s, applied to him a subtle and, in a sense, an admiring epithet when he wrote:

> People say that Jack Lynch is waiting to see which way the cat will jump. What they don't understand is that he is the cat, and will jump whichever way he wants.

Lynch faced a difficult period in opposition, between 1973 and 1977, and particularly halfway through that term, when Michael O'Kennedy proposed a policy change for the party, demanding a British declaration of intent to withdraw from Northern Ireland. The political cards were held by Liam Cosgrave and the Fine Gael-Labour Coalition. Cosgrave led this partnership Government with a remarkably deadpan aplomb which only became vulnerable at the end, with his "blow-in" speech, and with Paddy Donegan's "thundering disgrace" outburst, and the resignation of Cearbhall Ó Dalaigh.

With hardly a journalist aware of it and none, apart from myself, prepared to predict that he had a snowball's chance in hell of winning the general election called in the summer of 1977, Jack Lynch demonstrated absolute skill and authority in recovering power with an unprecedented majority.

It was a highpoint of achievement that he actively regretted. He saw the huge danger of such a large majority, the complacency it engendered, and the backbiting and treachery which built up against him and the majority of the members of his Government. It was a politically shameful period the full details of which have yet to be told. His downfall was coldly worked for, with different deputies recruited to embarrass him and work against him. This they did, on the baseless offer that Charles Haughey could give them a better deal and a prospect of greater power; he also offered involvement to those in Fianna Fáil who were disgruntled and peevish about being excluded from the party's achievements.

Jack Lynch told me at the time that the party needed to make up its mind. For better or worse, it had to choose its future way forward and live with the consequences. It was Brian Lenihan who told me, in advance of the event, that Lynch was resigning. Then followed the leadership struggle: curiously bleak and unhappy days in Leinster House which I shall never forget.

Lynch throughout his career was the object of an immediate and pervasive sense of trust and affection. It went beyond the normal human virtues for which he was admired and valued. He stood for integrity, courage and judgement; yet other politicians have done that and still remained remote. With Lynch there was another dimension to it. Deep down he was immensely strong, both physically and morally, and it gave him an inner confidence that is not always the lot of leaders. Though he had it he never seemed to display it. He was, to outward appearances only, fallible and vulnerable. In conversation he would characterise himself as one of the group, sharing the exploration of an idea and bringing to it no special wisdom or judgement. He listened to people and responded to them with inexhaustible patience and a polite respect which gave to the passing crowds a sense that he was their friend. He had an extraordinary capacity for this. He was rarely, if ever, ill at ease, no matter what company he was in. He could be angry and forlorn, and with good reason, but the expression of anger was swiftly controlled, and dismay or disappointment were of short duration. He trusted himself, and that gave him infinite capacity in judging and then perhaps trusting others. But he learned the hard way how little trust there can be in political life.

He was much more clever than anyone could conceive. Yet he exercised his brilliance in an instinctive way. He deliberately concealed the sharpness of his mind and the skill he had in judging situations. His intellectual judgements were sound and his legal training made him astute in the making of important decisions. He thought at length, and with great concentration, and was disposed by his deepest nature to delay decision-making until satisfied that he had exhausted the options and possibilities of the many grave challenges with which life presented him. Outwardly, he affected a homespun simplicity which made it seem that he carried the burden of office easily. He was the accessible sport-loving Corkman, easy and natural in conversation, affable, and always ready to joke with the people he met.

Jack Lynch honoured politics beyond its deserts. At no time in the country's history had there been a more stark contrast between the values he held and those that were then being attributed to his former colleagues and their successors. The emphasis on the contrast was an essential and an inescapable part of him in his active political career. It remained part of him after his resignation and has grown in proportion to the way in which those values he espoused have been diminished or besmirched, most notably by the man who succeeded him.

Jack Lynch was a leader who guided the country through crisis and who in the process changed its understanding of nationalism. It was a huge change, since it embodied a change for an enormous number of people in the way they understood themselves. Collectively, the country altered its views on Northern Ireland, on unity, on pluralism, on republicanism. He inspired new thinking about violence and the coercion of those of a different political persuasion. Throughout this process he exercised political authority with tact, skill and balance, and yet with a necessary thread of steel running through it. It embodied something else in him: strong convictions against sectarianism, bigotry and prejudice. He had such convictions about sport, religion, social attitudes and the role of the Catholic Church in Irish life. When he looked towards the North, trying to help our understanding of it, he was aware of shortcomings within the Republic, and it made him sympathetic and careful in his judgements and in his words.

His was a life of service. The taint of using politics for personal advancement or ambition, or relying on power to bolster deficiencies of character, were not only not part of his political make-up, they were the antithesis of it. Jack Lynch was characterised as a reluctant leader. This view of him was an illusion. It was largely, and indeed deliberately, created by himself. The degrees of reluctance expressed in his character and emerging in his supposed lack of action, or delay in taking action, are mixed with emotional and intellectual complexities, so that this part of his nature will never be completely understood. But he was a dedicated leader and his leadership worked. He was a man to whom power came naturally, but by whom it was used sparingly. He entered politics with the advantage of already being a national hero as a sportsman. He filled an allotted time with skill, judgement and dignity. He went out of politics without regret and without any loss of the high standing he enjoyed among the Irish people.

Lynch never cut a figure on the international stage nor did he seek to do so. His easy, relaxed style, unique in its way, did not adjust easily to collective displays of power which are artificial anyway as are many of the supposed achievements of international decision-making events. He brought to them an easy relaxed manner which made him a witty companion. The equals among whom he moved found it difficult to penetrate his real nature. But he presented himself as of the people, concerned for their welfare, and interested in what they did and said. In all this he encouraged a belief among people that they knew him and understood him. It was an essential part of his appeal. Other men in power affect paternalism and greater wisdom than the common man; Jack Lynch did the opposite.

He was not the only sportsman to enter Irish politics, but he was certainly the greatest to do so. He was the only player in the history of Gaelic games to win six senior All-Ireland championships in succession. He played both hurling and Gaelic football, and he maintained a lifelong involvement in sport. Liam Mulvihill, director general of the Gaelic Athletic Association, said of Jack Lynch at the time of his death:

> He was a great statesman who had a great love for his country, his people, the language, culture and the national games. He remained passionate throughout his life about the fortunes of his beloved Glen Rovers and Cork, but he was always generous in his appreciation of all teams.

Jack Lynch was a Corkman through and through. In a country where just being Irish is still a source of overwhelming debate and investigation, cultural argument and emotional exaggeration, the regional issues may seem of secondary importance. Yet the largest county and the second largest city in Ireland have a life of their own, a form of expression of their own, and a culture which obsesses the men and women of Cork. They looked on Jack Lynch as the greatest person they had ever nurtured, and exercised over him a benign collective patronage to which he responded with humour, tact and genuine feeling.

He came from the city. He was the son of a tailor, which perhaps explains his elegant, discreet dress sense. He was born in Shandon and knew the city in its time of poverty, knew its stories and its songs. He sang well. He had a deep mellifluous bass voice, and hearing him sing "The Banks of My Own Lovely Lee" was an unforgettable experience. Ken Whitaker, a major figure in Jack Lynch's life, records him singing it in a mood of great happiness on his last birthday, just two months before his death.

Twenty years ago, writing the biography of another great Irish man, William Orpen, the painter, I discussed Orpen with Seán Keating, who had been his pupil, and had then become his studio assistant. "I have been accused of hero-worship, in respect of Orpen," he told me, and paused. Then he said: "Whom should one worship, if not heroes?"

In writing about Jack Lynch my admiration has grown steadily. I think he was essentially happy because he was totally honest. I admire him for what he did and how he led us all. I admire him for his sporting prowess, and his loyalty. There is an attractive innocence about his love for Cork, his unflagging enthusiasm for good sport, his capacity for friendship, his loyalty to Fianna Fáil. But in the end the qualities one discovers in pursuing a whole life from start to finish reside within the man himself. They are not in his attitudes but in his inner being. Discovering that leaves one, at the end, with the greatest admiration of all for the fineness of his mind and for the integrity of his heart.

CHAPTER ONE

The Wild Boy

Jack Lynch was born in Cork on 15th August 1917. His parents were both migrants into Cork city in the early 1900s. His father, Dan, came from the west of the county, a townland called Baurgorm, east of Bantry, sixty miles from Cork. His mother, Nora O'Donoghue, came from east Cork, near Glounthaune. Her father became a publican and owned The Cork Arms in McCurtain Street.

Both parents were brought up on farms, but Dan Lynch, having moved to Cork for employment, became an apprentice tailor. He first worked at the firm of Daniel's, merchant tailors on Grand Parade, where his future wife as well as her sister already worked. She was a seamstress. The arrival of the new apprentice caused some stir. Her sister came to her to say: "Nora, come upstairs, a country boy has started work."

Dan and Nora were married in 1908. They had seven children, five of them boys. One son, Jimmy, died at two years of age, before Jack was born. Jack was the youngest of the boys. He had two younger sisters, Rena and Eva. He was regarded as "the wild boy in the family". It was a sporting family. His father had played Gaelic football in west Cork and, after he relocated, he continued to play with a city team whose members were mainly drawn from the drapery trade. In addition to Gaelic football and hurling, all other sports were keenly followed.

The family lived in a plain-fronted house in a laneway on the northern side of the city. It was a working-class area, not far above the River Lee. The river divides into two branches, making Cork what Edmund Spenser described as "an island fayre". The house was beside what was then St Ann's Protestant Church on the other side of the laneway known as Church Yard. This led down from the Church to Skiddy's Almshouses. These are immediately behind Shandon Church and date from the eighteenth century. The Church is famous for its pepper-canister bell tower, a landmark known locally as "the four-faced liar", not in disparagement of its parishioners but because the four clocks often disagree. Their chime is even more famous; loud, and ringing out every quarter hour, the clock bells kept country cousins visiting the Lynch house awake. The house, though plain, with four granite steps up from the laneway and a narrow fanlight door, was of a comfortable size and was nicknamed by the children "Grand Central Station" on account of the many visitors. It had a cellar in which the boys went on with their games of hurling when the weather was wet. Despite the considerable size of this basement room, "the play was very tight"[1]; nevertheless, Jack developed

[1] Finbarr Lynch, "Scoring Goals at the Butter Market: A Personal Reminiscence", in Liam

there the skill of controlling the ball during close play, and emerging from the clash with the ball in his hand.

Jack's parents both worked. As a seamstress, his mother was able to go on working at home after their marriage and this brought into the household what Jack has described as "a much-needed supplement to my father's earnings". Though regularly employed, his father was often on short time. Jack has said: "There was never any sign of wealth in the house, but the quality of life was good." His brothers have confirmed this. Charlie, who served as curate and priest in Cork, has claimed: "We were comfortable enough for the time. There was always enough on the table, and we were well-dressed with our father a tailor."[2] Finbarr, the closest in age to Jack, says that the family did well enough though the life was simple. They took a cottage each summer for a holiday by the sea.[3]

Dan Lynch remained keenly interested in sport after he had given up playing himself. He was strict and fair according to his youngest son who, as the supposed "wild boy" in the family, was often in conflict with him. Their relationship was a good one and his father, unsurprisingly, took an active and growing interest in Jack's sporting career. He was a "helpful" critic, though Finbarr Lynch says his father was a bit distant.

Nora Lynch was the main focus of attention in the family. All of them turned to her for guidance and direction, and Jack, the youngest, was particularly close. She was fussy about the turnout of her children and kept their clothes carefully repaired. But the family wore hand-me-downs and the general picture was one of careful austerity. These were frugal times anyway and Jack grew up during a period of husbandry. This was experienced countrywide and affected virtually all people growing up in Ireland during the period between the two World Wars. The experience of the Lynch family was paralleled widely in the population and, though not entirely governed by the spartan economic circumstances, these did play an important part in Jack's upbringing. The family, in both its difficulties and opportunities, is something of a paradigm for the Ireland of the times. This was a fact that Jack Lynch recognised and referred to in many of the interviews he gave, stressing that his own family life was normal for the times, even down to the dominance of sport. Yet there was an exceptional quality which surrounded and protected him as a child. It was derived from the care and prudence with which both parents ensured that the family remained together, free from the scarring of emigration, so widespread at the time. They were also unusual in that

Ó Tuama, *Where He Sported and Played: Jack Lynch, A Sporting Celebration* (Blackwater Press, Dublin, 2000), p. 8. I have drawn on Liam Ó Tuama's very rich account of Lynch's sporting career, which contains many press accounts of matches and specialist contributions by other writers. A championship player in Cork hurling, Ó Tuama was a member of Glen Rovers and St Nick's for fifty years.

[2] Quoted in *Jack Lynch: A Biography*, by T.P. O'Mahony (Blackwater Press, Dublin, 1991). This account of Lynch's life by a Cork writer gives a good account of the city and the family, relying on first-hand testimony from relations who knew Lynch from his schooldays.

[3] Interview with the author, August 2001.

they were financially secure enough to be able to keep all seven children at school. The family's strong moral values were combined with the instinct for success both at school and in sport.

The Church attended by the Lynch family was not the Protestant Church of St Ann's which overshadowed them, but the Catholic Cathedral Church of St Mary and St Anne at the top of Shandon Street; it was called the North Chapel.

Something of Lynch's later ecumenism derived from the easy association of Protestants and Catholics in this, the oldest part of Cork City. Finbarr Lynch remembers that when they were growing up there were eleven Catholics and eleven Protestants housed in Skiddy's almshouses. Their mother's doctor was Mrs Dr Hearn, wife to Dr Hearn, Protestant Bishop of Cork. The Sexton of Shandon Church, Mr Meredith, was a neighbour. The parish school, known as "Bob and Joan's", a name which some people applied to the area, had two Bateman sisters as teachers who lived beside the school.

*

The country's dreams, which had been engendered during the struggle for Irish independence – notably by writers like Padraig Pearse – had been based on idealistic promises of economic and social development of a high order. Freedom itself would see to this. In reality, the dreams quickly faded away in the face of the extremely limited economic resources being placed in the hands of relatively inexperienced politicians. They had, it is true, an elaborate and well-tried public service. But this had been set up, developed, and funded with the wealth, sense of power and prestige of a great imperial administration. Like the politicians, its members, who to a considerable extent stayed on in the service of the new administration, had to adjust to a new and essentially straitened set of economic circumstances, and the result was that conservative policies prevailed. This was reinforced in fields such as education, health, social development and culture by the power of the Catholic Church.

The highly important cattle trade was for some years in difficulty, adversely affected in the early 1920s by bad weather and a port strike. Much-needed industrial development did not take place, mainly, it must be said, because of the industrial strength of and competition from Britain. The country was handicapped by the very high dependency of the old and the young. This was an inescapable result of a rural and agricultural economy. Ireland had a disproportionately large professional class. Politically, there were deep divisions resulting from the Civil War.

Ireland was crushed by its own obligations. One of the results was that "the Government maintained a strict hold on the public purse, balancing the budget with an almost penitential zeal".[4] Understandably, the Government was also

---

[4] Terence Browne, *Ireland: A Social and Cultural History 1922–1985* (London, 1981), p. 151.

deeply security-conscious, rigorous in establishing and in upholding the rule of law. It saw the importance of a powerful Catholic Church, taking responsibilities seriously, but also acquiring even greater power as a force in the State than it had under the British administration. Economic hardship had other, deeper, more far-reaching consequences. One of these was that the tradition of late marriages, common in the country since the Famine, was maintained. The level of emigration, sadly sustained over decades as a basic economic and social ingredient of life, continued to be a central factor in the new independent Ireland. Rural life essentially dictated these national conditions, which included the alarming statistic that almost half (43 per cent) of Ireland's living population in the early 1920s had emigrated. The reality was that most farmers had holdings that could not support the large families they had, and certainly could not support marriages among the children. A combination of late marriage and emigration was the practical solution; the social and moral results were tangled and depressing, with families divided, life harsh and unrewarding, and sources of entertainment and enrichment of life very limited.

The most readily perceived impact of this on the Lynch family was that both parents were city-dwellers, but had come from rural backgrounds. They embodied, in a positive way, the social and economic developments of their time. Both the parents and the children were products of social inevitability and the material changes which took place at the end of the nineteenth century, then through the struggles in Ireland which led to independence, and on through the early, difficult decades in the State's history.

The surprise is how robust the Lynch family was in these years. The parents made ends meet. All the children went on to secondary education; Jack and one of his brothers each won secondary school scholarships, which helped financially. They all grew up and found their vocations in Ireland, Charlie as a priest, Theo as a National School teacher, and Finbarr in the Civil Service. Both daughters worked for local firms, married, and still live in Cork with their families.

*

It is hardly surprising that across Ireland sport played a huge role in social life. It went far beyond entertainment, binding together small communities around their local clubs and elevating or promoting the ambitions of talented sportsmen to a series of competitive leagues and championships. These were carefully constructed and, equally carefully, the leagues watched for emerging talent. This was then encouraged upward through the major county and provincial championships which loomed over community life. Nowhere was this more the case than with the Lynch family; no one within that family had a life more clearly shaped by sport than Jack. In his case it was overwhelmingly so. From childhood in the 1920s up to the time of his last matches for Cork in hurling and football, at the end of the 1940s, his career was a sporting one. It was remarkably successful. It placed him on the national stage. It gave him heroic qualities in the eyes of a population

4

where large sections were obsessive about following the games which he played. It also taught him a great deal about human behaviour and ambition, equipping him for the eventual leadership he would take up. He is unique in passing on from an outstanding sporting career to an equally prominent and successful second career as a politician. In understanding the man who led Ireland during a crucial period of its history, some understanding of the sporting hero is important. His early life is inextricably entwined with the sporting life, first of Cork, then of Munster, then of the country from the 1920s to the 1950s.

Jack's education began in 1923 at the local Sisters of Charity primary school, St Vincent's Convent, in Peacock Lane. He was there for two years. The school still holds the register recording his entry. He went on from there in 1925 to the North Monastery Christian Brothers' School in Cork city aided by a scholarship. He was at North Monastery for eleven years. Teaching was under the control of the Christian Brothers, though with some lay teachers as well. Brother Moynihan, known as "Tango", was one of those who taught him. He later became Provincial of the Southern Province of the Order.

From an early age Jack showed accomplishment as a sportsman, possibly to the detriment of his studies, though these produced adequate results. As children coming home from school, according to his brother Finbarr, who was closest to him in age, they played hurling out on the streets. When it got too dark to see the small ball, or *sliotar*, they played football. The pillars of the Butter Market were used as their goalposts. This fine structure, another of the historic buildings among which Jack grew up in Shandon, is a relic of the Cork butter trade out of Munster. Developed in the eighteenth century and a cornerstone of Cork's subsequent economy, it was at one time the largest butter market in Europe, its prices quoted on the world's commodity exchanges in the nineteenth century. The brothers borrowed the only football available from their uncle, Mick O'Donoghue, who was chairman of the Munster Football Association.

Jack was naturally a left-hander, but from early schooldays he trained himself to play as a right-hander and, by the time he came to play in organised, competitive games, he was better as a right-hander. As children they could not afford to buy the *camán*, or hurley stick, but bought what were called "shape-outs" from a local sawmill, O'Connell's in Leitrim Street, and then finished off the curves and edges themselves. It gave practical knowledge of what made a good hurley, including size and weight. This was important, since Jack was physically big, and a powerful player. Finbarr describes him as having "amazing speed and strength, which gave him enormous advantage, especially as a youngster."[5]

Sport was the most constant part of his life and of enormous significance, though they did sometimes go on wet weather occasions to film matinées, known as "fourpenny hops". From the sporting point of view, there were the Street Leagues, played on the hard surface of the Fair Field between rival teams in the

---

[5] Quoted in Liam Ó Tuama, *Where He Sported and Played: Jack Lynch, a Sporting Celebration* (Blackwater Press, Dublin, 2000), p. 10.

district. These were well organised, and a significant hunting ground for talent. They brought to notice many players who later became prominent sportsmen. In 1927, when Jack was only ten years old, he followed his brothers Theo, Charlie and Finbarr into the junior section of Glen Rovers, presided over by O'Connell. "He taught me so much," Jack wrote, "resulting in me playing on the Glen and St Nicholas – known as St Nick's – minor teams when I was fourteen." In 1931 Jack went to the All-Ireland at Croke Park with Paddy O'Connell, to see Cork play Kilkenny. Cork won after a second replay. On their next visit to Croke Park, in 1939, Jack would lead the Cork team out onto the field.

In the 1930s the Gaelic Athletic Association organised junior sport through schools and colleges. On a parish basis, local communities organised league and championship games for the under-sixteens. Jack was active in these under-age sporting events and figured prominently in them with much success. There is a photograph of the young Jack in 1930, sitting in with the senior Glen Rovers team at the time of their first county final appearance against Blackrock, which they lost. In the centre of the front row is the captain, P. "Fox" Collins, at the time a hero of Jack's and an outstanding player. He was the first Glen Rovers man to play for Cork in an All-Ireland final, in 1928. Cork won, and did so again in 1929 and 1931. Later, Jack was to play with him, both for the Glen Rovers team and for Cork.

Jack's first notable success was in 1929, at the age of twelve, when he played for the St Nick's under-sixteen juvenile football team. His brothers Charlie and Finbarr played as well, and the team won the North Parish championship. Jack developed fast at this time; a good player at thirteen, he was an outstanding junior by the time he was fifteen. In 1932 he figured prominently for St Nick's in the minor football county finals. They won in that and the following year. He was even more successful playing for Glen Rovers, whose minor hurling teams enjoyed considerable prowess throughout the 1930s. From 1932 to 1937 the team reached the county finals, winning the title four times, with Jack captaining the team on two of those occasions, 1933 and 1934. During this period he played minor hurling and football for Cork in the inter-county championships.

An important sequence of games, to which Lynch himself often referred, and which clearly represented a major achievement even when his later All-Ireland games are taken into account, were his senior school victories playing for North Monastery in 1934, 1935 and 1936. Paddy Deasy, writing on the four Harty Cup victories in a row between 1934 and 1937, describes them as achievements which were "never surpassed". Jack played in the first three of the four. "They place him among the elite of school or college athletes."[6] These were games that attracted huge attention. When North Mon played against Rockwell College in Mitchelstown in 1934, the first game was a draw, but the replay, on a weekday, had all the businesses in the town closed down, with two special trains coming

---

[6] Ó Tuama, above, n.5, p. 23.

from Cork bringing 1,500 supporters. Two town bands played for the teams as they paraded out to the playing field. The same thing happened the following year, though there was no replay this time. In those days there was no great emphasis on personalities in newspaper coverage of such games, but the *Cork Examiner* reporters singled Jack Lynch out as "prominent all through, scoring long-distance points and, from his stirring play, set up the movements for the Mon goals".[7]

*

In 1932 Jack Lynch's mother died. It was sudden, unexpected and it had a profound effect on the whole family. Nora had been in hospital with a kidney complaint and then suffered a heart attack. Lynch himself has spoken about the impact on him, then aged fifteen:

> My mother was a quiet person and, naturally, I was close to her when growing up. I was absolutely shattered when she died unexpectedly when I was in my early teens. She had gone into hospital because of what we believed to be a minor ailment, and we were expecting her home the day that she died. She had been fairly healthy up until then, and had been in hospital for only a week or two.[8]

The family moved from the Shandon house to live for a short time with Nora's sister, Mrs Statia O'Reilly, who lived on the Douglas Road, on the south side of the Lee, further out from the centre of Cork. But it was too far from the schools they were attending and both families returned to the north side, to a house at 22 Redemption Road. Jack wrote: "There were more than a dozen of us living in that house, but it was nevertheless a very happy home."

At this stage Jack was facing the significant final years at school, with Intermediate and Leaving Certificates likely to define his future. Even so, he pursued sport in a serious way, playing games which were the focus of huge public interest, despite the fact that they were inter-school matches.

The most important 1936 game, during his last year at school, was against Coláiste Na Mumhan in Fermoy. It was regarded as a classic and was played on St Patrick's Day, again with special trains bringing supporters out from Cork. Brother McConville, a teacher in the school, used to sell the tickets for the train in the classrooms at two shillings each. Jack captained the team from the centre half-back position he favoured at the time. John Lyons, a younger All-Ireland player for Cork, who was on the winning teams in the early 1950s, described Jack stepping up to receive the Harty Cup after that 1936 game:

---

[7] This and other descriptions, quoted in Ó Tuama, above, n.5 were largely the work of P.J. Mehigan, a noted Cork journalist who reported on games in the *Cork Weekly Examiner*, doing radio commentaries as well in the 1930s.

[8] Quoted by T.P. O'Mahony, above, n.2, p. 32.

He was our hero at that time and we all returned home happy and looked forward to the victory parade from the station to the school. Three bands were there to greet the teams and thousands lined the streets. Up McCurtain Street, down 'Pana', up the North Main Street and Shandon Street. Molly Owens, a Shandon Street trader, set the tar barrels blazing, one at the top of Shandon Street and more at the school gate. The usual day off from school was granted after the team was introduced to the students in the school yard next morning, amidst scenes of great jubilation.[9]

Jack sat his Leaving Certificate examination in 1936, after which he left school. He did not do well enough to get a scholarship, but he did sit for several other examinations. These qualified him for teacher training as well as a Civil Service clerical officer position. He also passed entry examinations for the Electricity Supply Board and the Agricultural Credit Corporation. He was faced with a relatively simple choice, between teaching and the Civil Service, and eventually chose the latter. But in the meantime he obtained his first job from Seán Brennan, chairman of the Civil Service Hurling Club who worked as private secretary to Dr James Ryan, Minister for Agriculture. At this time Finbarr Lynch, Jack's older brother, was a civil servant in the Department. Dr Ryan set up the Dublin District Milk Board in 1936 to regulate the supply of milk in the Dublin area and appointed Brennan as chairman of the board with responsibility for recruitment. Brennan asked Finbarr, who was working in his office, if Jack would like a job. "It required only one phone-call and Jack was in Dublin in double quick time." Jack of course was a promising asset to the Civil Service Hurling Club for which he played. Jack knew Dermot Twohig, who worked in the Civil Service Commission, and he often visited his house in Dublin. It was Twohig's job to allocate the jobs to the people who were successful in the Civil Service examinations. When a vacancy occurred in Cork Court House, Twohig asked Jack if he was interested, which of course he was. But he had a conscience about letting Seán Brennan down. Finbarr Lynch and Donal O'Riordan, who had played with the two brothers on the North Mon Harty Cup team in 1943, told him: "Don't be a fool, do what you want to do."[10]

He began working in the Cork Circuit Court staff as a clerk and was acting registrar on occasions. This was when he decided on a career in law. He enrolled in 1941 at University College Cork to study for the Bar.

As these years unfolded, they saw Jack's greatest sporting achievements, inevitably and above all associated with Glen Rovers. The Glen fielded a number of hurling "greats", the most outstanding of all, and perhaps the greatest player of the game ever, being Christy Ring.

Cork is a great hurling county. Its senior county championship is referred to as "the Little All-Ireland". It attracts huge attention; never was this more the

---

[9] Ó Tuama, above, n.5, p. 21.
[10] Interview with Finbarr Lynch, August 2001.

case than in the period from the mid-1930s when Glen Rovers emerged from relative obscurity and achieved an outstanding run of eight-in-a-row victories in county finals (1934–1941), which saw Jack begin his sixteen-year active association with the senior team. He played in a variety of positions: wing back, centre field and most forward positions. He captained the 1939 Glen Rovers team which beat Blackrock, and did the same in 1940 against Sarsfield. He was also captain when the run of successes ended with Glen Rovers' defeat by Ballincollig in 1942.

For concentrated sporting intensity and focus, this was a critical period for him. In it he defined those qualities of play and of style which decided his provincial and national career as a sportsman. He had, after all, a job to do and a career to pursue. By 1936, when Jack made his first senior appearance for Cork in the Munster Championship game against Clare, the most remarkable sporting period in that part of Ireland was taking place. Raymond Smith, in his history of the game *Clash of the Ash*, rated the Munster Championship final, at Thurles, even more highly than All-Ireland finals at Croke Park. All these occasions have produced high-flown writing of a florid and ecstatic kind, nowhere more so than in Smith's own remarkable journalism or his vivid and colourful spoken accounts of moments that have a pure and exhilarating magic in them. Coming from Thurles himself and distinguished by his Tipperary accent, which seemed in Smith laid on with exaggerated intensity, he was of course part of the Munster event.

Jack himself, ever the natural ecumenist even in sport, cautioned balance rather than fervour. He made the points, first, that not every Munster final was a classic and, secondly, that in his own experience many Leinster senior hurling finals had surpassed Munster as sporting spectacles. This seemed like a moment of near-treason for a leading Cork exponent of the game. Jack's comment was ameliorated by his claim that Munster finals drew their unique quality from the outstanding level of play. That quality was partly derived from the intense county rivalries which had been built up in Munster over a century. He became part of that rivalry from 1936, when he played in the game against Clare, which Cork lost after a replay. The dominant team during the 1930s was Limerick, but Jack captained Cork in their victory over that county in 1938, and he went on to captain the Cork team in 1939, 1940 and 1942.

In 1938 he had on the team one of his own hurling heroes, "Fox" Collins. But the Cork team, having beaten Limerick, was in turn beaten by Waterford. The following year Jack captained Cork to its first Munster championship victory under his leadership, and its first provincial success since 1931. He was, incidentally, captaining the Cork football team at the same time. No one watching that 1939 Munster final, a glorious game by all accounts, knew that it was the prelude to his great sequence of All-Ireland finals as well. As a game it inspired the *Irish Independent* reporter to deliver some wonderful sports writing that eminently captures the wild excitement spectators experienced. He wrote of the two teams:

9

[compressing] into one glorious hour everything that ever made southern *camán* clashes famous. It was a glorious, thrilling, all-exciting game, an event that set hearts throbbing madly and blood pulsating wildly. Class hurling at any time is the fastest ball game on earth. At Thurles yesterday it was 'greased lightning' and of such play, adequate description is impossible. On the forty-odd thousand that thronged Thurles, it left an indelible impression that can never be erased. It was a game that will live in memory, keenly but cleanly contested, the players showing a fine spirit.[11]

A Cork goal in the final minutes clinched the game. The same reporter singled Jack Lynch out as having played "one of his best games, scoring one goal and two points".

It qualified Cork for the All-Ireland final that year, their opponents being Kilkenny. The conditions before the game were appalling, with torrential rain all morning, and thunder and lightning storms in the second half. The Cork team was considered unlucky in their defeat and Jack was disappointed both in the result and in his own play, which reportedly tailed off towards the end. Despite their victory, Kilkenny's fortunes declined in the years that followed, while those of Cork began to flourish from then on.

An extraordinary story is told by Tim Horgan, quoted in *Where He Sported and Played*,[12] of a football game which took place in cold, wet November weather, between Clonakilty and Jack Lynch's Cork team from Blackpool, St Nick's, on a playing field called "the Bog of Bandon". It was a county final and St Nick's were leading. They had two footballs, one of which was punctured, and when the second was kicked into the nearby stream, swollen to a flood by the rain, there was fear that the game would have to be abandoned. This would have destroyed the Blackpool team's chance of an historic county double. Jack plunged into the water, swam towards the disappearing ball and retrieved it. He then returned, dripping wet, and resumed the game, which St Nick's won. He was made Cork football captain the following year, 1939, which was also his first All-Ireland hurling championship as captain, thus being the only man to captain both teams in one year.

*

It is worth recalling another critical game in the build-up of Cork self-esteem and sporting excellence. This was not an All-Ireland, but the great 1940 Munster confrontation between Limerick and Cork, known as the "Volcanic" Championship. Again, Jack captained the team. It ran to a replay and in this Limerick were winners, going on later in that year to take the All-Ireland. Liam Ó Tuama's book carries accounts of the match seen from the Limerick point of

---

[11] Ó Tuama, above, n.5, p. 42.
[12] *Ibid.*, p. 99.

view and written by one of that team's all-time "greats", Dick Stokes. Among other things, Stokes describes the strange concoction used by the team trainer, Martin Lawton, as a massage, and made up of olive oil, camphorated oil, and shots of whiskey and poteen. There were, however, very few pulled muscles. There was no seating; all stood, with the exception of the Archbishop of Tuam and senior GAA men. More importantly, he describes the kind of hurling played then, which Jack grew up with, and at which he excelled. "Running with the ball on the hurley was not a feature, with very odd individual exceptions". (This was to change, with Christy Ring one of the outstanding exponents of carrying the *sliotar* on the blade of the *camán*, on one occasion half the length of a full pitch.) "Bunching was rare and four or five players trying to catch a falling ball on the hand would never occur." It was very much man-to-man play, with overhead striking with and against the ball, and hurleys "used with skill and accuracy – all features which made the game very exciting for the onlookers."[13]

By all accounts the replay was an outstanding game, played in perfect ground and weather conditions, with an amazingly tight half-time score, Cork 0-3, Limerick 0-0. Limerick turned this around in the second half, leading Cork by two points with ten minutes to go. Dick Stokes writes:

> All hell then broke loose. Hurling, the greatest game on earth, reached a peak point in excitement that years will not dim or distance sever from the recollection of the 25,000 that [sic] were thrilled beyond measure. The play swiftly moved from one end to the other, chances were gained and flitted away, reputations lost and won, new heroes applauded.[14]

After an incident, Micka Brennan was removed on a stretcher, provoking an angry reaction from Cork supporters, who went on to the pitch, causing a suspension in the game which was close to time. When it resumed, Jack took a shot at the Limerick goal, but the Limerick goalkeeper, Scanlan, parried the shot, cleared the ball, and the final whistle went.

According to Finbarr Lynch, no defeat disappointed Jack as much as that one. The year became known as "the last year of the cars". After that, according to Mick Mackey, getting to matches was "like pilgrims to Mecca". But the disappointment felt by Jack was also the prelude to his outstanding years as a player. He played and played: club, county, province, All-Ireland, hurling and football, challenge games, tournaments, leagues and championships. "Whenever or wherever a match was played, Jack was there."[15] Mackey was something of a legendary figure in Munster hurling, and a major contributor to Limerick's outstanding performance during the 1930s. He had already played in successive All-Ireland finals between 1933 and 1936 when Jack first joined the Cork senior

---

[13] Ó Tuama, above, n.5, p. 45.
[14] *Ibid.*, p. 51.
[15] Mick Mackey quoted by Ó Tuama, above, n.5, p. 53.

team, and Jack recalled events from their sporting encounters in a tribute for *The Mackey Story*.[16]

With the coming of the Second World War, travel was a problem. With petrol and coal in short supply, and trains running with difficulty on turf from the bogs, it was difficult to make the very long journeys through Munster to attend games. It was even worse for the All-Ireland, involving the increasingly difficult travel to Dublin and back, and therefore impossible to achieve any mass turn-out of supporters. Nevertheless, the crowds did turn out, and went on making prodigious efforts to get to matches in the Munster championship. The 1944 final, first game and replay, at Thurles, between Cork and Limerick, became known as "The Bicycle Finals", although in fact all the Second World War finals could have been so described, so great was the dependence on this mode of transport for supporters. It was estimated that 25,000 supporters travelled to the match from all over Munster, "many of them travelling over 80 miles to the final and back home again for work on Monday morning".[17] Then it was a drawn game, with a replay. The later outbreaks of foot-and-mouth disease, threatening Ireland's greatest export and its central livelihood on the land, were a further complication, affecting not only supporters but leading also to cancelled matches.

The 1944 game perhaps merited the kind of hyperbole which Munster hurling attracted, particularly in its climax. Christy Ring, in the words of the *Irish Independent* sports reporter, "ran from his own half almost to the Limerick line with the ball bouncing merrily on his hurley, and then smacked it across for the goal that won the day". Jack played a powerful game on that day, his open play especially praised by the same writer.

But the final, triumphant phase in Jack Lynch's career as a sportsman, and his outstanding record as a hurley player, had begun well before this game, and well before the great Christy Ring emerged to transform play. It dates really from the All-Ireland defeat at the hands of Kilkenny in 1939. This was widely regarded as a turning point in the game, in Gaelic games generally, and in Jack's own career. It began a period which saw him taking part in nine championships. He played in seven All-Ireland finals, winning six in a row, five of them at hurling and one at football. It is a unique record never since equalled.

Jack, who had captained the senior Cork side in 1938, 1939 and 1940 was not captain for the first All-Ireland victory on 1941, in which he played mid-field, partnered by Paddy O'Donovan. This combination was to be a powerful factor in subsequent games. The match included a twenty-year-old Christy Ring, described in the *Irish Independent* as "one of the stars of the game". The Cork team as a whole turned out to be invincible and easily beat a strong Dublin side. The team, under Jack's captaincy, had more of a struggle in the 1942 All-Ireland, which turned out to be a closer game, with the Lynch-O'Donovan partnership

---

[16] Séamus Ó Ceallaigh and Seán Murphy, *The Mackey Story* (Limerick G.A.A. Publications Committee, 1982).
[17] Ó Tuama, above, n.5, p. 61.

contributing to mid-field strength, and with outstanding play from the young Christy Ring. Con Murphy became a member of the Cork team in 1942 and played with Jack in the back line in four of the six all-Ireland victories.

> I never really saw him beaten. Jack Lynch was tough, uncompromising and *extremely* competitive. He could adapt to any style. There was no set pattern to his game. He had great flexibility as a player and great manoeuvrability. He was a quick thinker on the field, and a good 'reader' of the game. He had a capacity for seeing where the flaws were in the other side, and tipping off his own players about this. It was part of his leadership and captaincy and it worked whether he was captain or not. On the field he *was* the 'captain' anyway.[18]

Murphy says that Jack Lynch's leadership developed rapidly. He was 22 when he was first captain of Cork and by 25 had settled into his own style and approach. "In any capacity he had a presence. He commanded attention and respect. And in his sport he made decisions in the light of the whole picture, never just for himself." At the same time, according to Murphy, Lynch had a wonderful sense of the parochial. He was referring in particular to his association with Glen Rovers, but also his loyalty to Cork. In a funny way, Glen Rovers could do no wrong. He took great exception to the admonishment of these players or the imposing of penalties on them, but whenever a rough encounter was over there were no grudges. Everything was forgotten once the game ended.

Murphy, who became a referee in many of those games in the 1940s and early 1950s, made it clear that Jack never sought to interfere in any refereeing decisions made in Glen Rovers games in the 1940s and early 1950s. He had, Murphy said, a great sense of responsibility and respect for authority and applied this in every aspect of his career as a lawyer, politician and statesman. "He was an example to everybody."

Cork began to dream of three All-Ireland victories in a row, not achieved by the county since the triple victories in 1892–1894. Their 1943 opponents were a surprise when the Antrim team defeated Kilkenny in a sensational semi-final, but were then trounced by the Cork team. Despite the wartime travel difficulties, a huge crowd attended the game, only 2,000 or so short of the record attendance in 1936. Antrim was overwhelmed in every way. One of their players, writing about the game afterwards, described Cork as "one of the greatest hurling teams ever", not without justification.

In 1943 Jack Lynch moved to Dublin, and lived there in lodgings. He was attached to the District Court's Clerks' Branch, and he transferred his studies to the King's Inns. His sporting career was largely unchecked by this development. He continued playing in the different championships.

---

[18] Interview with the author, August 2001. He is one of only three surviving players from those Cork All-Ireland victory teams. He played as full back and had a unique view of the game, and of both Lynch's play and his strategy as captain.

The following year Jack played in the memorable Munster final against Limerick which ended in a draw with Cork winning the replay but through injury did not play in the All-Ireland semi-final against Galway. Dublin had beaten Antrim in their semi-final and were Cork's opponents. He was back on the team for the final, and after a difficult and scoreless ten minutes, Jack secured a first point for Cork. He developed what the *Irish Press* commentator on the game called "a marvellously successful partnership" with Con Cottrell, and "their sound and spectacular feats paved the way for the forwards to get the all-important scores".

It was a remarkable achievement to win four consecutive All-Ireland victories. Both Lynch and Ring had played in all the games, along with seven other heroes from what the newspapers regularly described as "the Rebel County", and their return to Cork after that 1944 game produced a spectacular reception. But their invincibility was checked in 1945, when they were beaten by Tipperary.

A phenomenal, record-breaking crowd of 65,000 turned out for the 1946 game, also against Kilkenny. The gates were closed an hour before the start, with 5,000 spectators locked out. Ring captained the Cork side, and scored what Ó Tuama describes as "one of the greatest goals in the history of All-Ireland finals".

Jack Lynch always recognised and praised the skills of outstanding sportsmen. During his own era he praised the deeds of Kerry's Jim Langton, Limerick's Mick Mackey, Waterford's John Keane and Tipperary's Bill O'Donnell. He never wavered in his admiration for Christy Ring. As team mates from 1939 to 1950 with Glen Rovers and Cork, and on many Munster Railway Cup teams during that period, they were regarded as the best hurlers Cork ever produced. It was Jack Lynch who brought "Ringey" to Glen Rovers when he left Cloyne in 1940 heralding a very successful period for the club. It was Jack who spoke at Christy Ring's graveside: "His feats and skills were legendary. . . . As a hurler he had no peer."

*

Jack's career outside sport was unspectacular at this stage. The move to Dublin allowed him to complete his legal studies at the King's Inns. Because of his Civil Service job, he was quite restricted, taking limited time off in the afternoons to attend lectures. The course was three years if you had been to university; if not, it took four years to complete. He qualified as a barrister and was called to the Bar in 1945.[19]

Finbarr referred to Jack's integrity and said he was a very conscientious man. He recorded Charlie, who became a priest, once saying: "We all have tender consciences." This referred to the family generally, but Finbarr gave an

---

[19] Interview with Eoin Ryan, May 2001. Of the group of new barristers called to the Bar in 1945 only three were still practising law twenty-five years later, when they held a reunion.

example of it in respect of Jack. As clerk to the County Registrar he had to carry books and files to the train station for dispatch to Dublin, and to save money he used to take the bus or walk, though he claimed expenses for the taxi fare to which he was entitled. He had a conscience about this and went to his confessor, Father Dalton, explaining what he did and asking if it was wrong. The priest asked him: "Have you a lot of stuff to carry?" Jack described the County Registrar's books and papers and Father Dalton listened carefully. Then he said: "Yes, it's all right to claim expenses for a taxi."

Jack had not been entirely happy in the Civil Service. He said later, "the Civil Service as a career got me down", and having completed his legal training, the obvious decision was to practice law. He claimed he made it on the toss of a coin. Allegedly, he did the same in respect of his choice when it came to politics, not about following it as a career, but about which of the political parties to join. But this is an apocryphal story. In fact, it was in 1946 that Jack was asked by the Fianna Fáil organisation in Cork to join the party and stand in a Cork by-election in that year. The party had done well in the previous general election of 1944, winning an overall majority.

However, the 1944 election had been called by Éamon de Valera to rectify a fairly disastrous performance by the party in the 1943 election, the first held since 1938. With the war, there were shortages of everything. Foot-and-mouth disease had seriously damaged agricultural trade. Without a convincing platform, Fianna Fáil did badly, and dropped ten seats. There was some compensation in the fact that Fine Gael, despite quite a spirited campaign, had dropped even more, by thirteen seats. The problem for Fianna Fáil during the campaign had derived in part from some astonishingly scurrilous speeches by Seán MacEntee, attacking Fine Gael as fascist and the Labour Party as an off-shoot of Soviet communism. He had the good grace to offer his resignation after the result, but was ignored. The winners had been the Labour Party, under William Norton, and Clann na Talmhan, the farmers' party, which won fourteen seats. De Valera managed to limp along in Government, but took the earliest opportunity to seek a stronger mandate in 1944, returning with 76 seats.

Despite the assurance of a full term, it is not surprising that the Fianna Fáil organisation, on the lookout for promising new talent, had already noted the indisputable appeal of a highly successful Gaelic games sportsman, and the party would have approached him anyway. The by-election gave urgency to this in 1946. Jack Lynch declined, but suggested to the party that he might be available at a later date.

In 1947 another magnificent All-Ireland final, "a hurling classic" against Kilkenny, saw Cork defeated, and the run of outstanding victories came to an end.

Lynch was rated a very good footballer, and more than one of those who played with or against him made the point particularly that he played a strong but fair game. He was often provoked but was never seen to indulge in unfair tactics. Jim Murphy, a member of the Garda Síochána who captained Kerry in

1953, is quoted as saying: "He was very strong and able to use himself in the right way. When 'shouldering' an opponent, he was a topper, but he was always fair. He had a lovely temperament on and off the field."[20] Lynch missed the hurley stick in his hand. "I always felt at a loss on the football field. I didn't know what to do with my hands, being so used to holding a hurley. It was a strange feeling that one got over only after many, many matches."[21]

Up to the early 1940s Cork supporters had shown an indifference towards football as a game, a situation that was changed by Cork's victory over Kerry in the 1943 semi-final of the Munster championship, following a replay. Jack played a very prominent part in the win. It was the first defeat for Kerry in thirty years, and Cork went on to win the final against Tipperary. The Cork team went to Croke Park to meet Cavan, "football kingpins of their time", but were narrowly beaten, having made a number of early mistakes which caused them severe disappointment. It was a game they should have won. The Cork team recovered form in 1945, both in the Munster final, where they beat Kerry, and then in the All-Ireland, when they exacted a convincing revenge on Cavan. After 34 years, the Sam Maguire Cup returned to Cork. Lynch told a story about that game against Cavan, when he almost missed the beginning:

> I was doing my Bar finals in that year and I was in digs in Terenure in Dublin, which isn't far from the 16-bus route. This went right beside Croke Park, down under the railway bridge, and on to the road out to Drumcondra. I met the boys from the team in the hotel in Dublin the night before and we usually foregathered on the morning of the game, for a cup of tea and maybe a pep talk. I told Jim Barry that there was no need for me to go to that as I was living 30 yards from the bus, and that I'd be there in good time. So I did that. I went to the bus queue near Kenilworth Square. Several full buses passed, and there was a big queue. I was getting a bit worried, looking at my watch – of course, it didn't occur to me at that time to get a taxi. I was surprised that so many people from that area seemed to be going to the football final and after a while, when I got really worried, I broke the queue and stepped on the platform of the bus. The bus conductor put up his hand and said 'Oh, no you don't. You have to take your turn'. 'Look,' I said, 'I'm playing in the All-Ireland final today.' 'Oh,' he said, 'that's about the best one I ever heard. Stay on.' Obviously, he thought it was such a good one, he decided to give in to me. Anyway, I got there, and ran around the back of the Cusack Stand from the main Drumcondra Road, and came around by the dressing rooms. There seemed to be a deathly silence inside except for the sound of someone pacing up and down in the dressing room. Hesitantly, I knocked on the door. It was Jim Hurley who happened to be pacing up and down the floor, with nerves I suppose. He opened the door and he looked at me, and I thought he was

---

[20] Ó Tuama, above, n.5, p. 100.
[21] *Ibid.*

going to savage to me. He said, 'Hello Jack Lynch, you were great to come'.[22]

Jack lived in Dublin from 1943 to 1945. Glen Rovers resumed their winning ways again in 1948, 1949 and 1950 and Jack played a major part in these victories. In the 1948 county hurling final against Blackrock he was outstanding. This was regarded as one of his finest games in which he completely dominated the play. He was the moving force behind the winning tactics, and seeming to revel in the difficult conditions of the pitch. He played again in the following two years which brought his active career as a hurler to an end.

*

Blackpool was the main district in the constituency where he stood for election for the first time in the 1948 general election. This was to make his representation of the area lifelong; first in innumerable sporting contests, and then in politics. He was of course sought out for politics on the strength of his sporting career. Heroes are always hard to find, and make good emblems, but no one recognised at the time just what kind of hero had been singled out for the career that is open to the public representative. It would be many years before the full value of Lynch's sporting excellence would be realised in an equally heroic, conflict-filled political career.

Lynch was a good judge of how far he had come, and how rich and integrated were the experiences he had gained from sport. However, he did not regard his first political fight with any easy confidence. While those around him during the campaign, and even more so during the election count, were convinced he would win a seat, Lynch himself was doubtful. He kept seeking reassurances from election workers and others from the party who had campaigned with him. He was the sportsman, doing what he had done in so many games, which was to overrate the opposition and underrate his own capacities. This stood to him as an approach in his first outing into politics, as it had so often done in sporting engagements.

Though there was some overlap between two quite different careers, the watershed was the 1948 general election. Invited by the Glen Rovers team captain, Seán O'Brien, to come out of retirement in 1951, Lynch, who confessed in a letter to being sixteen stone in weight, declined. "There's nothing I'd enjoy better than to be able to pull on a Glen jersey and give an hour of the best that's in me."[23] But he made the point that it would be unfair for a "has-been" to dislodge younger players, and that it would undermine the enormously successful policy of the club in bringing forward young players. "We might as well throw our hats

---

[22] Ó Tuama, above, n.5, pp. 18–24. "Jack Lynch talks to Mick Dunne" in an RTÉ Radio Interview, 27th September 1982, published in full in Ó Tuama, pp. 172–188.

[23] Ó Tuama, above, n.5. Ó Tuama reproduces the hand-written letter on p. 37.

at our life-long policy of fostering our minors."[24] Lynch was a product of that tradition, and of close on two decades of enthusiasm for hurling above other sports.

Jack Lynch was a good all-rounder. Not only did he play hurling and Gaelic football, but also handball and athletics; moreover, he was a swimmer. He grew to be both physically big and enormously strong, and this shows in the photographs of him as Glen Rovers captain and later as captain of the Cork team, leading out his men at the start of matches. The ritual had an impressive solemnity about it, with kilted pipers and drummers and the solemn expressions on the faces of the players. He looked remarkably handsome, his full head of hair at that time carefully brushed, with a 1940s' quiff on the crown of his head. He had great energy. On one notable occasion he played three matches in one day. He has described the event himself:

> I was playing with Civil Service and doing a line with Máirín at the time and when she asked me what I was going to do, I said: 'I'll go to Croke Park, I don't think I'll play with Civil Service in the morning.' So, even though she wasn't a typical GAA person, she said: 'Well, surely, your club must come first,' and I said: 'Goodness, you're right.'[25]

He went to Islandbridge in the morning to play a match against Eoghan Ruadh. He was in goal for the first half, not very successfully, and then moved up field. He went on to Croke Park in the afternoon to play two matches for Munster in the Railway Cup semi-finals, the first in hurling, which they won, the second football which they lost. Jack confessed he was exhausted by the end of the second game at Croke Park and vowed he would never repeat the three-game undertaking. The date was 20th February 1944. He scored in all three matches.[26]

Lynch developed an intellectual gamesmanship that was much admired, "reading" the play, often brilliantly, and having total recall of the sequence of play in matches. His brother Finbarr describes him as "always very tense before a big game: his face would be drawn and he would be very nervous. All this disappeared once the match began".[27] Watching him in the Dáil, in the 1960s and 1970s, when he was leader of Fianna Fáil, the same characteristics were clearly apparent, both in power and in opposition. This was never more so than at the times of great stress when he or the party were in crisis, which occurred both at the beginning and at the end of his last ten years as party leader. He had a remarkable capacity for "reading" correctly the often very complicated political moves around him. He was tense in expectation of what he should do, but always clear and decisive when he acted.

---

[24] Ó Tuama, above, n.5.

[25] *Ibid.*, pp. 124–125, an article by Mick Dunne, RTÉ sporting journalist, taken from an interview with Jack Lynch.

[26] *Ibid.*

[27] *Ibid.*, p. 10.

His first love was hurling; football came second. But he was good at the second sport, winning an All-Ireland medal in 1945. He took a principled stand against all sporting bans and kept to it throughout his life. He disapproved strongly of the Gaelic Athletic Association's ban on its players taking part in so-called "foreign games", such as rugby and soccer. He maintained this attitude at all levels, including schools and colleges run by the religious orders where sporting bans were imposed.

The GAA ban reached ludicrous proportions at times. On one occasion a Glen Rovers team mate, Jim Young, was suspended for attending a rugby dance. He was blocked from being present for the Munster Championship award of medals, and Jack declined to attend out of sympathy. He was himself suspended for attending an Irish rugby trial in which his brother-in-law was playing in 1946.

His wife Máirín has said of her husband: "Jack was a good hurler, but always said it was because he played with great hurlers."[28] He later became celebrated and this added to his sporting reputation. Yet by any standards he was a truly great sportsman, both in his playing and in his leadership of other players. Leaving aside the comparisons with other players, which, given the era in which he played, are increasingly apocryphal, his outstanding play is attested to time and time again. He always brought to his play "the best that's in me", a phrase used in 1951 in a letter in which he expressed the wish that his generation would make way for "the new lads coming on".[29] This was part of his greatness. He saw and valued the life of the games of hurling and of gaelic football in terms of previous generations, of his own time as a player, and of the future. He loved the game not for himself and his own skill at it, but for the game's sake. Every word he uttered about it, every action he took, every stroke he played, from the games in front of the Butter Market pillars in Shandon as a child to the All-Ireland triumphs in the 1940s were viewed in that light. Perhaps, most memorable of all in the character of a great sportsman, were his qualities as a leader, as a captain and as man capable of inspiring others. As one of the few survivors of those great victories in the 1940s, Con Murphy, has said, Lynch understood the "play" of everyone else in the field and "read" the game for the team's benefit.

I never saw him play. My view of him was exclusively concerned with a very different "game", that of politics. Yet in photographs and in descriptions of him, in moments of pure magic when he lost his hurley and kicked the *sliotar* over the bar, I have been as electrified by the immediacy and the force of his action as those who were lucky enough to witness it in the way that I witnessed moments of grave political anxiety. In the truest and best sense, of playing the game, of understanding it, and of living for the sake of the sport itself, he was truly one of the greatest sportsmen Ireland has ever had.[30]

---

[28] Ó Tuama, above, n.5, in an Introductory Note, p. vi.

[29] *Ibid.*, p. 37.

[30] See the Appendix for details of his sporting career listing his awards and medals.

Despite Jack's move from Cork to Dublin in 1943 to follow his legal studies, he remained a player for the county and one of its high-profile heroes. He enjoyed this special relationship with Cork to the end of his life, having grown up in a period of intense inter-provincial and inter-county rivalries that were most extravagantly expressed through Gaelic games. Of all Ireland's provinces, Munster holds a very special place in Gaelic games. Of all the Munster counties, Cork, the "Rebel County", enjoys a special distinction. Additionally, it includes the southern "capital", a city of great beauty and appeal, and great in its rivalries, most notably with Dublin.

Being an Irishman outside Ireland is a distinction to be enjoyed. The hallmark is simple and unique. The common bond of language, wit, conversation, sporting, acting or musical ability, a desire to please, to be friendly, and to lay extravagant claim to the birthright are all part of it. But to be an Irishman in Ireland is to invite an immediate and inexhaustible examination of exactly where one comes from, which province, county, parish or townland, and after that which family and with what antecedents. For a people who have spent generations seeking an overall unity, the distinguishing factor within the land, and among its people, is diversity. If sporting prowess is added to blood, then the mortal ties that bind great players to their place of birth are like the cords that bound Cuchulain to the rock, cords that only death can release.

Jack Lynch was a lifetime member of the Cork race; an inhabitant, long after he left it, of that soft city with a sting in its tail. People who do leave it – and many have been forced to do so over the centuries, and notably in the twentieth century – pass their involuntary exile heaping praise upon its beauty, its life and its people. Padraic Colum described it as the city that gave Ireland her journalists, her schoolmasters and her civil servants. He could have added her sportsmen, but hardly her politicians.

In Jack Lynch Cork certainly produced an outstanding sportsman, and a hard-working civil servant. But in company with so many others, he moved away from the city, and took up work in Dublin. In doing so, he was taking the first tentative steps towards giving to Cork what Cork had not otherwise produced, a politician of the first rank.

Dev's Disciple

Jack Lynch met Máirín O'Connor while on holiday at Glengarriff in 1943. She was an only child and also worked in the Civil Service. Jack Lynch was on holiday with his close friend and fellow member of the Cork side, Paddy O'Donovan. Other friends were with them. Máirín was on holiday with her friend Beryl Fagan and was staying in the Golf Links Hotel with a group of other girls.[1]

There was some teasing. Since the young women, in keeping with the hotel in which they were staying, were putting on airs, Lynch and O'Donovan adopted exaggerated Cork accents. And initially Jack, who was attractive to women, took a liking to Noreen Dillon, who worked as secretary in the hotel. But between himself and Máirín when they met, according to his brother Finbarr, it was really love at first sight. They spent time together hiking and swimming, and in the evenings they danced. "Many a time we rolled back the carpet for an eight-hand reel and then settled down for a sing-song."[2] Then and later, Lynch was an easy man to persuade to sing, and did so in a fine baritone voice. In one of his favourite songs, "San Antoine", his rendition was a passable imitation of Bing Crosby, who had brought this piece to prominence in the early 1940s.

Máirín O'Connor was living and working in Dublin at that time, and shortly after the Glengarriff holiday Lynch also moved to the city where he combined his law studies with a job in the Department of Justice. He was Máirín's first and only boyfriend, and they went on seeing each other on a regular basis during the two years when Jack was finishing his legal studies. A year later they decided to marry.

Neither Jack nor Máirín had strong political traditions in their immediate families, but Jack's more distant west Cork relations, through his father's family, came from what is called a "strong republican tradition". Yet he was not completely unaware of the political life of the country. No pupil who had attended a Christian Brothers school could be unaware of Irish political traditions, and the predisposition towards Fianna Fáil was natural enough. As early as 1932, when Jack was fifteen, he walked beside Éamon de Valera's carriage in the crucial election which first brought the Fianna Fáil leader to power. Jack carried

---

[1] Beryl Fagan was the daughter of Bernard Fagan, Dublin City Analyst. She later married Brendan Smith, the dramatist and actor, who still later became director of the Dublin Theatre Festival.

[2] Jack Lynch, "My Life and Times", *Magill* (November 1979), p. 37.

a political banner during that march in Cork , and formed from that time a great admiration for de Valera. But then, and for the next ten years, he was far too busy with sport to become actively engaged in politics.

Máirín always had mixed feelings about politics and about Jack's involvement. She knew, from her husband's character and from his life as a sportsman, that the commitment would be a serious one, and that he would succeed in whatever career he took. She also knew that this would have a profound and lifelong impact on their marriage. It would decide her involvement, thereby affecting her own life and, ultimately, shaping his.

She had the choice, exercised as far as one can judge by the vast majority of the wives of Irish politicians, to stand aside from any overtly political role. Politics was almost exclusively male territory, and this was particularly the case in the 1940s, when the involvement of women in public life fell to its lowest level in the twentieth century. The tempestuous and revolutionary involvement of women in the fight for independence, and in the early years of the State's history, had given way to a quite different political culture. In very clearly defined circumstances, women stood for Dáil seats and won them during most of the period of Lynch's involvement in politics. But they did so as the widows or daughters of deceased politicians, exercising an emotionally compelling political right to what might almost have been considered a "family" seat. It was only much later that women came into politics on their own and with clearly defined party, and in some cases personal, objectives.

Máirín chose not to stand aside. She was involved in the making of decisions about Jack's career from an early stage, and developed skills and propensities of a lasting kind, though she never involved herself in his central political role. She became in time a unique figure, a byword for the monitoring and management of Lynch's public life, attracting both praise and blame for this, but establishing herself as a constantly concerned figure at his side. It became the shaping characteristic. At the time of their marriage Máirín seems to have preferred not to have politics interfere with the beginning of their life together. Jack Lynch left the Civil Service once he qualified as a barrister. From 1945 to 1948 he practised in Cork and he and Máirín lived there in a house they rented in Farrenleigh Park off the Model Farm Road. According to Pearse Wyse, who canvassed for him in 1948, later serving with him as a Dáil deputy, Jack joined the Local Defence Force after the Second World War and served three years in the 47th North Cork battalion. Wyse served in the 48th battaltion. According to him, military service gave Jack insights that proved valuable later.

Eoin Ryan knew both of them from early on and he and Jack Lynch had become good friends while studying together between 1943 and 1945. Eoin Ryan and the Lynches saw little of each other then, but were reacquainted in 1948. After Jack became a deputy, he and Máirín lived in Dublin during the week. Eoin was taking out Joan Dowd and the four of them got on. Jack and Máirín were not well off in marked contrast with Eoin Ryan, whose father, a leading figure in Fianna Fáil, owned a fine house in Wicklow. The Lynches lived in an apartment on the top of a house in Dundrum. Ryan remembered the relationship between them as a young couple. Máirín was fussy and bossy, always saying how things would be, directing Jack and telling him what to do. He, in marked contrast, was easygoing and accepted her directional instincts. "But it was only appearances," Ryan said. "Once he said anything would happen, it happened."

Máirín had no family except her mother. This was significant in their marriage, significant also in the relationship with the extended Lynch family. The contrast was very marked. The Lynches, with between thirty and forty first cousins, represented a large and sprawling clan. Máirín had no capacity for dealing with this. Her brother-in-law, Finbarr, who was probably closer to her than anyone else in the family, except Jack, realised this and understood why she did not always attend family weddings and the like and kept Jack away from some of them as well. There was a benefit in the inevitable detachment as his political career developed through major ministerial appointments to party leadership and the role of Taoiseach. He was neither lofty nor distant; the Lynch family affection was too strong for that. But he was increasingly protected by Máirín, and it was in her nature , as an only child, to be overwhelmed by the scale and exuberance of her husband's family and to draw back.

Máirín's mother, Mrs O'Connor, had been active in promoting Irish goods through the Dublin Industrial Development Association. Erskine Childers and Kevin McCourt were on its council. The promotion of Irish goods during St Patrick's week was one of its undertakings. She also organised the first fashion show in Ireland, to which she invited Elsa Schiaparelli, who attended. Schiaparelli's liking for the use of traditional fabrics had an impact on early Irish fashion design. When Mrs O'Connor suffered a stroke, Máirín and Jack moved her into the house they had bought in Garville Avenue. Jack's relationship with Máirín's mother was a good one. Mrs O'Connor had great admiration for her son-in-law and he dealt with her sympathetically, spending time in her company when she was frail and disabled by her stroke.

Eoin Ryan's view of Lynch as a lawyer was that he was a good man with people, easy, relaxed, able to talk with them. Professionally he was "a good operator", but in terms of legal promise he was not a particularly outstanding lawyer. Once he became a Minister, he was set on an irreversible course in politics and away from the law. Ryan questions Lynch's seriousness in ever saying otherwise. Similarly, he regards references to Máirín agitating for the law over politics as just talk. Ryan and Lynch's involvement together, though initially intermittent with one pursuing law and the other politics, was lifelong, as was their friendship. Ryan was put off active politics by what he had seen of his father's day-and-night involvement with the party, and the fact that there had been very little family life.

*

The person who attracted Lynch to Fianna Fáil was undoubtedly Éamon de

Valera. Lynch said of him: "I had always had a great feeling for Dev. I was conscious of him being a marvellous, romantic figure."[3] It seems that Lynch was disposed to enter politics in the mid-1940s; it was timing rather than reluctance that held him back. The fact that he did not accept the party nomination for the 1946 by-election helped to create the myth that he was somehow reluctant in his political career. There was also a myth of uncertainty over his choice of a party to join. This derived from rumours about him having considered the possibility of joining Fine Gael, and about the approaches made by Clann na Poblachta. All these circumstances have rational explanations. He was never approached by Fine Gael, and never considered it as a party which suited his brand of politics. He was approached by Seán MacBride's party, Clann na Poblachta, in 1946, the same year in which Fianna Fáil asked him to be a candidate in the same contest. His response to the Clann was an emphatic negative.

The truth behind his decision not to go for the 1946 by-election seat in Blackpool is a simple one. He was friendly with "Pa" McGrath, who was also seeking the nomination, and this caused him to hold back. "I wasn't going to stand against him."[4] Apart from this loyalty, he had no political experience in 1946 and already had a difficult choice to make between the pursuit of a legal career as a barrister, or of taking up a position as a civil servant in the Department of Justice.

In no sense was Jack Lynch reluctant to be politically involved and the by-election campaign proved this. It was in the Blackpool constituency in Cork, necessitated by the resignation of William Dwyer. Lynch campaigned for his friend "Pa" McGrath. He made his first political speech, sharing the platform at Blackpool Bridge with Frank Aiken, one of the senior figures in Fianna Fáil, who, much later, was to support Lynch for the leadership and then serve in his first Government.

In the absence of Lynch as a candidate, McGrath won convincingly enough. Commandant General Tom Barry stood as an independent candidate and there was a candidate from the Communist Party. The by-election had historic overtones because it was preceded by the hunger strike of Seán McCaughey, an IRA man, who died in Portlaoise Prison on 10th May 1946. A month later Clann na Poblachta was founded, with Seán MacBride as party leader, and a new force in Irish politics was unleashed.

It was an uncertain period. Virtually all political groupings in the country, including organised industrial labour, the Labour Party, republicanism, the two large parties, Fianna Fáil and Fine Gael, as well as the Catholic Church, were adjusting to the aftermath of the Second World War. This had devastated Europe, changed irreversibly the world balance of power, and, as a result of Irish neutrality, had largely excluded the country from any active participation in events. Economically, the conflict called the Emergency (that wonderful Irish euphemism

---

[3] Jack Lynch, "My Life and Times", *Magill* (November 1979), p. 37.
[4] *Ibid.*

for the destruction of Europe) had stultified Irish trade. Socially, there was a sense of isolation, and this also had a moral and religious dimension. The political philosophy of Ireland as a "protected territory", with its Christian, Gaelic and cultural identity saved from the dilution of foreign influence, was a real factor in the life of the country, and was to shape political life during the period of inevitable change which followed the war years. The safest bet, in these circumstances, for the kinds of radical reform which were needed in health, education, industry and agriculture was to clothe them in some form of republicanism. This in part explains the success, in the period between 1946 and the general election of 1948, of Clann na Poblachta. It grew in strength, at the expense of a disorganised and divided Labour Party. It also presented a dynamic alternative to the main political party in the country. Fianna Fáil had enjoyed sixteen years of unbroken power and had become complacent and uncertain. Unlike Clann na Poblachta, the party felt that its republicanism was secure. There was some emphasis on attracting younger men into political life; those who belonged to a post Civil War generation and were focused on the future were seen as a necessary leavening. It was more a gesture than a strategy.

One Cork politician and lifelong associate of Jack Lynch's, Gus Healy, has said that the choice of him as a member of the party and as a future candidate was part of Fianna Fáil's attempt at the time to attract a new generation for which he was an eminently well-suited candidate. The process was not widespread. Éamon de Valera was by nature a gradualist, respecting the older men who surrounded him, and the urge by men of talent and energy to enter politics, was, at the time, lukewarm. Intelligent, well-educated and a good sportsman, Lynch had a political style very different from that of the older generation. The majority of these were not only associated with the Old IRA and the historic events connected with the fight for independence, but were proud of the fact, and had not really thought through any alternative personal or political strategy. The more enlightened figures in Fianna Fáil recognised the need to attract young people, and Lynch epitomised the kind of thinking that met this need and countered the heavily republican tradition that permeated Fianna Fáil.

*

Whatever Máirín Lynch's misgivings might have been, she encouraged her husband at this time to pursue his career in law outside the Civil Service. She later described the first two years of their marriage as "the happiest years of our lives" and she would have preferred that he remained a lawyer. His early practice was, in his own words, "run-of-the-mill". It involved company actions, traffic accidents, claims and offences, and rent cases. It was too early for him to specialise. It provided him with a good training for politics and allowed himself and Máirín to enjoy themselves.

Máirín was naturally quite shy. She dreaded what she believed would be the loneliness of public life; the separations that were an inescapable part of men being successful in a man's world from which women were traditionally excluded. She successfully challenged that interpretation, but only much later. In the early years, whatever influence she exercised in relation to his career was done privately.

They did not have children. Quite early in the marriage, after seven or eight years, Máirín had a hysterectomy, and they thought at that time of adopting children. But by then Jack's political career had made sufficient progress for her to see the dangers of not being free to pursue their close and essentially companionable marriage in the world of political action. "I decided to devote all my time to him so that I could travel around with him everywhere."[5]

Máirín was an attractive young woman with an elegant dress sense. Despite her declared abhorrence for public life, she steeled herself to be as good at it as she could. Later, as Jack moved up the political ladder, she worked hard at being aware of people and of appearing relaxed in company. It was done at considerable cost throughout her life. In due course she took infinite pains over public events and her own participation. She felt her role was to be at Jack's side. Together, they always seemed entirely natural and at their ease. Jack was himself an elegant man in his dress, there was positive good nature in his demeanour, and he was always relaxed in his dealings with people. His tall, spare frame was a tailor's dream, and his father had ensured good judgement and care in the choosing and wearing of clothes. This was the case even in those raw and austere post-war days of the mid-1940s. He was never flamboyant. Those days may have influenced his actual approach, as his taste was modest and his style, on the whole, unassuming. In no aspect of his personality did he ever show excess. On the other hand, he had a natural grace in his movement. The two of them made a fine couple. Máirín seemed then and later to match him for determination and personal dynamism. In due course this was to acquire its own political authority.

*

Early in 1948, before the February general election, Lynch was again approached by the Brothers Delaney Fianna Fáil Cumann in Blackpool to stand for the party. He wanted to go for a seat in Cork. Máirín did not want this.

On their way to the party office to put in his papers for the selection convention, they were still discussing whether he should run. Eventually Máirín said: "We'll toss for it." The coin, which she tossed, fell in his favour. His political career was decided as though in a game of chance, his good fortune and the nation's measured in the spinning of a penny in the air.

Lynch was not at the time a member of Fianna Fáil, nor did he attend the Cork Borough selection convention. He was at a law dinner in the Metropole Hotel in Cork, and only went on to the party event after he had heard of his nomination. He joined the party that night. On the ticket with him was his friend

---

[5] Interview with Sheila Walsh, *Sunday Press*, quoted by T.P. O'Mahony in *Jack Lynch: A Biography* (Blackwater Press, Dublin, 1991).

and the then sitting deputy, "Pa" McGrath. Lynch had widespread support in the campaign, not least from those who had followed his sporting career. Glen Rovers supplied many election workers.

At the end of the campaign, Éamon de Valera came to Cork for final rallies, and it was at one of these in the city that the two men first met. Lynch's admiration for de Valera, dating back to his youth, was confirmed and strengthened by the personal encounter, and to a large extent it was mutual. Lynch saw a man who had inspired a majority of the Irish people during difficult times, and had governed the country firmly and fairly during the greater part of his growing up. There was no alternative political hero, and his loyalty was to remain unswerving until de Valera's departure from active politics ten years later.

Jack Lynch won the seat convincingly, topping the poll with 5,594 votes. However, the 1948 general election was not a happy one for Fianna Fáil. The party dropped to 68 seats and went out of power. Two parties which have since disappeared from Irish politics, Clann na Poblachta and Clann na Talmhan, got a total of 17 seats, more than Labour's 14, and Fine Gael won 31 seats.

The Government that resulted from this, led by John A. Costello of Fine Gael, was inherently unstable. Costello was not the Fine Gael party's leader; this was General Richard Mulcahy. Objections to Mulcahy as leader of the mixed-party administration led to the compromise choice. Five political parties shared power, including two Labour parties. Seán MacBride, the leader of Clann na Poblachta, was from the start a source of tension. Shades of liberalism were in potential conflict with devout Catholicism. Issues of health, social welfare and education were susceptible to the impact of conflicting ideologies, and they emerged most obviously and most damagingly in the widely examined "Mother and Child Scheme" on which histories have been written.

For Lynch, who had not had much direct involvement with Fianna Fáil in power, the following three-year period of opposition represented a relatively quiet introduction to the business of politics. In that first period as a deputy, Jack Lynch used to travel back to Cork with his brother, Finbarr. They would stop in Cashel having given Mick Davern, Noel's father, a lift. Finbarr remembers the two deputies talking about the political life to which both had been elected at the same time. "A year after that election both felt that they did not want to be in politics."[6] De Valera made Lynch secretary of the party and gave him a job as a political researcher, but he was also able to continue with his legal practice.

Jack Lynch had a constituency helper who worked for him from the very beginning. He was a bootmaker in Blackrock called Séamus O'Brien. He would have nothing to do with the Fianna Fáil party. He would just do the constituency work with Jack, bringing all the problems to his attention. Because he was in the business of mending people's shoes, everyone knew to come to him when they had problems. Jack reportedly used to spend considerable time with him in the back of his shop talking about what was happening in the constituency and who

---

6 Finbarr Lynch interview with the author, August 2001.

needed help. He worked very hard as a constituency TD. Eric Peard, who was employed by Gouldings, the fertiliser company, and was subsequently chairman of the Harbour Commissioners in Cork, knew Jack Lynch well from the 1950s and remembers him asking for employment on behalf of constituents. When the Corpus Christi parade was on in Cork, Eric Peard, who had become chairman of the Harbour Commissioners, had a leading part in the parade. He was somewhat more important, in Cork's eyes, than the Lord Mayor. He remembers walking up the parade with Jack, who was inevitably being cheered by the crowd. Some remark was made about this, and a Fine Gael man shouted out, "Why wouldn't they cheer? Weren't you throwing them pennies on the way down?" "That's more than you would have been able to do," was Jack's reply.

He had reason to share in the sense of disillusionment that swept through Fianna Fáil following the 1948 election. Not enough had been done to revitalise the party, and this remained and indeed grew as an objective. Though it is not always the case, there was an inescapable instability about this particular coalition holding on to power, and a growing probability of its disintegration before it completed a full term. For the Fianna Fáil party in opposition, with Jack Lynch playing his first modest administrative role, there were major questions to tackle.

Perhaps the greatest of these, and the most intractable, concerned the continued leadership of Éamon de Valera. The party did not know how to address it. By a common, unspoken consensus, the "Chief" was given his own time to reflect. Whether he did so, and what the nature of that reflection might have been, is not recorded. But de Valera's own reading of the national consensus in respect of himself was positive; the result was his decision to soldier on. There were lesser questions about the party's candidates, the presence of too many older men, and the inadequacy of policies and ideas. Given the lead which came from de Valera's decision to stay on, these were not tackled either.

The reality for the party, now of direct concern to its new member, was that it had become complacent after sixteen years in power. Jack Lynch, as well as being new to political life in Leinster House, was also party secretary and researcher. In this latter capacity he was responsible for the kind of investigation of party morale, electoral strategy and economic and social policies which had been found to be less than adequate in the February election. There had been misgivings about the readiness of the party to fight that election. They had lost two out of the three by-elections in 1947, both to Clann na Poblachta, one to Seán MacBride himself. The party had appeared to recognise, in the nomination of Lynch among others, that new, dynamic talent was required, but not a great deal was done to develop that talent. More importantly, not enough of it had been recruited. The party was unquestionably in the hands of the revolutionary generation, and, in the opinion of one senior member of the party, they were careless, lazy and badly briefed.

Not much could be done about those who controlled Fianna Fáil at the top. There were too many of them, and they were to remain there for the next decade. It was evident to all that the party's principal electoral tactic had been to attack the concept of coalition as inherently unstable and to present the undoubtedly revered leader, de Valera, as a father of the country whose wisdom was of greater value than ideas or policies. Seán MacEntee was a brilliant exponent of the anti-coalition demonising, by characterising the left as communist, and the right as fascist. But wiser minds in the party saw the limitations of this. "This will not do for waverers", Erskine Childers told MacEntee.[7]

*

The political instability, not just of this early period after the ending of the Second World War, but of the whole decade of the 1950s, has been extensively examined. Those who governed the country have been criticised for their failure to solve economic "problems". Yet there were not, nor are, any easy solutions to poverty, and industrialisation takes a long time. Ireland was, both morally and socially, a deeply conservative country. The attitudes resulting from this were combined with an equally deep respect for democracy. This in turn explains the intense interest in politics. It also reinforced concerns for basic freedoms which at that time were contrasted pointedly both with the evils of fascism that had devastated Europe, and with those associated with communism, now seen as the great threat overshadowing the free world.

Jack Lynch was a product of that period. He was and remained throughout his life a practising and devout Catholic. He was liberal about his belief and pluralist on wider Church interests as they affected Irish society. He had similar views on republicanism and nationalism. As we have seen, he was opposed to the GAA ban, and saw at first hand that the instinct for sporting excellence crossed all barriers, and that this should always be respected. He was a good democrat, and neither had, nor developed later, any obsessive view of himself as capable of a contribution to the country's welfare that was special or unique.

In much of this he followed de Valera. For all the difficulties of this period, the essential stability of the country, its dependence on a solid constitutional and legal foundation, owed much to the politics that emerged and developed under his leadership. No comparable figure existed on the other side in politics. What is remarkable is that this powerful, indeed awesome, leader was at heart protective rather than in any way threatening of the essential freedoms Irish men and women associated with the birth of their country's independence.

When the "Mother and Child Scheme" brought about the abrupt disintegration of the Inter-Party Government in the spring of 1951, the result in the subsequent general election was inconclusive. Fianna Fáil added only one seat to their miserable outgoing total of 68, and formed a minority Government. Fine Gael improved its position – a mark of its appeal to Catholics, who feared the liberalism

---

[7] Dermot Keogh, *Twentieth Century Ireland, Nation and State* (Gill and Macmillan, Dublin, 1994, p. 183. The quotation is from a long and candid letter about how Fianna Fáil underestimated the political opposition and relied too heavily on de Valera.

29

of its partners in power – but Labour dropped seats. Small parties and independents, which in 1948 had held 29 seats, won 22 seats, in itself a destabilising phenomenon, and an indicator that far from adequate electoral measures had been taken by Fianna Fáil. In the general election in June 1927 there had been 40 independents and small party deputies. That Dáil was the shortest in the State's history, being dissolved three months later in September 1927. On three other occasions where Fianna Fáil had failed to get a convincing majority – in 1932, 1937 and 1943 – de Valera had gone to the country within twelve months. But circumstances in 1951 did not present him with the opportunity for this, and the climate of economic stagnation and emigration was too risky. Furthermore, the necessary internal party changes designed to tackle the social and economic issues in advance of another election were not well advanced, nor were they easy to construct.

Jack Lynch was offered a junior role in the administration, that of Parliamentary Secretary to the Government and to the Minister for Lands. He had particular responsibility for the Irish-speaking areas. The job was newly created by de Valera. It involved, in Lynch's own words, "roving responsibility for the Gaeltacht and congested districts". Accepting the appointment was his first occasion to visit the Taoiseach in his office. The relationship between the two men is of considerable importance in charting the future progress of the young politician, and also in explaining why he stuck consistently with Fianna Fáil and the life of politics, giving up his prospects as a lawyer. Jack became very close to Dev. More senior men in the party were in awe of him. Jack, who had no experience of the "Chief" in earlier times, developed a man-to-man approach. Years later, this bridging of generations characterised Lynch's relationship with Desmond O'Malley.

The appointment was highly significant since de Valera was slow to take in new people. The job meant that Lynch travelled and he did so in relation to an area of responsibility that was of particular interest to de Valera himself. On one occasion during this period in power, the Taoiseach travelled with his junior Minister to Donegal for an Irish-speaking celebration. This was the silver jubilee of Coláiste Bhríde at Rannafast. Pádraig Faulkner, not then a Dáil deputy but later a Minister in administrations led by Jack Lynch, was treasurer of the college. Even though de Valera prided himself on his knowledge of Irish, and although Jack Lynch had been given the job on account of his reasonable knowledge of the language, neither was at ease with the Donegal dialect. As they left the hall, where a play in Donegal Irish had been performed, de Valera said, to Lynch's great relief: "Bhí sé sin go h-iontach, an té thuigfeadh é" (That was wonderful, if only one could understand it).

*

The appointment as Parliamentary Secretary meant that Lynch had to suspend his legal practice; it was the watershed between a professional and a political life, despite returning to practice law during the subsequent period in opposition.

It was as though he had accepted a political destiny, one that was in part preordained by the success of his sporting career, making him an attractive proposition for a political party. Once he was committed to it and had entered the Dáil, withdrawal apparently ceased to be an option. But the difference in attitude between them, slight though it was, contributed to two important perceptions. Firstly, there was the idea that Maírín was the more dynamic partner, the decision-maker, the wife who knew what she wanted while her husband did what he thought was correct and dutiful. Secondly, there was the idea throughout his political career that he was somehow a reluctant participant in politics. He seemed unwilling to enter in the first place – although we know now this was because a friend was running – and then he seemed reluctant to go on. The purported reluctance was probably noted most publicly of all some years later, at the time of his succession as leader after Seán Lemass.

The pleasant side of the job was that it involved essentially positive actions on his part. He was responsible for assessing the needs of remote, Irish-speaking areas, as well as those areas which had been identified as economically depressed. The two were often common. Their needs had been the substance of government reports and special aid programmes since well before Independence. The methods of help had been controversial in the past. The plight of the congested districts had attracted considerable attention, and a great deal of sympathy. This was probably disproportionate. In part it resulted from the cultural appeal of the language and the way of life. The poorer parts of Dublin, in many respects worse off economically, could not compete with the attractions of Connemara or west Cork or the Dingle peninsula for public sympathy. Moreover, the restoration of the Irish language was part of the ethos of Fianna Fáil and one of its fundamental political objectives. This gave a huge advantage to the commitment.

The resources were not excessive. Nevertheless, a State board for the promotion of industry in the west and south-west of the country was set up in 1952, as was the fisheries board, Bord Iascaigh Mhara. Jack Lynch was in part responsible for initiatives in these sectors. He was also responsible for various infrastructural projects.

It was a time of heavy emigration which went on throughout the 1950s, increasing as the period went on. The west and the Border counties were badly hit. The previous emigration high point had been in the 1880s, when large numbers had left Ireland for America. In the 1950s the majority went to Britain and, in the main, were from rural parts. They were unskilled agricultural labourers who were able to adapt to building work in England. Women who went obtained employment in hotels or as domestic servants. It was a sad phenomenon, this economic recruitment that broke up families and was at its most extensive at the bottom of the economic scale, something which induced a good deal of anger and envy directed at those who could afford to stay. At the same time it provided an important source of money in the remittances which many of the sons and daughters of families faithfully sent back to help the meagre income from the unproductive fields of the west.

Jack Lynch's perspective on the early years of the 1950s came from his first appointment. It was therefore based on what was essentially a west of Ireland view of the operation of politics in Dublin, an extension in its way of his view of Ireland from the very beginning: that of a Corkman and a provincial. Economically, the parlous state of the country as a whole had the effect of putting the west of Ireland on an equal footing with the east, and even with Dublin itself. Emigration may have flowed more thickly from Mayo and Leitrim, but it also flowed out of the capital. This was a universal tide of people flowing eastward into England, and it represented a judgement on those who governed, and who had failed to grasp opportunities, or make them, in the aftermath of the Second World War.

*

In broad terms the grim period of the 1950s was inevitably associated with the instability of all of its three Governments and with the fact that power had changed with each election, because neither side was able to come up with effective solutions to the general despair. In their successive platforms for fighting the general elections from 1948 to 1957, Fianna Fáil had understandably, if a bit unfairly, created a view that the economic distress was a product of coalitions in power. Writing about it later, Kevin Boland claimed that the Irish people in 1954 needed "a further experience of the Coalition to really get it out of their system," and claimed that what achieved this was the spectacle of "the unemployed sitting on O'Connell Bridge."[8] As a result the people turned to Fianna Fáil, and "the nine years period of indecision was over".

It was far more complicated than that, though the essential focus was certainly on unemployment. But the inability of either side to turn the economy around was evenly shared throughout the decade. When it was appropriate, the earlier policies of guarding the fledgling economic resources by the means of tariff walls worked. But as a scheme for national development after the Second World War, when trade liberalisation was providing the energy for growth in the rest of Europe, it had only limited potential. Unfortunately, no-one in politics knew what to do next.

At this time, as Garret FitzGerald has pointed out:

> Fianna Fáil remained wedded to its inward-looking protectionist stance, which had ceased to yield any dividends in industrial employment or output once the post-war process of developing new industries behind these barriers had been completed around 1950. Industrial stagnation was the result, temporarily masked in the early 1950s by some short-lived opportunistic exports to Britain.[9]

---

[8] Kevin Boland, *The Rise and Decline of Fianna Fáil* (The Mercier Press, Cork, 1982), p. 65.

[9] Foreword to *Planning Ireland's Future: The Legacy of T.K. Whitaker*, edited by John F. McCarthy (Glendale Press, Dublin, 1990).

Western Europe had recovered from the terrible aftermath of the Second World War. It had transformed its fairly painful recovery programme, involving great hardship, into an aggressive period of economic expansion and increasingly competitive trade. There was still much protectionism. But essentially what was to become the European ideal, that of a market of allies put in place by the signing of the Treaty of Rome early in 1957, was being worked out in practical terms at this time. Ireland was not part of it. While the economies of other European countries were expanding at record rates in historical terms, Ireland faced economic stagnation. The country had protected itself from Europe too well. In war it had done so by neutrality, a de Valera legacy; in peace it was achieved by protectionism, a Lemass legacy.

Garret FitzGerald claims that few of the survivors of what he terms the "nationalist revolution" had been "either radical social thinkers or people with an economic bent." Among the few he places Lemass and Patrick McGilligan, but finds that in general the country's leaders "were even more conservative a third of a century later".[10]

With Fianna Fáil in power, Jack Lynch was learning to be a politician in the best way possible: by the exercise of ministerial discretion in the junior appointments de Valera gave him. The discretion was not extensive. Power, as we have come to see, was of a different order then, circumscribed by lack of money. Furthermore, of his first ten years as a politician barely four were spent in power. One of the lessons was that politics was a service to the community involving financial sacrifice. The privilege lay in this, not in any personal advantage. De Valera was an austere leader, and this belief came from him. The tone he set was one of personal sacrifice. It was combined with a firm belief in single-party government, and in the pre-eminent advantage of Fianna Fáil as the provider of that Government. The state of the country was no real endorsement of this belief. But other Governments were not really any better.

Furthermore, in the figure of Seán Lemass, who in due course was to become de Valera's successor, Ireland benefited from an equally impressive but quite different political force. The power Lemass exerted was economic, and he was effectively Fianna Fáil's spokesman on economic affairs, despite the fact that he never occupied the position of Minister for Finance. Apart from a period during the Second World War when he was Minister for Supplies, his entire ministerial career was in the Department of Industry and Commerce. There is some sense in this. Money was a budgetary commodity, but not a great source of wealth. There wasn't much of it in the State coffers, and it was treated with profoundly conservative and bureaucratic restraint. The country's "wealth" lay in the land, the people, the capacity of nature to feed and fatten livestock, and the future prospect of creating an industrial structure. There was also the vitally important

---

[10] *Ibid.* McGilligan served in several early administrations, as Minister for External Affairs and for Industry and Commerce. He was Minister for Finance in the first Inter-Party Government of 1948–1951.

resource of remittance money, which was a product of generations of emigrants sending money home to assist family life.

The key to economic policy, as Fianna Fáil saw it during the years when Lynch was growing up, lay in tariff protection. This looked after the wealth that did exist, and allowed for a gradual growth and development of the more sophisticated industrial society that operated elsewhere in Europe, even in countries which had comparable rural societies and a heavy dependence on agriculture. Once the party entered the Dáil, the theory of an economy developing behind the protection of its own tariff walls became Lemass's political message. From the start he believed in Ireland as "a self-contained unit... Until we get a definite national policy decided on in favour of industrial and agricultural protection and an executive in office prepared to enforce that policy, it is useless to hope for results."[11] When he came to power he enforced this policy, and it served the country, indeed shaped its development for the next thirty years.

It was controversial and painful. Some aspects of it were seen as revolutionary and it embraced the Economic War, in which Ireland's refusal to pay certain agreed land annuities to Britain resulted in high tariffs on Irish imports. In a sense, though for totally different reasons, the two countries, during an era of free trade, applied strict controls. Ireland was an important market for Britain, one which supplied a huge amount of the country's needs, despite Lemass's policy of protection. But Britain was absolutely vital as a market for Irish goods, and this made the Economic War particularly difficult.

Lemass's own thinking developed and changed. In terms of economic strategy he was innovative during the years from Lynch's entry into the Dáil, but he was handicapped by the political instability, the periods out of power, and the failure of any consensus between Fianna Fáil and the Inter-Party Governments. As Whitaker pointed out in his book,[12] the indications – and they are little more than that – of the closely reasoned changes in Lemass's thinking are evident in a Bill he brought before the Dáil in 1947. This would create powers for the supervision of the industries created behind Ireland's tariff walls, it proposed measures both to help and to regulate, and even provided a ceiling on profits. "The Government was empowered to set the maximum profit which a firm could make and if the firm made any excess profit then the Minister could claim that excess."[13]

At the time, of course, Lemass was researching and fashioning an industrial structure, in some respects from the dust under his feet. In his mind he was constructing a comprehensive system of industrial development which would harness the collective energies of many different interests and forces in the State. These included the firms themselves, many of which were still fledgling

---

[11] Seán Lemass's Dáil speech in 1928, quoted by T.K. Whitaker in *Interests* (Institute of Public Administration, Dublin, 1983), p. 58.

[12] T.K. Whitaker, *ibid.*, pp. 66–67.

[13] *Ibid.*

enterprises. Also, there were considerations relating to the workers, investment money, the State's regulatory and development aids, the trade union movement, a system of grants for modernisation and adaptation, and the surveying and research work that in time would involve State bodies and the universities. He had a sense of this collective, corporate thinking, and he recognised that Ireland's needs would best be helped by such an approach. The legislation, the Industrial Efficiency and Prices Bill, came to nothing. Fianna Fáil went out of power, and the measure was dropped by the incoming administration. Today it remains an indicator of the man's thinking, and of the tentative debate going on in the party at the time.

Lynch's political character owes a great deal to the unwritten contract that existed within the party's dual leadership. Others who were influential included Frank Aiken, James Ryan and Seán MacEntee. During those first ten years as a deputy Lynch was privileged enough to enjoy junior ministerial office during the 1951 to 1954 Fianna Fáil administration, which led to his becoming fully committed to political life. Inevitably, he returned to the practice of law while in opposition between 1954 and 1957, though continuing to represent his Cork constituency.

*

The decade of the 1950s, which was to shift and change in its final three years during which the foundations for the future were to be laid, was a sad decade for many unavoidable reasons connected with poverty and loss of confidence. But it was also a period in which real opportunities of thought and planning about the nation's future were fumbled and misjudged. Some knowledge of this is essential to an understanding of political evolution during the period, and of how it influenced Jack Lynch. He was, after all, to spend much of the next ten years in political appointments that dealt directly with the practicalities of planning the Irish economy. Perhaps, more importantly, in all this he was to be drawn into increasingly close contact with the pivotal figure in Irish economic development from the mid-1950s onward, Dr T.K. Whitaker.

Whitaker was appointed Secretary of the Department of Finance in 1956 on the recommendation of Gerard Sweetman, Minister for Finance in the outgoing second Inter-Party Government. It was an unprecedented choice in that Whitaker was moved into the most powerful position in the Irish Civil Service ahead of more senior officials in the Department. It concluded the remarkable early trajectory of an outstanding career, placing Whitaker at the centre of the country's future development throughout a substantial part of Lynch's own career.

Sweetman justified his proposal of Whitaker for the top job in the Irish Civil Service in a brief but pithy observation: "Whitaker was the most qualified man for the position. It was that easy."[14] Here was an enlightened politician whose

---

[14] Interview with Gerard Sweetman on 6th August 1969 by John F. McCarthy, editor of

35

thinking was not too far removed from that of Seán Lemass acting in a way that Lemass himself might have found eccentric. Sweetman had witnessed, during his own somewhat frustrating and sterile period in the Department, the emergence under Whitaker's direction of the necessary thinking and planning for the future which was now to come to fruition. It was on the strength of this that he acted.

Whitaker's personal strategy went back some years. As early as 1950 he had put to the then Secretary of the Department, J.J. McElligott, the idea for a new post – designed for himself – of assistant secretary with a roving brief essentially aimed at the formulation of policy. Whitaker actually phrased it more adroitly in his memorandum: "that of assisting the head of division and yourself in any problems you might set me."[15] It meant that he gained the freedom to study and prepare for economic development and planning when the circumstances for action arose.

Unfortunately, other circumstances intervened affecting the country's economic strategy, and the kind of national development programme which Ireland needed did not emerge. The politics of the period were only one of the factors contributing to this. On the one hand there were the unavoidable strains within the two Inter-Party Governments. On the other hand, during both periods of office, 1948–1951 and 1954–1957, the ideological flexibility and range of thought and ambition were too great for the kind of concerted and focused thinking that was needed.

Ironically, the earlier Inter-Party Government produced a kind of prototype for later planning documents in a White Paper entitled *The European Recovery Programme: Ireland's Long Term Programme (1949-1953)*. But this was in reality a formal reflection of the view taken by the United States of Ireland's post-war needs, and its real function was to ensure that the country obtained at least a share of the dollars flowing into a Europe ravaged by warfare. Whitaker was quite frank when he said:

> [It was] never conceived as a programme for policy. It was conceived as something to satisfy the Americans so that we could get Marshall Aid... We were putting together the most plausible memo we could...[16]

In a limited way, the outlining of a national programme of much-needed investment worked, and for a period the dollars flowed into Ireland. But the Marshall Aid money was directed into capital investment almost certainly of the wrong kind. It went to land reclamation, rural electrification and fertilisation. It did not go to the creation of industrial development, and therefore failed to create jobs, with the result already outlined, of widespread unemployment and chronic emigration.

Planning Ireland's Future: The Legacy of T.K. Whitaker (Glendale Press, Dublin, 1990), p. 14.
[15] Author's interview with Dr T.K. Whitaker, August 1986.
[16] *Ibid.*

It had all ended by 1951, when American aid ceased. Perhaps because of this, perhaps simply because its policies at the time were dominated by a conservatism reflecting fear of radical innovation from the mixed parties opposed to them, when Fianna Fáil came to power in 1951 they did nothing about planning. An independent, private enterprise plan for Ireland was produced, but no action was taken.

Sweetman himself was enlightened and forceful but quite conservative. He served in the second Inter-Party Government, as Minister for Finance, with colleagues of widely different political thought, included men such as Seán McBride, arguably more radical than any member of the Labour Party at the time. Without the benefit of United States monitoring, and even more importantly, without the funding which had motivated the policy in the period 1948–1951, Sweetman could do little in respect of development planning beyond his inspired choice of a future leader for the Civil Service.

This rather complicated background was familiar enough to Lynch, cutting his political teeth on the turbulent first ten years as a Dáil deputy. He was witness to the strange phenomenon of de Valera and Lemass presenting two sides of a party's ideology; one of them in keeping with the old traditional ways of governance, the other seeking new departures.

The drama of change and reform presented in the period before the 1957 general election tends to place heavy, even disproportionate, emphasis on the contribution of Lemass. It is sensible to see that it was not exclusively his thinking that brought about the great transition towards effective government planning. For one thing, Whitaker was a significant contributor, working with chosen officials and having the freedom to act which his own special appointment in the Department gave him. Even before his appointment as Secretary of the Department, he had been working quite consistently on the kind of detailed measures that would be needed to effect the process of capital formation and its investment. Whitaker influenced the establishment of the Capital Investment Advisory Committee 1955, and read a paper to the Statistical and Social Inquiry Society in May of 1956; by stressing the need for more productive investment, it laid down part of the groundwork for the more comprehensive survey of national needs and potentialities that was to follow in 1957–1958.

By the time Fianna Fáil faced the watershed election of 1957, "Dev's Disciple", the sportsman from Cork with his good looks, his well-built frame, his undoubted and proved qualities of leadership and of sporting prowess, had accommodated himself to the new and challenging deputy leadership of Lemass. He had broadened his experience and his understanding to embrace the future needs of Ireland as much as he had adopted the political and historic traditions of the country's largest party and its role in Ireland's future. He had a profession and a modest career at the bar. He was happily married, with a home in Dublin and a base in Cork. He was ready for larger challenges and greater responsibilities.

CHAPTER THREE

"The most calm man I have ever dealt with"

– James Dukes

Jack Lynch was in his fortieth year at the time of the 1957 general election. He had been part of an earlier administration, consisting mainly of old men. He had then shared the opposition benches in the Dáil chamber with the same founding figures of the Fianna Fáil party. Together, they had witnessed the crumbling of the second Inter-Party Government during a period described by Ken Whitaker as "a dark night of the soul, shared by the principal politicians both in and out of office and by concerned citizens and public servants".[1] Whitaker wrote about the sense of despair at the time, that "after thirty-five years of native government people are asking whether we can achieve an acceptable degree of economic progress".[2] When he reconsidered it many years later, it was to add that "the years 1955 and 1956 had plumbed the depths of hopelessness".[3]

Nevertheless, the process of politics was producing action. Seán Lemass in opposition, as at all times, read voraciously and thought a great deal about worldwide economic change that seemed to be leaving Ireland behind. He developed a Keynesian prescription of increased public investment to generate jobs. He set publicly a target figure of 100,000 jobs, and gave an undertaking that these would be delivered in five years. He made a speech in October 1955 to a party meeting in the restaurant of the Dublin department store, Clerys, which had become a kind of Fianna Fáil club for major Dublin party meetings. The speech is part of the folklore of economic planning, and was dubbed at the time "the 100,000 jobs speech". It broke one of those time-honoured rules of political promises in that it offered a specific target within a specific time frame. The rule is one or the other, but not both. Lemass also announced it in the early months of 1956, in an *Irish Press* newspaper supplement.[4]

---

[1] Interview with the author, August 1986.
[2] John F. McCarthy, ed., *Planning Ireland's Future: The Legacy of T.K. Whitaker* (Glendale Press, Dublin, 1990), p. 50.
[3] Interview with the author, August 1986.
[4] Lemass later laid it down as a political maxim that all electoral promises become invalid on the day of the count. But on this occasion he was too deeply and too publicly committed.

It came at a critical moment for the Inter-Party Government. The country had run into serious balance of payments difficulties. Increased importation of consumer goods had not been matched by revenue from agriculture. Tourist earnings were static, and so were the remittances which now formed a staple element in national income but which were not growing sufficiently in line with the actual levels of past emigration. Twice in 1956, in the spring and in the summer, Gerard Sweetman, the Minister for Finance, imposed levies on a range of imports and these had the desired effect, giving Ireland a trade surplus in the following year. But the immediate results were a further rise in unemployment, an increase in emigration, and a succession of protests by the unemployed. Uniquely for the country, this collective "dark night of the soul" was palpable for everyone. Many of those who emigrated did so not because they did not have employment, but simply because the atmosphere of black despair about Ireland's future was too much to bear. The population of the country reached its lowest level ever during these closing years of the 1950s, down to 2,818,341 in the 1961 Census.

The election itself was sparked off by Fianna Fáil tabling a motion of no confidence in the Dáil in January 1957. Seán MacBride had effectively pulled the rug from under the Inter-Party coalition by withdrawing support. He, with two other party members, had not been part of the administration, but generally had endorsed its policies. He now opposed Sweetman's handling of the economy and what he saw as his right-wing and oppressive measures during 1956, a very difficult year. He also reacted negatively to John A. Costello's handling of the renewed IRA campaign against the security forces in Northern Ireland, which had resumed in 1956. Rather than face the no confidence vote, Costello sought a dissolution on 4th February choosing a month-long election campaign.

Lemass had prepared himself and his party on the economic front. de Valera was equally ready for a campaign which everyone knew would be his last. His message was simple and uncompromising: coalitions did not work. At the age of 75 he barnstormed the country, delivering the word to huge mass meetings, to the accompaniment of brass and pipe bands and torchlight processions. It was a prodigious performance.

Almost in the background, but no less effectively, Lemass was following up on his own reasoned and, by now, well-developed arguments in favour of public investment designed to create "100,000 new jobs". This "policy" was now repeated, in amended form, in various other speeches, statements and documents. It was a Keynesian prescription. Designed to allocate sufficient public funding to productive investment, its overall purpose was to reduce the chronic unemployment.

The combination of Lemass, the economic pragmatist, and de Valera, the Father of the Country, effectively leading Fianna Fáil side by side, worked in

His successor was in a parallel situation after the 1977 election, with far more damaging results.

electoral terms. The party won a record 78 seats. Fine Gael won 40 seats, Labour 12. There were 17 independents or small party deputies. Four of these were Sinn Féin and had run on an abstentionist ticket, winning in Monaghan, South Kerry, Longford-Westmeath and Sligo-Leitrim. Clann na Poblachta was virtually wiped out, with Seán MacBride losing his seat, while Clann na Talmhan, the farmers' party, took 3 seats.

Lemass, who was Tánaiste, exercised a certain measure of control over the appointments in that last de Valera-led administration, and was responsible for sidetracking Seán MacEntee into Health and away from Finance, the portfolio he had held in the previous Fianna Fáil administration. Instead, James Ryan took over this position. Lemass also vetoed the reappointment of Gerald Boland; his son, Kevin, newly elected to the Dáil, was given a place in the Government. He was one of the very few deputies in the Dáil to be appointed a member of the Government on his first day.[5] De Valera was able to give the father the rather dubious excuse that he could not have two generations of one family in the same administration. He could reinforce this by pointing to himself; his own son, Vivion de Valera, a man of some ability, had by then been a Dáil deputy for twelve years and he never saw ministerial office.

The size of the new administration was slightly expanded to fourteen from the twelve men who had served under de Valera between 1951 and 1954. That had been smooth and unchanging; this new Government was to contain several alterations leading up to the changeover from de Valera to Lemass in June 1959. An early upheaval was the death in November of Seán Moylan, Minister for Agriculture. He was succeeded in that position by Patrick Smith. In addition to Kevin Boland, other new Fianna Fáil Ministers were Neil Blaney, Micheál Ó Moráin and John Ormonde. Erskine Childers, who had already served a full government term while Lynch was a Parliamentary Secretary between 1951 and 1954, was in charge of Lands briefly, then became Minister Without Portfolio, and finally was responsible for Transport and Power. Lynch, Ó Moráin, Blaney, Boland and Childers, together with Frank Aiken, were the only Ministers to serve through from de Valera's last Government to Jack Lynch's first Government, formed in 1966.

*

Jack Lynch became Minister for Education in the new Government. He also held the Gaeltacht portfolio briefly which then went to Micheál Ó Moráin. Lynch later claimed, in another of the many references on which is based the idea of his reluctance about a political career, that both he and Máirín would have preferred the development of his legal career at this time. He does not mention the stronger pull that de Valera had. He offered Jack a ministry and Jack replied:

---

[5] Two others were Noel Browne and Martin O'Donoghue.

"My wife wouldn't like it." Dev said: "We all have trouble with our wives."[6] The details of the appointment were not discussed, just membership of the Government. Only on the day the Government was formed did Jack ask: "What Ministry to you have in mind?" He was told Education. The action that he took in accepting this influential ministry with its high profile, which would involve a great deal of hard work, effectively meant he was burning his boats as far as a legal career was concerned. The decision was of fundamental importance in determining his future in politics. It meant that he had entered the highest level of power, as a member of the Government, and had accepted one of the more onerous workloads at the time, in a Department that had huge significance throughout the country.

Education was a major challenge for Lynch, but an attractive one at an otherwise rather grim time for Ireland. The country had undoubtedly gone through a period of despair and hopelessness in the mid-1950s, and this final election of the decade was very much a watershed. Economic progress, which had been at a virtual standstill, was being offered in the election campaign as the central issue of practical politics. It was presented side by side with the more emotional message from de Valera that a single, united party, with clear aims and unity of purpose under a strong father figure, would be able to achieve a comprehensive national recovery. Public investment was the engine for change and for growth.

Lemass was linked in the public mind with policy intentions designed to bring down unemployment and end the equally high levels of emigration. What he had been proposing now seemed to be the only solution. At least, that was the judgement of the electorate. Unemployment was the humiliating nub of Ireland's stagnation. It had reached very substantial numbers during the previous ten years. Its character was complex; a proportion of those who went abroad were married men who simply could not provide for their families and so they took jobs in Britain, sending funds home. But many of the emigrants were young people who, on completion of their education, simply went abroad. They were not tied to the idea of remittance; they were not committed to return. They were simply looking for a worthwhile life for themselves. If it was to be found across the water, then they would pursue it there.

At that time the main direction of emigration was into Britain. The jobs market there was healthy and, as many of the Irish immigrants were well-educated, Britain's economic growth gave them unparalleled prospects for the future. "The common talk among parents in the towns, as in rural Ireland, is of their children having to emigrate as soon as their education is complete in order to be sure of a reasonable livelihood."[7] Inevitably, the impact of this was to debilitate the economic circumstances at home by taking away from the economy the initiatives and skills it so badly needed and further undermining confidence in the future.

When Jack Lynch joined it, in the spring of 1957, the Department of Education

6 Finbarr Lynch, interview with the author, August 2001.
7 T.K. Whitaker, *Interests* (Institute of Public Administration, Dublin, 1983), pp. 67–68.

could be characterised cynically as an intellectual passport office for emigrants to Britain. More realistically, and whatever the destiny of the young people passing through the system, education was one of the country's real strengths. It clearly had to be managed in the light of overall government policy which was to reverse the dismal economic conditions and introduce effective planning. It was critical that education should become a part of this.

Though Lynch's time in the Department was relatively short, it was important for him in proving himself as a capable Minister and good working colleague within the government team. He took to the work with enthusiasm and displayed a prodigious energy. At that time he travelled to Cork every Friday evening, returning to Dublin early on the Monday morning in time to be in his office in the Department in Marlboro Street at around nine-thirty. His private secretary in the Department, James Dukes, remembers him always bringing back a substantial amount of work for him, including constituency and departmental correspondence. He spent an hour, sometimes two hours, each morning with Lynch. When the Dáil was sitting he would go over the River Liffey to Leinster House.

At that time government Ministers had offices in a corridor along the curving wing of the building. They were small and cramped. When the Minister was seeing anyone, the private secretary, who had nowhere else to go, stood outside. The corridor became an uncomfortable ante-chamber for private secretaries. "We were a kind of Mafia."[8] Much of the private secretaries' work involved communicating with other Departments on behalf of the Minister to sort out constituency queries. It meant the rapid acquisition of a working knowledge of all Departments. "Jack Lynch was the most calm man I have ever dealt with in my life. He hated anything that was done wrong. He always planned his time well and fitted in a lot of work."[9] Dukes remembers him as a kindly man, not as electric as Donogh O'Malley, and not particularly humorous:

> He was immensely courteous to everyone. He didn't give his opinions easily. He liked to mull things over. He liked to consider every bit of evidence – a product of his legal training – and he was good on legislation.[10]

The impression is of a man who did not have any very close relationships with other Ministers. He kept largely to himself. While Lynch was in Education Dukes remembers that Erskine Childers, who had little enough to do in the Department of Lands and who read a great deal, used to send Lynch cuttings from magazines and newspapers about educational matters. Memo tags were attached, offering the documents as helpful or useful. Though it sounds rather officious it was meant to be co-operative and Dukes knew that these Childers missives were sent

---

[8] Interview with James Dukes, June 2001.
[9] *Ibid.*
[10] *Ibid.*

in other directions as well. "Lynch never read them! An immense pile grew in the corner of the office, and was ignored."[11]

Lynch at this time formed a close relationship with Paddy Hillery, and Dukes attributes to this the fierce support given later by Hillery when the Arms Crisis developed. Lynch and Padraig Faulkner, according to Dukes, also became close. Though Faulkner was a backbencher, newly elected in 1957, he was a teacher and an Irish speaker, and he had first met Lynch in Donegal when Lynch, then parliamentary secretary, had visited an Irish-speaking school for an event with de Valera.

Initially, confidential correspondence to the Minister was given to him unopened, but in due course Dukes had access to everything, and when Lynch was indisposed on a couple of occasion Dukes went out to the Garville Avenue house to work with him there. He formed a high opinion of Máirín Lynch's abilities.

Education at the time was not without controversy. The Department had an image of conservatism. Within the teaching profession there was widespread recognition of change and reform in other countries not matched in Ireland. Within the news media generally the Department was criticised for this lack of progress. But the controversy was not particularly public. There was unease, but the teachers were not prepared to side with public critics in the newspapers, and the Catholic Church was decidedly reluctant to side with anyone. If changes were to be made they would be achieved by a comparatively quiet revolution within the Department.

Jack Lynch met with a broad measure of good will on his appointment. He was faced with budgetary cuts which he chose to leave in place, emphasising the hard times the country had come through, but at the same time offering an amelioration if possible the following year, giving a special emphasis to the undertaking as it applied to vocational education. He gave his speech in Irish. This was normal at the time, though some Ministers still split up their addresses, using English for certain parts. Lynch's previous ministerial experience working in the Gaeltacht had by now equipped him to deal comprehensively in the traditional way. He was well received.

Negative speeches were made by Dr Noel Browne and P.J. Lindsay. The latter savaged him using statements about education made by the teacher organisations. Lynch was selective in his reply, identifying aspects where criticisms could be answered, but by no means giving any undertakings he could not honour. It was a course of prudence. Though the education issues at the time were numerous, they centred essentially on the Catholic Church's role and the degree to which it was in charge. This point was made by John J. O'Meara, Professor of Latin at University College Dublin, and its format seemed to combine a fairly trenchant attack on the Department of Education while at the same time warning those who wanted reform to recognise the Catholic Church's position:

As long as the vast majority of the people of this country continue in such

43

loyalty to the Church and while the Church holds, as she will continue to hold, a very special viewpoint in connection with the end of education in any community, the influence of the Church here in education will not only be paramount, but decisive.[12]

O'Meara also proposed a link between his own university and Trinity College. It was neither the first nor the last time that such a proposal would be made.

The deference to the Catholic Church was intense and in certain circumstances led to excesses where the requirements of the law became secondary to the supposed influence of the bishops. There was an unwritten law that new schools in any diocese had to have the approval of the bishop. It was reversed only by the courage of individual founders of schools going ahead anyway, thereby forcing the recognition of the Department. Neither the bishops nor the Department had created this situation. The Department acted on the basis that if the bishop's approval had not been gained there would be no pupils. The bishops never insisted on departmental collaboration.

While Lynch kept his own counsel on these Church-related matters, he did become involved in the Irish language controversy that developed, again not for the first or last time, around the teaching of Irish. Serious criticism developed out of an address to a conference in Dublin of the British Association for the Advancement of Science in September 1957. An academic from University College Dublin, Father E.F. O'Doherty provoked an angry response from the language lobby when he claimed, not without considerable justification, that the promotion of Irish in the country was being done by means of "pseudo-bilingualism". He also claimed that it was "psychologically, emotionally and educationally bad for children".[13]

Lynch was understandably supportive of the Irish language, not only on account of his dual responsibility for the Gaeltacht, but also because of his earlier appointment as Parliamentary Secretary with Gaeltacht responsibilities in the 1951–1954 administration. His ministerial response on this occasion was to regret in general terms the attacks being made on the language and the hostile attitudes towards the language movement. It was a huge issue and went far beyond the field of education in which Lynch himself was directly involved. It was to be some years before government policy gradually changed. But Father O'Doherty both sustained and narrowed his criticism, drawing a line between the teaching of Irish in national schools, of which he approved, and the use of it as an exclusive medium of instruction. He disapproved of this in terms that were impressive

---

[11] Interview with James Dukes, June 2001.

[12] Lecture by John J. O'Meara entitled "Reform in Education", March 1958 (published later that year by the Mount Salus Press, Dublin, p. 5). The passage is quoted in Seán O'Connor's *A Troubled Sky, Reflections on the Irish Educational Scene 1957–1968*, on which I have drawn for the purposes of this chapter.

[13] *Ibid.*

enough – though he was in general ignored – to begin the important process of reconsideration.

It was not a schools problem. If Irish were to be restored as the vernacular of the country then the doctrine, widely held at the time, that this would be achieved through the schools, was not only nonsensical but was gravely unfair to the pupils in Ireland's national schools where the language burden lay most heavy. There was a virulent streak in the revivalist lobby; it was easily antagonised and very vocal. It was not to be removed at one stroke. The natural order of things suggested by Father O'Doherty was to reverse the sense in which schools were creating a false environment for children who found on leaving that the world outside was not as Irish speaking as they had been taught to expect. The schools were not preparing the child for an environment but creating one that was deceptive.

de Valera, a dedicated lover of the language, saw the sense of this dispute. The decision to have an inquiry into Irish teaching in schools came from his Parliamentary Secretary. Only later did Lynch announce the widened terms of reference to look at the "position in general" making it a matter, as he told the Dáil in May 1958 "for the Government, possibly for the Taoiseach". The widening of the scope was a mistake. Ideas were kicked around; nothing much happened and many other inquiries were to follow. However, Lynch did introduce the sensible measure of oral examinations in the subject, which was a more realistic approach to all language teaching and one that was widely recognised and praised.

It was not until January 1965 that the Government issued a White Paper on the language issue. This effectively represented the change for which Father O'Doherty had fought so fiercely. It was published in response to a Commission on the Revival of the Irish Language. As it happened, the source of the White Paper was largely the Department of Finance and the work that went into it was done in part by Dr T.K. Whitaker, who had a personal commitment. He was substantially the architect of the new policy. The aim was to restore the Irish language as a "general medium of communication" but to do so in a reasonable and reliable way. Whitaker's words were ameliorative, not confrontational. "To preserve and cherish Irish as the national language" was his interpretation of the White Paper's response to the Commission:

> ... to strengthen the Gaeltacht and extend the use of Irish as a living language, oral and written; and to give everyone growing up in Ireland, through knowledge of the language and its literature, wider access to our cultural heritage.[14]

Jack Lynch was not dynamic about the language; nor did he do well on the other

---

[14] With these words a long-standing but unachievable language policy was transformed, to the country's and to Fianna Fáil's benefit. These quotations are from *Interests* (above, n.7), p. 231.

highly controversial, emotive and publicly debated issue at the time which was corporal punishment. His legal training led him to make a proposal to change the way in which the *method* of corporal punishment was defined. This brought more criticisms down on his head, emphasising that he was failing to respond to the real and damaging existence in certain Irish schools, notably those run by the Christian Brothers, of fairly savage regimes of physical punishment. By delimiting methods he was allowing for the use of instruments of punishment like the strap. It was a blunder from which he was rescued by the anti-corporal punishment lobby pointing out the mistake and pressing on with a campaign for abolition. But he did less than he should have and it was to be many years before the disgraceful situation was put right.

The problem was the conventional but futile search for an alternative to corporal punishment instead of the recognition that it was quite simply unacceptable. There was the equally questionable convention of seeing the teachers *in loco parentis*. This was a cliché allowing for responsibility to be shifted around. Finally, there was the constitutional handicap of the State's inescapable requirement to give education to all children, thus precluding expulsion of the unruly. Jack Lynch was of his time. Huge battles, in which the Catholic Church had defeated the State for control, made the very idea of fundamental reform effectively impossible other than on a long-term basis, and Lynch was not the only Minister to be defeated by this assumption.

Another significant and potentially controversial reform was the removal of the ban on married women teachers. A negative reaction was anticipated from the Catholic Church. The view of the bishops, reportedly, was that they thought it unseemly for pregnant women to be seen by children in the classroom. There was also the wider conflict of the perception of working women undermining marriage and, therefore, family life. But the real issue was the shortage of trained teachers and the unnecessary draining of the supply by the ban. Lynch was aware of the dissatisfaction in the profession. When he announced the change his predecessor, General Richard Mulcahy, was incensed that he had not been informed that such a change was possible. It went through without objection Lynch, handling the issue calmly, was widely praised. There was one notable exception. Dr Noel Browne attacked him, deploring what he claimed was a reprehensible tradition of appointing intellectual lightweights to the Department of Education. In a classic example of his elegant thunder against neglect, weakness, prevarication and inaction generally, he cut a swathe through the otherwise benign debate.

Lynch introduced a major building programme for St Patrick's Teacher Training College in Drumcondra, identifying this as the main centre for development. He also increased the per capita grants in both primary and secondary education, all part of the development programme which represented the implementation of Fianna Fáil election promises. At third level he established a commission to look into student accommodation, resulting in increased levels of student grants.

The close integration of education in the wider programme for economic development became a reality within the terms of the new programming. Reforms in general had the guarantee of civil service support, and of its key figure, the Secretary of the Department of Finance.

Lynch's adviser on primary education in the Department, who later became its Secretary, was Seán O'Connor. His book is the best published account of the relationship between the critical role of education and the political impact upon it.[15] Though not published until almost thirty years later, *A Troubled Sky* is almost certainly the product of contemporary notes or journals, and is detailed and lively. He describes Lynch as:

> ... a young man with ambition; it was his first post as Minister; he had a reputation to make... We felt that education was a staging post in his career, with Industry and Commerce as his next immediate objective.[16]

O'Connor's judgments on Lynch and policy are interesting. Lynch's immediate predecessor, General Richard Mulcahy, has given as his view that the State's role was minimal, and did not include the initiation of reforms. Its job was to fund the operation and leave everything else to the uneasy contract between the Church, the teachers, the parents and the pupils. This of course was an abrogation of duty. Lynch altered slightly this view while in the department, making it notionally a co-operative business, but stressing that the State "did not hold all the shares". He later claimed a modest directional role for the State as well as a responsibility to protect its financial interests. But neither Lynch nor de Valera, nor indeed the Government or the Fianna Fáil party, wanted a confrontation with the most powerful organisation in the country, the Catholic Church. Control of education was a primary principle on the Church's agenda, echoed, it must be said, by the Church of Ireland.

---

[15] Seán O'Connor, *A Troubled Sky, Reflections on the Irish Educational Scene, 1957–1968* (Fallon, Dublin, 1983).
[16] *Ibid.*

CHAPTER FOUR

"A dawn in which it was bliss to be alive"

– Ken Whitaker

For the first time in a decade the country was beginning to have a coherent and reasonably comprehensive programme for political action. It was not immediate, but from the 1957 general election on there was a new presentiment of good fortune and of recovery. Despite de Valera's age, or perhaps because of it, and well before the actual changeover to Lemass, a smooth and invisible transition began. It was already taking place without the pieces being moved. Though a member of the Government, Jack Lynch played no part in what happened in the leadership changeover. "I wasn't involved in Dev going to the Park," he flatly commented.[1]

This was a neutral expression of the fact that Jack Lynch's first political hero, the very reason for him being a member of Fianna Fáil, was Éamon de Valera. During the 1950s there was much agonising about the long-delayed departure of this septuagenarian. Some of those who agonised were more brutal about it than others. Never had W.B. Yeats's line "[t]hat is no country for old men" been more apt to the circumstances that prevailed in Ireland throughout this decade, and it now became even more pointed. The country required change. It demanded younger men to revitalise it.

The greatest servant of the State, at this time, was undoubtedly de Valera. He was surrounded by men of his own vintage, the tried and trusted team he had built up since coming to power in the early 1930s. Frank Aiken, James Ryan, Seán Lemass, Seán MacEntee and others were the backbone of that team. They had occasionally been moved from one portfolio to another. Since 1932 all the de Valera led administrations, which in each case constitutionally meant a Government of fifteen people or less, had only featured an overall total of twenty-two different personalities, all of them men. Since five of the changes in the make-up of these Governments had been occasioned by death or illness, this meant that de Valera had soldiered on with the same team. This says little for his sense of duty about bringing on new talent; although it does say much for his loyalty to old colleagues in arms. It can be excused more easily for the sixteen

---

[1] "My Life and Times" in *Magill* (November 1979), p. 40.

years of unbroken Fianna Fáil rule between 1932 and 1948. It is far less excusable that he continued as before after the period in opposition and in the light of the dismal circumstances of returning to power with a minority administration in 1951.

Professor Joe Lee has written movingly and with great perception of this period, and particularly of the dilemma surrounding de Valera and his party. "The Chief", a title and a role in which de Valera took such pride and pleasure, was, for all his subtlety, an innocent and even, perhaps, a harmless man. Comparing de Valera's dedication to the cult of being "Chief" with the sinister threat of dictators such as Hitler and Mussolini, Lee writes: "In few countries has so powerful a personality cult proved so relatively harmless as in de Valera's Ireland."[2] Harm, if it was inflicted, was of a peculiar kind. De Valera did create a myth, not just one surrounding himself, but surrounding his party as well. This, while it may have worked under Lemass and even Lynch, came to be a threat and led to political distortions under the personality cult developed by Charles Haughey.

De Valera's more obvious shortcomings manifested themselves particularly in his failure to grasp the realities and implications of an age in which industrialisation and commerce were dominant. "It was in one sense his misfortune that his career should coincide with an age of accelerated economic change whose causes and consequences largely baffled him."[3] That they were allowed to baffle him through two administrations, until the leadership changeover to Lemass in 1959, was a reflection of the benign circumstances of his leadership and heralded the immense problems of replacing him. If de Valera stayed, other old men stayed as well.

Within Fianna Fáil a central issue of the 1950s was that of leadership. It was not inevitable that it would go to Lemass. Seán MacEntee was originally a serious contender, though his performance as Minister for Finance had led to a loss of confidence in his judgement.

In assessing Jack Lynch's political character the importance of de Valera is central. It was he who initially inspired Lynch to follow Fianna Fáil and then to enter politics. He gave Lynch his first job in the party. This was during the period of opposition that followed Lynch's first election. de Valera went on to give him his first taste of political office. In a man as complex as de Valera, it is difficult to draw the strands of influence upon another man who, in his way, was equally complicated. Certainly, de Valera's continual search for a consensus within Fianna Fáil was central also to Lynch's political character as it developed. Like de Valera, Lynch worked within a conservatism that was inherently Irish, and with an understanding of the limitations, economic, social, moral and religious, imposed on the country by its position in the world. As a judge of character, de Valera has been faulted in terms of appointments, particularly in appointments from his

---

[2] J.J. Lee, *Ireland 1912–1985* (Cambridge University Press, 1989), p. 340.
[3] *Ibid.*

own generation and for delays in changing these, yet he created and maintained an entirely stable team of colleagues whom he could trust and rely on, and this enhanced his own standing. Lynch had the same approach. He faced a wholly different set of circumstances, and different interpretations of trust and loyalty within the party, particularly from the 1960s on, but he derived his essential working methods largely from de Valera.

The significance of de Valera as a formative influence has since been underrated, perhaps understandably, with Lynch presented as someone who grew up politically in Lemass's shadow. The argument is complicated by Lemass's position during the 1950s. Although it was clear that he would not become leader of Fianna Fáil until de Valera was ready to move on, Lemass bore the brunt of responsibility for whatever dynamism was going to direct the affairs of the country. He did not do this, as one might expect, from the Department of Finance, but as Minister for Industry and Commerce. This was his portfolio from the first Fianna Fáil Government, in 1932, through all the Fianna Fáil led administrations until he took over from de Valera as party leader and Taoiseach on 23rd June 1959.[4] He was the principal architect of the protection mentality. At the same time he was committed to the industrialisation of Ireland. He bore the burden of making what little the country had, in terms of resources, work properly. He was also the engine for its change and reform. A great deal depended on this man, but he needed to be in charge.

The party had conflicting views over its own future without de Valera as leader. He had been so clearly identified in the public mind with the party that its successful future without him seemed inconceivable to many people. He had overshadowed the undoubted talent and good judgement of his most obvious successor, Seán Lemass, while at the same time tolerating lesser men on the grounds that they were tried and trusted followers from the past. Given the uncertain performance of the party during the 1950s, de Valera must have seemed an even more important asset than he had been in earlier periods. Yet he was an old man, almost completely blind, and his time in active politics was up.

Jack Lynch's loyalty to de Valera was not in question; yet he must have looked with a faintly jaundiced eye on his leader from the perspective of the Department of Education. As Lee has pointed out, de Valera, though a teacher, was less than generous towards the aims of higher education:

> The inadequacy of the resources his government devoted to higher education helped sabotage the pursuit of that intellectual excellence which would seem to be a prerequisite for fostering the cultivation of the mind that he was so fond of proclaiming as Ireland's mission in the modern world.[5]

---

[4] From September 1939 to July 1943 he was Minister for Supplies, and Seán MacEntee wàs Minister for Industry and Commerce. Lemass combined the two portfolios, Industry and Commerce and Supplies from July 1943 to July 1945.

[5] Lee, above, n.2, p. 332.

His departure coincided with the end of Seán T. O'Kelly's second term as President, and de Valera was put forward as Fianna Fáil candidate to succeed him. Combined with the presidential election, the Government also introduced a referendum to replace proportional representation with a straight vote. This would have ensured sizeable majorities for Fianna Fáil, cementing them in power for the foreseeable future against a mixed bag of opposition parties. The electorate put de Valera in as President, but rejected the proposed change in the voting system. Seán Lemass took over as party leader and formed the country's ninth Government, promoting Lynch to the ministry he had occupied himself, Industry and Commerce.

*

Perhaps unusually for a newly elected Government, from 1957 Fianna Fáil surpassed its election promises. Instead of sitting back with some relief after the substantial election victory, the party took action. There was the steady transformation of the country's economic circumstance from despair to hope. It was achieved, as Lemass had said it should be, by the stemming of emigration, and the creation of jobs. It may not have precisely followed Lemass's "100,000 jobs" blueprint, nor was it done immediately, but, from the beginning of Fianna Fáil's period in office, the process of economic recovery proceeded relatively smoothly and according to plan.

Central to economic recovery generally, and to economic planning as it had evolved in the hands of Dr T.K. Whitaker, was the move from protectionism to free trade. Whitaker has made the point that "nobody but the ultimate protectionist, the architect of it all, Seán Lemass, could have brought us from protection to free trade."[6]

The evolution of the plan had a curious chronology. The process actually began in January 1957, *before* the dissolution of the Dáil and the general election. In that month Whitaker commenced work on a study of Ireland's economy in its broadest context. He continued to work at it during and after the general election. Although he regularly saw his new Minister, Dr James Ryan, during the early period of the new Government, he did no more than mention economic planning in general terms. He was, of course, operating at two levels: he was responsible to his Minister for the running of a large and complex Department at the heart of the country's financial administration; he was also attempting a comprehensive planning process which required vision and foresight.

Not unnaturally, in the first year in office, the Minister was concerned primarily with what was happening, rather than with distant promises. But towards the end of the year Whitaker handed his Minister a memorandum which

---

[6] Interview with Andy O'Mahony for a programme on Seán Lemass in series of programmes entitled "Na Taoisigh: Leaders of the State", broadcast by RTÉ on Saturday, 23rd June 2001.

summarised the document which would eventually be published as *Economic Development*, and from which would be extrapolated the material for the government White Paper. Ryan gave Whitaker his support and urged the Government to do the same. It was agreed that all Departments would co-operate in the work of Whitaker's team, the two principal figures of which were Charles Murray, who succeeded him as Secretary, and Maurice Doyle.

It is hard to overestimate the significance of this publication in terms of medium and long-range political strategy. There was unity of purpose within a civil service structure often enough characterised by rivalries. Perhaps most important of all, there was the integration of politicians and public servants in a common cause that transcended the normal workings of the Executive with the administration and very different responsibilities of each Department. Agriculture, for example, was given a high priority, with much debate and redrafting of its sections. Industrial development was already well advanced in Whitaker's thinking. He himself took over the role of discussing with key Departments, including the Department of Education under Lynch, how their work would all be fitted together.

Economic Development in its draft form came to the Government on 17th December. Lynch's recollection was that Dr James Ryan was not particularly enthusiastic about the plan, but added: "Ryan was not too enthusiastic about anything."[7] This may have been deliberate on Ryan's part. An interesting cross-section of men around that government table had to be brought to a consensus over planning. The first year in power had not been easy, and pressure was on to go public with a strategy that would be new and different. The support of de Valera was critical. This was done by making him believe that Fianna Fáil was engaged in the fulfilment of policies which were at the heart of the party's political beliefs *and had always been there*. Years later, he claimed: "We set out those policies in 1926 at the formation of Fianna Fáil."[8] The party did no such thing. There was nothing in that original founding manifesto remotely connected with what Whitaker had written, and what Ryan presented, on that fateful day. But de Valera was brought to believe in *Economic Development* by the presentation of it as the embodiment of a deeply held and traditional evolution of what had gone before.

Lemass was already committed. The Government backed the draft. There were months of wrangling over the format and whether it should be anonymous or identified with its true author, the Secretary of the Department of Finance. Eventually, Whitaker's role was identified. The draft became his published economic strategy. From it a committee extrapolated the material for the shorter official government White Paper, with the title *Programme for Economic Expansion*. This was later to become universally known as "The First Programme", since it was eventually succeeded by a second and a third.

---

[7] John F. McCarthy, ed., *Planning Ireland's Future: The Legacy of T.K. Whitaker* (Glendale Press, Dublin, 1990), p. 50.
[8] *Ibid.*, p. 51.

There was a good deal of argument about how best to publish the plan. Lemass prevailed over some members of Government who did not want Whitaker identified. The crucial figure was Dr James Ryan. Ostensibly he wanted public recognition for Whitaker and his team. "The civil service never gets the credit it deserves."[9] However, there were other reasons for his strategy. Responsibility would be shared, with public servants being pushed out in front to take the credit, but also, if planning failed, to take the blame. Moreover, Whitaker, as an appointee of Sweetman, drew the source of his power from mixed political origins.

The White Paper was rapidly prepared and published on 11th November with individual copies going to every member of the Houses of the Oireachtas. Whitaker was invited to attend the Dáil for its formal presentation. He said of the work which he and his team had done:

> It was a kind of dawn in which it was bliss to be alive. There were a few small teams working on different aspects, such as industry and tourism. We worked into the night and were early to work, with real enthusiasm, the next morning. We were refreshed by our release from a purely negative role and the feeling that we were doing something constructive and worthwhile.[10]

Publicity was negligible: *The Irish Press* praised it; *The Irish Times* said there was nothing new in it; the *Irish Independent* did not comment. Eleven days later, on 21st November 1958, *Economic Development* was issued by the Government. Its grey cover and the need to distinguish it from the White Paper caused it to be nicknamed "The Grey Book". Its author was identified simply as "the Secretary of the Department of Finance". It was characterised as "a study of national development problems and opportunities". This time the press reception was different, with *The Irish Times* acknowledging the document's near-revolutionary importance and "the singularly independent, farsighted, and progressive" contribution of its author. The paper recognised publicly what had happened: economic planning had been effectively transferred to the Department of Finance and the shape of things to come had been placed in its Secretary's hands.

During the five years that followed, a period in which Jack Lynch became a central figure in the economic affairs of three administrations, the country's gross national product grew at a rate of 4 per cent a year which was twice the targeted growth. Unemployment dropped by one-third. The emigration rate of the second half of the 1950s was halved and the population once again began to increase. National investment doubled.

---

[9] Letter from Ryan to McCarthy, quoted in *Planning Ireland's Future: The Legacy of T.K. Whitaker* (Glendale Presss, Dublin, 1990), p. 56.

[10] McCarthy, above, n.7, p. 57.

*

Even before Lemass took over as Taoiseach, he indicated to Lynch that the younger man would become Minister for Industry and Commerce in the new Government. Lynch's own view of this, expressed later, was apparently unenthusiastic, but he felt he had little choice. Given that Lemass had spent nearly all his ministerial career in the one Department, the choice of Lynch to succeed him was a clear indication of trust and of admiration. Lemass had viewed it as a critical responsibility during the preceding quarter century. He certainly viewed it as a job that any future leader of the party would need to have experienced. While circumstances had changed sufficiently to give greater importance to the Department of Finance, a tendency reinforced by the new authority Whitaker brought to the economic planning process which was now concentrated there, Industry and Commerce was, and remained, a heavyweight responsibility. Its own status, in the critical new era of planning, was that of implementation. For a Minister with only two years' government experience, the appointment was onerous, and Lynch's reluctance is understandable. At that time all labour relations matters were dealt with by the Department of Industry and Commerce, which element caused Lynch some difficulty; later they were to be transferred to a newly created Department of Labour. In a typically human reflection on this, Lynch referred to "a number of occasions when I was called back from holiday because of strikes, and my wife and I lost a few holiday deposits during that period".[11]

His energies were mainly deployed, however, in the implementation of the First Programme. Its rather chilly press reception was followed by a slow and uncertain sequence of events. Despite his very real admiration for Lemass, Whitaker was at pains to ensure that the planning process would stick to public service rules rather than to the less stable political ones. Lemass had understandably linked economic planning to the creation of jobs, and by this means to the reduction of emigration. Admirable though this objective appeared to be, it was not really appropriate to the kind of planning which the First Programme sought to initiate. Whitaker specifically, and correctly, ruled out the setting of a target for so many jobs. He also excluded the construction of suitable plans to meet those goals, since disillusionment would be the likely result of such an approach. Setting targets was, however, characteristic of Lemass, and needed to be watched by those closest to him.

The implementation of the programme was delayed. *Economic Development* and the *Programme for Economic Expansion* were slow to be accepted, both in terms of public support and in practical implementation within the Civil Service. The original period for the planning was delayed. In the end it coincided closely with Lynch's time in the Department of Industry and Commerce. Because of delays, the fiscal years involved were 1959/1960 to 1963/1964. Some of the

---

[11] "My Life and Times" in *Magill* (November 1979), p. 41.

more controversial thinking in Whitaker's original document was modified and the Government, in its White Paper, introduced measures to sustain the agricultural sector, notably in favour of tillage over cattle, contrary to the theories propounded for a developing sector. Whitaker had also put forward the idea that industry should be encouraged in urban areas, whereas the Fianna Fáil Government, again responding to its traditional position, wanted industrial development to be rural. Apart from these minor, and understandable, political amendments, the plans which Whitaker had thought out and presented to the Government were generally followed. In the broader sense, a working and dynamic relationship was established between civil servants and politicians based on a level of idealism and vision not previously experienced and certainly not sustained in the same way in later years.

When Lynch moved from Education to Industry and Commerce, he had much more to do with Whitaker, and the two men had some involvement together in economic planning and its implementation. This relationship became even closer when Lynch moved to the Department of Finance in the Government formed in 1965. It would be fair to say that a good deal of Lynch's economic thinking, and some of his social and other views, were shaped by Whitaker, who was a considerable figure in Ireland's development in the second half of the twentieth century.

It would also be fair to say that Lynch on his own was never an original thinker in terms of policy, nor naturally disposed to innovative action. He was not a reformer. He saw the best in what existed and generally he liked what he saw. He was a hard worker and always dealt with his ministerial briefs efficiently. He took time to make decisions. His legal training made him judgemental and he sought a balanced, overall view on issues and on legislation. He was conscientious, and, as has already been reported from his time in the Department of Education, "the calmest of men".

*

The broad national targets that emerged as a result of realistic planning were all of direct significance to Lynch in his new appointment. What Whitaker had intended, which was "a substantial change in the direction of policy", involved, in his own words, "a purposeful co-ordination of development effort".[12] This meant in effect that industry had to confront the removal of tariff protection and the challenge of free trade. If this were successful, it would lead the country inevitably towards international partnerships. If jobs were created, in the wake of the growth rate forecast in the programme, then the management of industrial relations would require greater political involvement and in due course the creation of formal working relationships between labour, management and the State. In all this, as Lemass intended, Lynch was to play a significant role.

---

[12] McCarthy, above, n.7, p. 51.

Lemass had achieved the transition through Ryan, his Minister for Finance, who had handled so adroitly the revolutionary transformation deriving from Whitaker's planning. In the first period of its implementation, up to the 1961 general election, the Taoiseach relied heavily on Ryan (and through him, of course, on Whitaker) to maintain and stimulate the growth and the many changes that it heralded.

Lemass was not a particularly good party manager. Whitaker, who worked closely with him and was a great admirer, came to the conclusion that the role of the leader of party and country "did not appeal to him as much as being a progressive crusader on his own." On the other hand, he was decisive:

> [Decision making] was the thing he could do best of all. To postpone, to delay or not to take a decision was the worst decision of all. I think that the role of the chairman, or judge, didn't appeal to him as much as being a progressive crusader on his own.[13]

There were figures, including some very senior members of Fianna Fáil, who disapproved of the upheavals which economic success would bring. Sure enough, there was industrial unrest and a real fear of the impact of free trade, but the critical control of activity was in the hands of four Departments: Finance, Industry and Commerce, Agriculture, and, to a lesser extent, Foreign Affairs. The Secretaries of these Departments and in the case of the first three their Ministers, provided the core activity, with the civil servants reporting to a government sub-committee chaired by Lemass. The major exchanges, many of a highly practical kind, were between Finance and Industry and Commerce, and Lemass, who had a clear grasp of its implications, saw much of this material.

A great deal was put in place between the delivery of the First Programme and *Economic Development* in 1958 and the general election in 1961. It climaxed in the Anglo-Irish trade agreement of April 1960, and the decision to follow Britain into the European Economic Community if the UK's application for membership went ahead. This in turn raised many defence and neutrality issues, and produced from Lemass a sensible and enlightened approach that clearly characterised his "European" disposition on the main questions about Ireland's future.

His political platform, when he called a snap election in September 1961, was not without defect. There was industrial unrest and even a sense of crisis, and Lemass was not a dynamic campaigner on the hustings. Issues other than the economy intervened, and the declared purpose of the election – to clear the way for Ireland's application to join Europe – was faintly unconvincing. It raised the very issues which had emerged as a result of Ireland's new view of itself in Europe, including NATO membership – on which Lemass had decidedly positive views – and, of course, neutrality. But an additional problem was the absence of

---

[13] T.K. Whitaker, in RTÉ programme on Lemass, above, n.6.

de Valera. The party had always feared the reliance placed on the shoulders of the Chief, and it had been a compelling reason to allow him to stay as long as his judgement so indicated. Under a new leader, the old magic was replaced by something rather different: a pragmatist without much charisma.

As one historian of the period put it: "When the votes were counted, Dev's successor had suffered a serious rebuff from the electorate. He was denied an overall majority."[14] Fianna Fáil had in fact lost eight seats and was destined to remain in power as a minority administration, a situation subsequently repeated in the following general election, which confirmed Lemass's limited public appeal. It also confirmed something slightly more positive, which was the stabilising of the party's support sufficiently to end the party merry-go-round of Irish politics in the 1950s. Though they were not to know it, Fianna Fáil was set to enjoy a second sixteen-year term in office. Despite the poor result, commentators who have written about the period have described the Government formed in 1961 as arguably the best the State has ever had.

Immense thought and vision had gone into the raising of economic planning to a central and dominant role in political life; and the energy and experience brought real rewards. These were evident in economic growth, employment, industrial expansion, greater entrepreneurial skills in trade and a confidence in the country that was equally balanced between the two main social partners, the employers and the unionised workers. But it did not bring undiluted harmony. The burden of dealing with problems that in time became either intractable or endemic, including the exercise of trade union power leading to lengthy and damaging strikes, fell on Jack Lynch's shoulders. It took the shine off the country's sense of its new-found worth.

Lynch returned to the Department of Industry and Commerce and it placed him at the centre of political action from the 1961 general election onward. Until he took over from Lemass as leader of Fianna Fáil and Taoiseach in mid-November 1966, he was in this powerful Department and then in the even more influential Department of Finance.

For those involved in public life there was a glorious quality to those years. They were by no means perfect, in any material or social sense. Much was still wrong with the country. It was still finding its way. But the period was coloured by a quite palpable optimism. Whitaker's "dark night of the soul" was over. The expression captures the mood of despair in the 1950s so well. The sense in which those years had been suffered, and suffered deeply by so many people, belongs exclusively to them. Whatever subsequent historians have discovered, including many new grim features that have come to light in recent years, only those who lived through the period, tried to find work, brought up families, emigrated and then came back to start again, can fully appreciate how hard it all was. Now it not only lay in the past, it was quite literally replaced by an atmosphere

---

[14] Dermot Keogh, *Twentieth-Century Ireland: Nation and State* (Gill & Macmillan, Dublin, 1994), p. 248.

characterised in Whitaker's equally compelling description of recovery taking place in a "dawn in which it was bliss to be alive".

The factor that changed all was the belief in the future. The country had a role and a purpose. It had a programme of action. It had targets for trade and for trade association. It was shaking off the armour of protection and putting on instead more civil clothing of enterprise and competition. Huge challenges remained, but they were challenges the country was confronting.

The centre of action was industrial and economic development, and a considerable part of this was directly Lynch's responsibility, now in his second term as Minister for Industry and Commerce. Within the Government itself he ranked somewhere around the middle in seniority. Lemass still had around him four very senior colleagues from the past in Seán MacEntee, Frank Aiken, James Ryan, and the slightly distant and reserved Cavan politician, Paddy Smith.

MacEntee, a brilliant thinker and an aggressive politician, had for long been regarded by his colleagues as a somewhat intemperate and extreme party figure, and had been retained in the comparatively controlled environment of Health and Social Welfare. He was Tánaiste or deputy Prime Minister and still a formidable figure in the Government, but he was less part of "The New Age". Aiken was similar in place and attitude, occupying the slightly isolated Department of External Affairs. His name had become synonymous with the "international" side of Ireland's affairs; a natural result of the fact that he had occupied this Department in every Fianna Fáil administration since the Second World War. External Affairs, however, did not include Anglo-Irish relations in the areas that now mattered so much, concerning free trade and market access. Nor did it directly impinge on Ireland's forthcoming application for membership of the European Economic Community, which Lemass rightly retained in his own portfolio. Finally, and wisely as well, Aiken was not involved in what was to emerge during this important period as a change of direction in respect of Northern Ireland. Instead, Aiken concentrated increasingly on representing Ireland in the free world. Even here, it must be said, Lemass dominated in terms of the definition of broad policy matters.

It was he who was endeavouring to shape a foreign policy that embraced an international commitment to the preservation of western democracy. The theory of it was expressed, and indeed observed with interest by the American administration, in the light of President Kennedy's visit to Ireland in the summer of 1963. Earlier, during the Cuban missile crisis, Ireland had demonstrated the country's support for the West, in the potentially devastating context of East-West conflict. The practical problem was that direct participation in any defence pact involved NATO, and this meant Ireland joining militarily with Britain. Lemass, and those who followed him, saw the political difficulty of this, and the support for democracy remained deeply principled but no more than that.

Paddy Smith was sixteen years Lynch's senior and had been a battalion commander of the IRA in 1920. He was first elected to the Dáil while in prison. He held government office from 1939 onward, was first appointed to the

Department of Agriculture by de Valera, and then reconfirmed in that position by Lemass. Lemass and Smith did not get on well, but Smith carried some weight in the party.

The fourth senior figure in this group of veterans around Lemass was Dr James Ryan. He was much more at the centre of action. He had presided shrewdly and well over Whitaker's economic revolution, and was a significant figure in the small ministerial team now directly involved in turning the economic plans into real advance and progress. They were a team, and they were making their way through stimulating economic territory that had its difficult side, both in terms of money and people.

*

Lemass himself became stigmatised by his expression of a belief in the rising tide that lifts all boats. This broad approach had a certain pragmatic appeal; but in essence it was laissez-faire. The reforms were concentrated in the realm of industrial action; much less so in terms of social change. Reform generally was directed towards those who were engaged in profitable and productive enterprise whose welfare was raised by the economic tide. Lemass was responsible for initiating national wage rounds. The national pay settlement of 1964 was introduced in the face of two by-elections that were critical to the minority Government. The political gesture created greater demand than the economy could justify, and a period of instability threatened. There were respects in which the careful planning of economic recovery began to unravel as demand exceeded growth. Despite the introduction of the generous 1964 wage round, there was a serious strike in the building industry in the autumn of 1964 that lasted some eight weeks. The Government sought to resolve this in a mollifying way. This approach angered the Agriculture Minister, Paddy Smith, who resigned abruptly.

His grounds for doing so were that the trade unions were running the country, with farmers suffering as a result. Lynch disapproved of Smith's resignation, which provoked what he saw as an unnecessary crisis, but he did recognise that a widening gap between the industrial and agricultural sectors was creating tensions which needed careful handling. Smith's resignation was handled adroitly by Lemass, who viewed the action as public trouble-making, and pre-empted Smith's attempt to explain himself in a press conference by swiftly appointing his own son-in-law, Charles Haughey, to the Agriculture portfolio.

Though Lynch's position was pivotal within the Government, those early years of the 1960s were characterised by the rise of a new generation within Fianna Fáil. These younger men who had been appointed to ministerial office during the unbroken succession of Fianna Fáil administrations from 1957 included in their number several key figures who would dominate the party for two decades. Lynch's view of them was benign and co-operative. As in sport, so in politics: they were part of the team, and all had a purpose and a role. He got on well with them. He was popular. Along with all of the others, he had the clear view that

Lemass was in power as leader for the foreseeable future, and that he had no inclination to hand over the reins of power.

Central to Lemass's nature was a visionary quality. He did seek to explore in his mind ideas about development and the refinement of economic and social life. But he had gone through a long and tiring political career, and in the early 1960s his hand on the tiller was slack enough. He allowed, even encouraged, views and opinions within his Government and inside the party that were both diverse and inventive. Inevitably, this liberality, which largely excluded the moralistic political attitude of his predecessor, led to a new materialism.

*

As a potential leader of the party, Lemass had marked Lynch's cards in respect of Northern Ireland. He did this by the initiative he took in visiting Stormont and meeting with the Northern Ireland Prime Minister, Terence O'Neill. The meeting took place on 14th January 1965, with Lemass driving up to Belfast and lunching at Stormont. Later in the afternoon other members of the Northern Ireland Cabinet met with Lemass and a joint statement was issued. The talks were amicable. They avoided constitutional or political issues and concentrated on matters of possible co-operation. All of this was expressed in cautious language, but it did not conceal the momentous nature of the occasion. Forty years had been bridged. A great gulf, probably at its greatest during the Republic's neutrality in the Second World War and also when the 1950s' IRA campaign on the Border was taking place, had been bridged. Classic, too, was the abruptness of the decision. It was not until Whitaker pointed out to Lemass the omission of informing the responsible Government member, the Minister for External Affairs, that Frank Aiken was informed of the invitation and its acceptance. Only on the day of the trip, after Lemass had picked up Whitaker from his home in the official car, was their driver informed of their destination. Lemass, at all times a brusque man, simply said: "Belfast, Henry."

The idea for the meeting came from O'Neill. He was an admirer of Seán Lemass. He saw him as the kind of person whom he would wish to emulate. Lemass, in O'Neill's eyes, "was a person of progressive instincts, of capacity, of energy. He would like to have been that kind of leader in Northern Ireland."[15]

Such a meeting would not have been possible with O'Neill's predecessor, Lord Brookeborough. It was an indication of changing times and an acknowledgment that free trade necessitated better relations between neighbours. It pointed the way towards better Anglo-Irish relations, and the promise of European integration. It seemed that a previously divided Ireland, in which the two communities had so little to say to each other, was being brought together. This gesture by Lemass and O'Neill, unprecedented in its dramatic impact, set a number of different agendas, but all of them were important.

---

[15] T.K. Whitaker, in RTÉ interview, above, n.6.

The first of these was an indication to the world at large of how the two parts of Ireland would see each other for the future. Lemass had certain international targets in his sights, and had developed a sense of the interests of the free world and of Ireland's place within that wider context. He had already redefined Ireland's attitude towards the United Nations and towards NATO, where he recognised its role in achieving international peace. To this he added the two closer objectives of redefining the political relationship between Ireland and Britain as a confirmation of the fresh initiative being taken on the trading front. An agreement built on the principle of freer trade between the two countries would be hollow without a more enlightened relationship between the two parts of Ireland. In a mood that was relaxed and harmonious, Lemass was offering guidelines as to how Northern Ireland might bring together its own divided communities, the Unionists and the Nationalists. He was well advised on the problems. What he could not know was how far ahead the agenda stretched.

Other meetings followed. In February Jack Lynch and Brian Faulkner met in Dublin to discuss economic co-operation, and Charles Haughey and Harry West met to discuss agriculture.[16] The cautious start ran into minor difficulties, with first O'Neill and then Lemass being pushed into definitions, Lemass having to make a rather nationalist, "one State, one Nation" speech. This was then further debated in the Dáil. It brought a statement from the British Secretary of State, Patrick Gordon Walker, that the problem was one to be settled by Irishmen.

It was a necessary political safeguard, in order to straighten out any uncertainty over where Lemass stood on the "National Question". Though the economy was in good shape, and growing at a fast rate compared with other European countries, the spectre of the 1950s, politically speaking, hung over the electoral landscape. The position taken by Lemass was a prelude to the early general election, brought on by the death of the Fianna Fáil deputy, Joseph Kennedy of Westmeath, that left the Government relying on the support of independents.

The Dáil was dissolved in February 1965 for a mid-March poll. Lemass came back to power, though again without getting a comfortable majority. He was dogged by the limitations of the proportional representation system, and this was clear enough in the result. Fianna Fáil seats increased from 70 to 72, but with Fine Gael at 47, Labour with 22, and with independents, the balance of power was uncomfortably even. The results were very close in some constituencies. The High Court refused a Fine Gael appeal for a recount in Longford-Westmeath which was successfully appealed, and the recount then went on for five days. It resulted in the election by fourteen votes of P.J. Lenihan, the father of Brian and of Mary O'Rourke. Another lengthy recount took place in Dublin north-east, with four votes dividing the last two candidates. Two

---

[16] Lemass, ever the pragmatist, advised Lynch to meet an adverse comment by Brian Faulkner over trade levies by granting Northern Ireland special status for products originating there. Lynch went ahead with the announcement of this (see National Archives document S162721.) I am indebted to John Horgan, who drew my attention to this.

independents, one of them Seán Loftus, who was to have an interesting, somewhat marginal role in politics for many years to come, considered challenging the constitutionality of not being able to have the name of his party, the Christian Democrats, on the ballot paper.

Before the Dáil's reassembly for the formation of the new administration, Lemass said that perhaps it was time to look again at the Irish voting system. It was, he said "not very efficient".

He then went on holiday, leaving the Tánaiste, Seán McEntee, in charge. Characteristically, Lemass made few changes. With James Ryan's departure from politics, Jack Lynch was an obvious choice to succeed him and, thus, was moved from Industry and Commerce to Finance. Paddy Hillery succeeded Lynch in Industry and Commerce. Others stayed where they were. New members of the Government included George Colley, who replaced Paddy Hillery in Education, and later Seán Flanagan, who became Minister for Health.

New men came into Government. One of these was Pádraig Faulkner, who was already close to Lynch and who was made Parliamentary Secretary to the Minister for the Gaeltacht, Micheál Ó Móráin. Paddy Lalor was also picked by Lemass to serve as a Parliamentary Secretary in Agriculture. He presents a good picture of the tensions then surrounding promotion and the awe in which Lemass was held.

Before the party meeting Lalor was sitting with Paudge Brennan and Jim Gibbons. On his way into what was the first parliamentary party meeting following the 1965 election, Lemass passed the table where the three of them were sitting. He asked to see all of them after the meeting. When the time came, Lemass gave Lalor his job, which was Parliamentary Secretary to Charles Haughey, already appointed to Agriculture. Then he added: "If you see Pádraig Faulkner tell him to come and see me." It was an intimation that Faulkner, too, was in line for promotion, and quite properly in Lalor's view, since Faulkner was some four years his senior. Lalor went to find him, and saw his wife, Kitty, sitting in their green Volkswagen. He gave her the message. Faulkner thought it was a leg-pull, and indeed it was a favourite way of teasing colleagues. Faulkner told Lalor he would only go to Lemass if Lalor went with him. Under the circumstances Lalor did just that, explaining to Lemass why he was there a second time. Faulkner was made Parliamentary Secretary in charge of the Gaeltacht.

Paudge Brennan went as Parliamentary Secretary to Neil Blaney in Environment (then called Local Government). He became a dedicated follower of Blaney's, later taking his side in the Arms Crisis, and resigning in sympathy. Jim Gibbons was made Parliamentary Secretary to the Minister for Finance, Jack Lynch. It was the beginning of an association that remained close but became less cordial in later years as Gibbons displayed signs of uncertainty. Yet in character there were similarities between them, Gibbons being something of a solitary figure in the party.

Lynch introduced his first Budget in May. In July negotiations began in London on an Anglo-Irish free trade agreement, in which he was a leading participant. A ten per cent reduction annually in Ireland's trade tariffs was agreed in exchange for British concessions on Irish agricultural imports into the United Kingdom market. It was signed in December, although the main employer organisation was gloomy about its impact on factories and businesses.

The economic circumstances over which Lynch presided did not really reflect the mood of hope that had prevailed in the aftermath of the First Programme. As a result of organised wage rounds, designed to ameliorate industrial agitation, there developed a more active mood among the social partners. In July a separate Department of Labour was established, designed to cope with worsening industrial strife. Paddy Hillery was appointed Minister. The change coincided with moves to introduce a wage freeze. In fact, in the aftermath of the 1965 election the Budget had to confront expenditure rising over revenue and an unacceptable level of unemployment, at 50,000, combined with 25,000 citizens a year emigrating. In the event Lynch did not change direct taxation, but introduced higher indirect taxes to fund a weekly rise of ten shillings for pensioners. He was suffering from a terrible cold, and wheezed his way through the long speech.

Worse was to follow. The 1966 Budget was a tough one, with increases in income tax and indirect taxation, including raised road taxes. There was even a tax on dances! Within three months a supplementary Budget increased taxes on tobacco and petrol. There were serious industrial disputes, including a crippling bank strike and a power workers' strike.

This was the country's mood in the late summer of 1966, with Seán Lemass arriving at the decision to hand over leadership of the Government. To outward appearances, Jack Lynch was not well positioned to succeed. Charles Haughey was in ministerial trouble as the same time, his position in Agriculture threatened by a growing mood of militancy among farmers. One report on his confrontation with the Irish Farmers' Association, that also alluded to the possibility of him being a contender in the leadership race, carried the jingle:

> Charlie, Charlie, Buttery Legs,
> Sold his mother for two Dutch eggs.
> The Eggs were rotten, Charlie got nothing,
> Charlie, Charlie, Buttery Legs.

Chapter Five

Departure of Seán Lemass

Becoming leader of Fianna Fáil was a momentous event in Jack Lynch's life. It was a life that would have more than its fair share of drama and excitement in the future. Party and, indeed, government leadership defined all that he did from that point forward until his death. It made him a national icon. In due course it led to the perception of him as a hero, and in this respect it placed him in terms of popularity beside Michael Collins in the twentieth century and, according to Liam Cosgrave, on a par with Daniel O'Connell in the nineteenth.

The popular view of him is that he was a "reluctant" leader. It is a view to which Lynch subscribed, at the time and later, in quite dramatic and florid terms. It must be questioned fundamentally. It is, and it was, a myth created by the man himself for reasons he saw as entirely valid.

It has already been shown that his supposed reluctance about entering politics at all had a well-reasoned argument behind it. It was not reluctance at all. Uncertainty over his career in the 1950s, drawn as he was by the rival claims of politics and the law, has to be seen in the context of the political doldrums represented by that decade of unemployment, emigration and general despair. After that he became committed, and ministerial appointments defined his future. When we come to his transition from senior Minister to leader of the party and Taoiseach of the country, we are faced again with the old dilemma: how much did he want the job and when did he decide?

The handover from Seán Lemass should have been a textbook transition. Instead, it became a mess reflecting badly on Lemass himself, who from the initial decision seems to have been uncertain how to proceed. For so long the assured deputy and then leader of the party, Lemass did not grasp the political significance of announcing his impending departure as though it were an issue for debate and consensus. More seriously, he did not fully grasp the varied ambitions of those who were waiting to take over. The nature of power is simple enough: once a leader decides to go, the focus shifts to the possible successors. In Lemass's case the decision in principle, without any fixed timing, had a destabilising impact.

Lynch had been schooled for the job. He had done all the right things. His acceptance of the sequence of ministerial appointments was the equivalent of an acceptance speech in advance. On all the evidence, it seems that Lemass had favoured Lynch right from the beginning, and that even de Valera saw Lynch as leadership material from a very early stage. It was a process in which Lemass had favoured Lynch overtly. The appointment to the Department of Industry and Commerce, that he had occupied with such distinction himself, and for so long, placed Lynch undeniably at the centre of the political stage. Lemass had been personally close to Lynch during crucial negotiations with the United Kingdom on the Anglo-Irish Free Trade Area Agreement. He had ensured that Lynch's political experience suited him to the broad-ranging negotiations for joining the EEC, which demanded the combined experience of two major Departments, Industry and Commerce and Finance. By the time he came to the leadership, Lynch had spent valuable time in both.

Lemass appears in retrospect to have crowded into a short period in power a substantial range of defining objectives for the country's next leader. Reflected in this is also what Whitaker has described as a less than wholehearted enthusiasm for the job. It was not that overall power came too late; it was that he was not entirely at ease with the broad nature of the responsibility. He liked specific action and concrete decision-making. After seven years Lemass was content and ready to hand over. Perhaps he did not give enough time to those who shared the responsibilities of government to allow them to adjust to his departure, which mixed precipitation with procrastination. Or maybe this, like so much else he did, was deliberate.

Lemass decided to give up the leadership on age grounds rather than on the health grounds which were discussed at the time. He did suffer from heart problems, and as a heavy pipe smoker had breathing difficulties. It was thought at the time that he had throat cancer. But there was a clear denial by Lemass of health as the reason. Instead, it was described as "a political decision". His own words are straightforward on the subject:

> My decision to relinquish office is a political decision, uninfluenced by any personal considerations. There is certainly no question about my general health, which is quite good. I am convinced that it is in the interests of the country, the Government, and the Fianna Fáil Party that responsibility should now pass to a younger man. The one consideration that is important above all others, as far as I am concerned, is the success of the Fianna Fáil Party at the next and subsequent general elections and I believe that a change of leadership at this time will help to ensure this. The celebration of the fiftieth anniversary of the 1916 Rising reminded me that I have been on active national service during all these years, almost thirty of them being spent in Government, and over seven as Taoiseach. I regret that time would not stand still for me so that I could go on indefinitely.[1]

---

[1] Official "Preliminary Statement" issued at the press conference held at Leinster House on Tuesday 8th November 1966 (attended by the author). By then the many leadership options had been exhaustively explored. The choice of a successor was fixed for the party meeting the next morning, and the resignation was to be given to President de Valera on the following Thursday. (Author's archive.)

The words about the future of Fianna Fáil were central to the character of this brusque man; short on words, short on charm, but totally committed and focused. "He lived with the Party all his life and promotion of the Party was his main objective apart from the Government. The Party was his life."[2]

In deciding on a long, drawn-out leadership transition, Lemass undoubtedly favoured Jack Lynch and would clearly have preferred a changeover by agreement. It is almost certain that, in the early stages, he expected this to happen, since this was how the party had proceeded on the previous occasion. Lynch was more experienced and occupied a more central role in the Government than any other Minister, with the possible exception of Frank Aiken. He also occupied a more central position in the party. He had political experience, appeal and charisma. In any of the discussions which went on among party members in the Dáil, it was always clear that Lynch had a commanding level of support. But somewhere along the way Lemass lost the textbook on how to proceed. The problem was not simply that Lynch was cautious about going forward; it was the uncertain basis on which this was being contemplated.

Jack Lynch was in his fiftieth year. He had the support, the experience, the ability, and the stature. He also had public appeal. There was a natural warmth and grace in his personality and a special appeal in his sporting achievement. There was also appeal in his relatively simple and uncomplicated background. To many within Fianna Fáil and, more importantly, to the large numbers outside the party whose support nevertheless was vital, he offered in human terms the new departure for which Lemass, in many of his late decisions, had set the timetable. He had served under two powerful party leaders who had historically heroic backgrounds. There was no third figure of that kind, and in any case it was inappropriate to be looking for a historic framework for the set of problems which Lemass had defined. The demands of the future required the dropping of such baggage, not its renewal.

More deeply, however, for a leading political player confronted by the leadership issue rather earlier than had been expected, there was a broader question. Did Lynch, who had already defined his own life as a politician and had ruled out the alternative of the law, see within Fianna Fáil anyone under whom he could serve for the foreseeable future? The answer has to be emphatically in the negative. Of the eventual contenders who came forward – Charles Haughey, George Colley, Neil Blaney – none was in the same class as Jack Lynch. He knew it and so did they. He had the job for the asking, and that was the central issue behind a leadership contest that for a time took on a machiavellian colouring.

---

[2] Michael Mills in discussion with Andy O'Mahony for a programme on Seán Lemass in a series of programmes entitled "Na Taoisigh: Leaders of the State", broadcast by RTÉ on Saturday, 23rd June 2001.

Lemass knew who *should* lead the party. He wanted Lynch to succeed him. The leadership contest itself went on for a period of two months. In reality Lemass had been engaged in a survey of party potential with a view to handing over from shortly after the 1965 general election. He gave indicators to possible candidates. He told George Colley, for example, that he should think about himself in the context of party leadership, and should "go out and make republican speeches." He meant this in sober, doctrinaire terms. He explained it to Colley as a necessary pulling back from the heavy emphasis which he, Lemass, had applied to programmes for economic recovery and business incentives. Lemass thought that in general these had been "bad for the party" though he did not specify to Colley in any detail how this had been the case. Lemass told others of his intention, and indicated his feelings about their chances.[3]

Colley took Lemass at his word, though in the speeches he made he offered a rather more rounded characterisation of himself. Haughey was a declared contender from early on. Lynch quite wisely played a waiting game. By doing so he drew out and tested all the leadership candidates on offer, and this confirmed their unsatisfactory standing. Colley and Lynch discussed the leadership issue more than once and Colley's expressed view was that Lynch had the capacity to bring together the increasingly divided elements in the party. Lynch's response to Colley was to offer him support. In the party, during the summer months of 1966, there was a belief that Lemass would not resign, and that the contrary rumours were a product of newspaper speculation. Kevin Boland, for example, simply could not take the idea of a leadership change until Erskine Childers rang him and told him that two government Ministers, Brian Lenihan and Donogh O'Malley, were canvassing for Haughey and that others were supporting Colley. Boland considered Colley a "nincompoop" and thought that Haughey was not to be trusted. He was bitterly opposed to both men and came to the view quite quickly that they had to be stopped "at all costs", and so he expressed himself to other party members. He was also annoyed at the very idea of having to campaign. He rang Frank Aiken, to discover that Aiken was supporting Colley.

Lemass, in an uncharacteristically slow and deliberate way, had introduced the idea of his departure from the leadership of both party and country and had then begun to lose control of the situation. He took action in mid-September 1966, telling Lynch in a private interview of his decision to go, and asking if he would be interested in succeeding him. In a later version of what happened, and in accordance with the general view of how the succession took place, Lynch said: "I told him emphatically that I was not and he seemed to accept it."[4]

But it was by no means as clear-cut as this. New evidence indicates that Lynch and Lemass exchanged views on the succession that were far less emphatic

---

[3] George Colley in interviews with the author, June and July 1979. The subsequent articles about George Colley were published in *The Sunday Independent* on the 16th and 23rd of September 1979.
[4] Jack Lynch, "My Life And Times" in *Magill* (November 1979), p. 42.

than Lynch claimed. Two weeks later, at the end of that month, Lynch, as Minister for Finance, was in New York for a meeting of the International Monetary Fund, with the Secretary of the Department, Dr T.K. Whitaker. One night in New York they attended a performance of *Hello Dolly*, with Ginger Rogers in the lead part. They were at this stage good friends with a degree of personal trust unusual between senior civil servant and senior politician. Lynch told Whitaker what Lemass had said. Whitaker asked him what response he had made, and Lynch said he told him he wanted time to reflect.

"What will you do?" Whitaker asked. Lynch told him that he would accept. Whitaker's response indicates a close understanding of Lynch, for he then asked: "What will Máirín have to say?"

"I'll talk her round," Lynch said.[5]

Some time after this, Lemass summoned Lynch again, this time in the company of George Colley and Charles Haughey, and told them all that they should be thinking about the future leadership of the party. Lynch says that he repeated his earlier comment about not being interested. The other two indicated that they were interested in succeeding Lemass.

We now know that the background to this was a decision in principle by Lynch that he would in fact do the opposite, and take up the leadership of the party and of the country. What we do not know is at what stage Lemass was told. Neither do we know whether Lemass engaged with Lynch in what was clearly a tactic designed to bring out all contenders, thereby exploring the whole leadership issue and involving the future direction of the party, in the way that then took place.

Recent books on Lemass and on the Fianna Fáil party shed no light on this. To this day there is considerable disagreement about Lemass's views. Michael Mills has expressed the view that George Colley was Lemass's first choice. John Horgan has stated that Lemass supported Colley before Lynch, but that there is evidence that Paddy Hillery was "the person he would first of all have preferred." Dermot Keogh concurs with this view, adding that there is some evidence, not conclusive, that Lemass turned *first* to Hillery. Mills is emphatic that Hillery *never* came into the reckoning. Hillery did come into the reckoning, in the sense that Seán Lemass indicated his suitability and invited him to consider himself for the position. Early on, though, Hillery decided against it. As far as Haughey and Colley were concerned, they were regarded within the Dáil, according to Mills, as "a joke".[6] Of how much Lemass was made aware was not known then or later by the main protagonists, with the exception, that is, of Lynch. Typically, he kept his counsel.

---

[5] Author's interview with Ken Whitaker, April 2001.

[6] From a discussion involving Michael Mills, former journalist with *The Irish Press*, John Horgan, biographer of Seán Lemass, and Dermot Keogh, historian, with Andy O'Mahony on Seán Lemass in a series of programmes entitled "Na Taoisigh: Leaders of the State", broadcast by RTÉ on Saturday, 23rd June 2001.

Everything that happened at this stage was consistent with the tradition of *omerta* within the party, that Sicilian vow of silence to which many other attitudes and patterns of later behaviour in Fianna Fáil may also be attributed. Things were not written down. The party, after all, came from a revolutionary background. In the earlier days of Sinn Féin subversion and rebellion, records had been minimal, for obvious reasons. Decisions were recorded, but not details of those who made them or even of those who attended meetings. Equally, that became the pattern in Government from 1932 on. Government minutes never recorded discussions, only decisions. Neither was there any procedure laid down for the process initiated by Lemass when he decided to resign.

Lemass was almost certainly complicit in a political exploration of a complex nature and with unfathomable motivation. How it was explained or discussed is not likely to be ever known, but it is highly unlikely that Lynch, having made the decision in principle, would have kept Lemass totally in the dark. It is just as unlikely that Lemass, if he had been kept in the dark, would have continued to consult with Lynch on the matter. There was a benign stand-off between them while other options were either explored or witnessed. All the circumstantial evidence suggests that there was a genuine attempt to discover the weaknesses and strengths of Lynch's position in the party. His sporting experience would have conditioned him to be sure of victory before engaging in the full conflict of a leadership battle. At the end of this long exploration Lynch rang Paddy Hillery to see whether he (Hillery) wanted to put his own name forward. Hillery responded by offering Lynch his support.

*

In due course three candidates put their names forward. Two of them, Colley and Haughey, acted immediately. Both men were out of the country when Lemass's decision to resign was made more generally known in the party. Colley was on IDA business in the United States, but Lemass had given him an undertaking that he would summon him back, which he did through Frank Aiken at the United Nations: "The position has changed; your return should not be long delayed."[7] The reason given by government sources for Colley's surprise return was that there was a crisis with the farmers, the Department of Agriculture was being besieged, and that the deadlock was going to be resolved by a government reshuffle. Both Colley and Aiken surmised that Lemass, who unsurprisingly had little experience of what he was about, was losing control in Dublin. The Haughey canvassing, led jointly by the ebullient and self-confident Donogh O'Malley and by the agreeable party man Brian Lenihan, was already getting out of hand.

Colley enjoyed the backing of Aiken who as Tánaiste was the most senior figure in the party after Lemass. This was coloured by the fact that Harry Colley,

---

[7] Colley interview, above, n. 3.

the candidate's father, had been in politics under de Valera, and had been involved in the 1916 Rising. It was a traditional candidacy and Colley was well-suited as its representative. He was a solicitor with conventional Fianna Fáil republican views, and he was a fluent and enthusiastic Irish speaker. His experience was limited. His first government appointment, as a Parliamentary Secretary, was part of Lemass's minor reshuffle in 1964, following Paddy Smith's resignation from Agriculture. Colley got his first full government appointment, as Minister for Education, from Lemass in April 1965. When the Department of Labour was created, and Patrick Hillery moved to it in the summer of 1966, Colley was made Minister for Industry and Commerce. Nevertheless, like the other contenders, he was a victim of the short space of time given by Lemass to his potential successors, and there was a degree of panic in his response to the Taoiseach's surprise decision.

Haughey represented a quite different faction in the party. Though he had married Lemass's daughter, Maureen, in 1951, his antecedents were pro-Treaty. He had even less of the Fianna Fáil anti-Treaty tradition in him than Lynch. His father, John Haughey, was an ardent supporter of Michael Collins, and distrusted and disliked de Valera. It was not until after his father's death that Haughey went into active politics and from then on he denied the earlier record.

Not surprisingly, he supported and sought to control the new and modern grouping in Fianna Fáil which established the Taca organisation and came to be associated with the "mohair suits" affected by those who relied on the new business wealth that the party attracted.[8] He was publicly close to Brian Lenihan and Donogh O'Malley; the former a follower and supporter, the latter more gifted and courageous than Haughey, but fated to have only a short political career. Haughey was slick and self-confident, paying only superficial attention to the older traditions of the party, and identifying himself with industrial and business development and economic planning. His own father-in-law had misgivings about him as leadership material. Others in the party felt the same. He had, however, more ministerial experience than George Colley. He had been appointed Minister for Justice in the 1961 administration, and had done well there.

Haughey was caught out by the timing of Lemass's departure. He was not experienced enough and had not sufficiently prepared his support in the party. Moreover, following his satisfactory performance as Minister for Justice, he had been thrown into the difficult role of dealing with the farmers. His appointment to the Department of Agriculture after Paddy Smith's resignation was not a success. He did not understand the farming mind and in any case the farmers, who were very militant at the time, had demonstrated aggressively against government policy. They rapidly turned their anger against their new Minister's handling of his brief. The difficult time they gave him was sustained over many months. Nevertheless, his very evident ambition for leadership, and his smooth

---

[8]   Taca was a fundraising organisation. Irish businessmen – the target was 500 – met monthly for dinner, paid an annual subscription, and were given access to Ministers.

political manner, which concealed his devious nature, made him a serious contender. He had not at that stage developed the later flamboyance with which he clothed himself in the attributes of a wealth quite out of balance with his earnings as a politician. He did not buy Abbeville, his eighteenth-century house and estate on the north side of Dublin, until 1969, but he courted public attention and had a following that included a number of journalists who were treated with flattery and indulgence.

Neither of these two men satisfied Fianna Fáil, however. Haughey was viewed with deep suspicion and eventual dislike by Frank Aiken. Paddy Smith and other senior men had similar views. Colley, despite bringing the right moral and republican standards, was seen as too limited, too rigid and too ambitious. In fairness, his declared candidacy was inspired in part by the fact that Lynch was thought not to be a contender in the early stages, and that Paddy Hillery and Donogh O'Malley had ruled themselves out. It was Hillery who was critical of what he called Colley's "zeal" to become leader. But in reality Hillery recognised that Colley was really stepping forward because of the vacuum. This view of Colley is endorsed by Bobby Molloy, at that stage a newcomer to the Dáil, first elected for Galway west in 1965. Molloy's first choice would have been Lynch and, after him, Colley.[9]

It was Colley's main purpose, politically, to represent the republican tradition in as modern and forward-looking a way as possible. He needed to have this view of himself in the light of a third candidate, who put himself forward when it appeared that the contest would be confined to Colley and Haughey. This was Neil Blaney. He was a republican, but with none of Colley's zeal to be seen as modern and forward-looking. Instead, backed strongly by another hardline Fianna Fáil nationalist, Kevin Boland, Blayney sought to develop support out of the various strands of party tradition, personal ancestry and an antipathy to the British in Ireland. Both Blaney and Boland, who came from a similar background, saw the Colley-Haughey race as a media-promoted contest. This view was endorsed when Colley came back from America and was greeted in a blaze of publicity. Faced by the prospect of the party being in the hands of one or other of these two younger men, Blaney and Boland moved in. They both preferred Lynch and thought that he could be managed; in short, if they could put him in, they could take him out. When he failed to co-operate, Boland put Blaney's name into the ring. Arguably, this was one of the moves anticipated by Lynch in his waiting game.

Blaney's background was Donegal. His father had preceded him in a Dáil seat for that constituency and was an old IRA man from the War of Independence and the Civil War. Moreover, the son had succeeded his father in 1948, the same year that Lynch had entered the Dáil.

Blaney had been appointed to the Government by de Valera in 1957. His first

---

[9] See interview with Bobby Molloy in Stephen Collins, *The Power Game* (O'Brien Press, Dublin 2000), p. 35.

ministry was in the Department of Post and Telegraphs. He had gone on from there to the key Department of Local Government, which made him responsible for Dáil constituencies and electoral matters. Blaney had thrown himself enthusiastically into party organisation and had shown himself to be a shrewd and efficient electoral expert. Bobby Molloy said of him at this time: "Blaney was driving the party; he took over the organisation. He ran by-elections and drove people very, very hard. He was a bit over-enthusiastic, we all thought."[10] Though five years younger than Lynch, he was of an equal seniority in Dáil and ministerial terms, and arguably a more convincing choice than either Colley or Haughey.

Blaney enjoyed the support of Kevin Boland, who had been appointed to the Government in 1957 as Minister for Defence, giving him also seniority and weight equal to that of the man he was supporting. His first appointment, by de Valera, had been used by the party leader to avoid putting Boland's father, Gerard Boland, into yet another Fianna Fáil administration. Both Kevin Boland's father and his uncle, Harry Boland, enjoyed almost mythic status in the party. From them Gerard's son had derived a remarkable level of political arrogance about the party's divine right to rule. Not alone was he dismissive of the very idea of coalitions having power, he was also on his guard against the dogmatism of Fianna Fáil being undermined by softer and more liberal versions of what the party believed. To him, both Haughey and Colley were watering down what Fianna Fáil was, and he objected to them both. He backed Blaney and pushed him within the party as the best option.

The emergence of Blaney, with Boland's backing, had effectively brought all the potential leaders except Lynch out into the open, catering to all shades of opinion, and in the process had demonstrated the shortcomings of all three candidates. None of them would do and this was clear to many in the party. It is even clearer now. But it was unusual to the point of being publicly alarming that Fianna Fáil was being exposed to wide public examination and speculation about its leading figures, its policies and its organisational behaviour. This would not do either. Some kind of resolution was required urgently.

*

The public and much publicised version of what happened next has become part of the folklore associated with Jack Lynch. It further emphasised his supposed uncertainty and procrastination. He repeatedly told Lemass that he was not interested in the leadership and Lemass repeatedly invited him to think again. Part of Lynch's reasoning is always overlooked. He had a genuinely happy marriage and he and Máirín clearly enjoyed:

---

[10] Quoted from an interview with Bobby Molloy in Stephen Collins, *The Power Game*, above, n.9.

... our own company in the privacy of our home, listening to music, watching television, reading or just chatting. Ministerial life didn't leave much time for private life and we knew that being Taoiseach would leave even less time.[11]

He then turned to quite another problem, the difficulty of "assuming the mantle of the likes of Éamon de Valera and Seán Lemass. They were both towering figures in my mind and the thought that I could adequately fill their place seemed to me the height of presumption." The first reason, not entirely convincing however much one admires the quality of the Lynches' marriage, represents a static state of affairs to which all life's developments have to adjust. The second was changing as the leadership situation developed. It was becoming increasingly clear to Lynch that to look at the issue in the light of the standing of the predecessors was illogical. If he was presumptuous, the others were even more so. He was the best candidate; that was how it was to be judged and he had to consider that fact with less concern for his evening chats with Máirín than had been the case.

Lemass was, generally speaking, a determined and decisive man. He had put the issue of his continued leadership beyond speculation and had, it might be surmised, brought out into the open probably the most important event in Fianna Fáil's history. He was pursuing, for the second time in the party's life and indeed in his own, a process which, if it had any tradition at all, should have been part of the secretive and almost introverted behaviour of this political organisation. He had schooled Lynch for the job, giving him key appointments and intended, as far as one can judge from all the evidence, that Lynch would take over. Lemass seems to have knowingly invited a contest involving not just two other candidates but also a third, and presided over protracted reaction from deputies throughout the country. This cannot have been other than deliberate. It is difficult to see it other than in terms of a desire on Lemass's part to modernise the party's understanding of itself. He had, after all, reformed attitudes on the economy, Northern Ireland, the United Kingdom, defence, neutrality, the United Nations, and on Europe. Why neglect Fianna Fáil?

All this supposed jockeying for power was taking place against an unusual background – that of a new and unbridled ambition for control within the party. In the short period of seven years since Lemass had replaced de Valera as leader – a smooth, internally focused and non-contentious transition – a quite new mood had developed. The party had been energised at several different levels, and those responsible wanted to become involved. Blaney, on party organisation, Haughey, overtly on the issue of "style", and Colley, as an expression of traditional values, were all limited in what they offered. All had been brought out into the open. All had been judged as less than what Fianna Fáil needed. Politically, it was a necessary and valuable exercise. For any new leader it was a vital process, demonstrating where power lay within the party ranks and how it was disposed towards him.

[11] Jack Lynch, "My Life and Times" in *Magill* (November 1979), p. 42.

Lynch was contemplating, in his fiftieth year, a future that was inextricably bound up in Irish politics. There was a possibility that he would find himself serving under a leader whom he knew to be a lesser man. In effect, he would be rejecting a party that had demonstrated reasonably clearly that it wanted him as leader. This view was coming right through from the very top. Lynch was the party's first choice and in his life at that time he had no real alternative. He had spent too short a period practising the law, had developed no business interests, and had accumulated none of the wealth that would have permitted him to look elsewhere. Confronted by Lemass's logic, he had to admit to himself that he had nowhere else to go. Lynch, who had already demonstrated his skills and had handled his career up to that point without giving any hostages to fortune, was faced with a choice he could not reject: he was the one to ride this aggressive and voracious tiger into Ireland's political future.

Lemass allowed himself too much time in the drawn-out process of succession. It had got out of hand. If there were a design to it, then the leadership contest should have delivered up a united political weapon of invincible strength and purpose to the new leader. It did not fulfil this necessary purpose. In fact, it did the opposite. But the catastrophes that lay ahead cannot, in all fairness, be laid at either Lemass's or Lynch's door, nor can they reflect on the open and exhaustive deliberations that coloured Lemass's departure.

In these final stages, pressure on Lynch again began to mount, with Fianna Fáil deputies from Cork supporting his candidacy and organising a "Draft Jack" campaign. This attracted support from other parts of the country. Lemass once more approached the man himself and asked him to reconsider. Lynch's later description of this is precise:

> Lemass again invited me to his room, informed me that several backbenchers wanted me to run and that the party generally favoured me as his successor. He pointed out to me that I owed the party a duty to serve, even as leader. He gave me to understand that the other contenders, to whom he had already spoken, were prepared to withdraw in my favour.[12]

At this stage, for party consumption, Lynch indicated that he would reconsider his position and discuss the matter with Máirín. He consulted with his wife and ostensibly, as far as the public was concerned, this was when he changed his mind. The process was "long and agonising", but finally he told Lemass that he would allow his name to be put forward. Lemass's own consultations with the other candidates, according to Lynch, had achieved agreement from all of them that they would withdraw. Lemass obviously meant this to be an additional incentive. But the Taoiseach had got it wrong. In the event, Haughey and Blaney did withdraw, but Colley decided to contest the leadership.

Lynch gave no flavour of the bitter and divisive party meeting which decided

---

[12] "My Life and Times", above, n.11.

his leadership. Seán MacEntee sharply criticised Lemass for stepping down at all. Kevin Boland attacked Frank Aiken with "a barrage of abuse", according to Bobby Molloy. Molloy was very new to the party, and he had agreed to second Aiken's nomination of Colley. He was astonished at Boland's outburst. "I had never seen this side of things in Fianna Fáil up to then. It was cussedness on his part that the man he was supporting was being opposed."[13] But it was also probable that Boland felt that the withdrawal of his own nominee, Neil Blaney, had been achieved under false pretences, weakening the prospects of the Donegal deputy for the future. Molloy also suggests in the same interview that there was a pact between Haughey and Blaney to postpone what they saw as a later agenda to replace Lynch as leader with whichever of the two of them could win majority support. This was unhinged by Colley's decision to sustain his candidacy, and understandably it made Boland livid that he had been cast in the role of a supporter of Jack Lynch. In the light of later events, the fact of Blaney, Haughey and Boland voting for Lynch has an entertaining irony about it.

To trump all that, George Colley had demonstrated the strength of his own standing in the party, endorsing Lynch subsequently, and becoming a close and loyal colleague. He brought with him his nineteen supporters, further strengthening Lynch's position.

Lynch was not unhappy afterwards at this development. "I rather welcomed the opposition for it gave the party an opportunity to express its support and in the event the count was 52 votes to 19."[14] It was the first time Fianna Fáil had held such a vote. It did not know what to do. In the event the party's secretary, Hetty Behan, went out and got a shoe-box and the ballot papers were collected in it and then counted. After his election Lynch said he was sorry to see Lemass leaving the Government. "No man has put a greater mark on the progress of the Irish nation than Seán Lemass."

In his autobiographical essay, published in *Magill* thirteen years later, Lynch elaborated persuasively, not without a degree of imaginative invention, on how it happened.[15] Subsequently, on this as on other issues, he embroidered his own story and the character and behaviour of those involved. Generally speaking, his interviews have an historical richness, much of which cannot be contradicted. There is a story-telling and anecdotal quality that is disarmingly attractive and convincing. Nevertheless, in his public statements, Lynch both settled and raised questions. The long process of a leadership election for the first time within Fianna Fáil was not going to be wrapped up and put away easily. Nor was it going to be agreed on the basis of consensus. This may have been the way the previous leadership changeover had been agreed, but Fianna Fáil had altered

---

[13] See interview with Bobby Molloy in Stephen Collins, *The Power Game* (O'Brien Press, Dublin, 2000), p. 37.

[14] Jack Lynch, "My Life and Times" in *Magill* (November 1979), p. 42.

[15] *Ibid.*

dramatically, and Colley's decision to contend the leadership had set the stage for a further display of how different Fianna Fáil had become.

*

The actual transition gave Lynch a full Dáil term in which to assert his authority and to shape Fianna Fáil in accordance with his own ideas about the future. In age and experience, when he took over in November 1966, he straddled the old and the new. The old was reflected in the re-appointment of Frank Aiken as Tánaiste and as Minister for External Affairs, a position in which he had become virtually institutionalised, rather to the detriment of the Department's development. Aiken was a solitary relic of the past; other members of the Government were Lynch's contemporaries in politics or were junior to him.

Lynch faced a number of problems and was aware of them from the start. The first concerned the appointment of his Government. He acknowledged that Lemass had pre-empted any radical reorganisation of government appointments by bringing in the younger men of promise during the relatively brief period he was in power. In de Valera's previous administration, Lemass had played a hand, demonstrating his power as the most powerful person after de Valera , and the leader presumptive. Now he was in the position of having left a legacy that allowed his successor little room to manoeuvre. In vacating the Department of Finance Lynch appointed Haughey, moving him out of the unhappy experience in Agriculture and placing him in the most influential job of all. It was an expression of trust. It designated Haughey as a likely successor. Two other senior Ministers whose new appointments were effectively promotions were Neil Blaney, who took over Haughey's job in the Department of Agriculture and Fisheries, and Kevin Boland, who replaced Blaney in Local Government. George Colley stayed where he was, in Industry and Commerce. The only newcomer was Pádraig Faulkner, who took over Lands and the Gaeltacht.

This strong team, already in place, and likely to remain around Lynch during his time as leader, did not really give Lynch an ideal balance. Lemass had achieved too much. His relatively successful economic thinking had gone a good way towards transforming the country, attracting into Fianna Fáil a number of ambitious and energetic men who had risen to positions of ministerial authority in the party and who were anxious to flex their political muscles. They had done so only to a limited extent while Lemass was leader, as he had held them in check. Now the situation changed.

It was perhaps aggravated by the almost universal perception that Lynch would be in the job for only a short period. Those around him could be excused for taking this view in the light of the long and involved process of persuasion through which Lemass had apparently led the party between September and November 1966. De Valera had been re-elected President during 1966, but at the age of eighty-three seemed unlikely to serve the full seven-year term. The early assumption was that his natural successor as President would be Lynch, thus clearing the way for a new party leader. It annoyed him:

> One of the irritations I encountered at the time was that people, knowing of my reluctance to stand for the leadership, assumed that my first wish would be to get out of the job. They used to say things like 'Don't worry, you won't need to be there long – there is always the Park.' The fact was that from the moment that I became Taoiseach I was determined to serve my stint there and not to run off at the first opportunity. I had no intention of being merely a caretaker Taoiseach.[16]

Lynch's view of the way he would handle the job was not unlike his attitude all those years earlier, when he had been both a sporting captain and a sporting hero. It was incumbent on him "to create a team spirit among the Government ministers, to impose a greater cohesion on the operation of the Government as a whole and to exert my personal authority." Given the strength and talent available to Lynch at the end of 1966, he should indeed have been able to mould a powerful and effective team. But it did not happen. In their different ways, senior men in the party, notably Kevin Boland, Neil Blaney, Charles Haughey and, until his death in 1968, Donogh O'Malley took fairly independent lines. The consensus view was that Jack Lynch was not tough enough for the job. The reality was that he governed effectively, dealing best with economic and development issues, and making progress on Northern Ireland, Anglo-Irish and European relations.

That first year went well for Lynch, and seemed to fulfil many of the promises he had made regarding good team work. Donogh O'Malley was particularly in the public eye with his policies of reform in education. These ranged from changes to Ireland's primary school system to a decision announced in April for the amalgamation of Dublin University and University College Dublin into a single University of Dublin. This was contrary to the recommendation of the Commission on Higher Education, but it was characteristic of O'Malley to take an independent line. He was the most colourful of Lynch's Ministers, but died suddenly in March 1968 while campaigning in a by-election in his own constituency, Limerick east. His nephew, Desmond O'Malley, succeeded him six weeks later.

Ireland reactivated its application to join the European Economic Community (EEC). This had first been made in 1961. It was only successfully concluded at the end of Lynch's second term. Everything in his early political career stamped Lynch as an exponent of Ireland's need for EEC membership and he was an active worker to that end. In Industry and Commerce and in Finance, and indeed within the whole series of economic programmes which guided political and business thought throughout the 1960s, Lynch had been a central figure. Now, as Taoiseach, and following the reactivation of the British application for membership, he engaged in a tour of European capitals that resulted in sympathy and support for Ireland's entry. It was not enough; Ireland was too closely allied

---

16 Jack Lynch, "My Life and Times" in *Magill* (November 1979), p. 43.

with Britain to be able to enter the EEC on her own. The application was again abandoned as a result of de Gaulle's veto of Britain.

At the very end of 1967 the Committee on the Constitution, which Lemass had set up in August 1966, issued a report with a number of interesting recommendations, including those for constitutional changes affecting the law on marriage and the position of the Catholic Church. It was an all-party committee, and not unnaturally there were some unanimous recommendations and some on which committee members were divided. A significant example of the former concerned the claim over Northern Ireland expressed in Article 3, where the committee unanimously recommended a less emotive wording than "pending the reintegration of the national territory". An example of a recommendation where the committee was divided dealt with the proportional representation system of elections (P.R.).

The deputies and senators from the two parties in opposition were in favour of maintaining P.R. Fianna Fáil was keen to get rid of it, and Lynch himself was very much in favour of this course of action. He had been persuaded by de Valera's arguments on the previous occasion in 1959. In 1965, well before the setting up of the committee on constitutional reform, Jack Lynch, speaking at a meeting in Trinity College, made the case for this system:

> [and against] the positive clampdown on all attempts to re-open it. This, to my mind, is completely wrong. The existence of a substantial minority favouring the abolition of P.R., as was shown in 1959, economic, social and political developments since that time, the possibility that the electorate may have erred for one reason or another in 1959, not to speak of its inherent importance, all these require that this matter should not be lost sight of.[17]

He felt the case for change was strengthened. He favoured "a Government to rule" rather than "every shade of opinion in the community" being represented. Lynch in the speech gives a very persuasive view of an alternative system, including in his remarks an examination of the wastefulness of the time and energy of deputies in the multi-seat constituency under the P.R. system.

The arguments were arguably less relevant in the mid-1960s. Nevertheless, the Government now engaged in another attempt to introduce a "first-past-the-post" form of election, similar to that in Britain and other parts of Europe. Because Irish politics still had the pro- and anti-Treaty divide, combined with the existence of a left-wing party in Labour, the change would have effectively ensured Fianna Fáil in power for the foreseeable future. The campaign to change the electoral system, which of course involved Kevin Boland as Minister for Local Government, and Neil Blaney in his role as party organiser on the National

---

[17] Speech to the Inaugural Meeting of the Philosophical Society, Dublin University, Thursday, 28th October 1965.

Executive, also had a significant impact on Northern Ireland, where the minority community were seeking the exact opposite. They looked with disdain on the desire of Fianna Fáil to cement themselves in power which coincided so closely with the beginning of a much more militant expression of nationalist pressure for reform.

To take the P.R. issue out of the constitutional committee's report and act on it was an error of judgement. It ran counter to the interests of the minority Nationalist community in Northern Ireland, and demonstrated to them a callous disregard for their campaign. Politically, it turned them against Fianna Fáil. It appeared to play into the hands of the hardliners in the party. It was a policy move which suited Blaney and Boland, and this further encouraged the idea that Lynch was being ignored by them as leader. But it was also an error of judgement in electoral terms. It was called for in the Fianna Fáil Árd Fheis in 1968. Even with Lynch as leader, there was sufficient distrust of the party in the country to ensure defeat over this electoral change, and it was defeated. In the Árd Fheis a year later, at the end of January 1969, a delegate described the P.R. referendum as "Fianna Fáil's darkest hour". It was reckoned that about 150,000 supporters of Fianna Fáil voted against any change in the voting system. Michael McInerny, the *Irish Times* political correspondent, claimed that the grass roots had turned against the leadership of the party generally. There was dissatisfaction with Taca, with the Criminal Justice Bill and the White Paper on Health, and "against the attitude that inspired the Referendum".[18] "The leadership – or most of it – had betrayed or complacently abandoned basic principles and objectives of the Grand Old Party." It was not the message to be receiving at the last party conference before a general election.

*

Jack Lynch's characteristic calmness, in his approach to a number of issues at this time, including Northern Ireland, was increasingly at odds with the situation on the ground. But he went on delivering speeches on a wide range of topics. They represent a series and they were clearly designed to strengthen his leadership. They are remarkably good texts. He spoke in detail about the character and aims of Fianna Fáil. He dealt quite bravely with the declining impact of economic planning and the ways in which practicalities upset theory. He contributed to the debate on European entry, and dealt patiently, even exhaustively, with the democratic mandate.

In April 1967 he gave a comprehensive speech to a Fianna Fáil gathering in Dublin on the Government's social responsibilities. It covered a number of issues, including "itinerants" (now referred to as "travellers" and then the subject of extensive proposals on housing and sites), proposals on small farms in the West, and more generally on housing. The speech was extraordinarily radical. There

---

[18] *The Irish Times*, Saturday, 1st February 1969, p. 13.

were elements of socialism in it combined with Christian thinking that was much of its time, but particularly reflected a sympathy and understanding in Jack Lynch himself about the services properly offered by politics but inspired by Christian thinking. He gave the impression of a country that worked because it combined in a balanced way the work of the individual, the voluntary body, the religious working in the community, and the public authority underpinning it all. "A sane view of the common good" was how he concluded, quoting the words of Pope John XXIII.

Lynch also took on the burden at this time of publicly presenting Ireland's case for entry to the EEC. The issues were complicated and controversial. They were also highly political. There were wide divergences between the political parties over what Ireland wanted, and there were demands for detail that would have exposed Ireland's negotiating position. Though it was still to be some time before Ireland would achieve actual entry, the spadework for gaining public support and removing unreasonable fears was achieved during the second half of the decade.

As the 1960s drew to a close, clouds began to appear on the political horizon. These were mainly associated with the North. From the beginning of his leadership, Lynch had dealt with Northern Ireland rather as Lemass had done. Better relations between the two parts of the country had been established and these were signalled in practical terms when Erskine Childers, Minister for Transport and Power, agreed with Brian Faulkner, the North's Minister of Commerce, on sharing electricity systems.[19]

In December 1967, a year after becoming Taoiseach, Jack Lynch had gone north for a meeting at Stormont with the Northern Ireland Prime Minister, Terence O'Neill. At the time there was optimism about O'Neill's premiership. He had espoused economic development, influenced in this by the success of Dr T.K. Whitaker in the Republic. In the 1965 general election in the UK an increase in Unionist representation in Northern Ireland seemed to be an endorsement of his policies. But the policy of reconciliation between the two communities was more apparent than real. The location of the second university for Northern Ireland in Coleraine, a staunchly Protestant community, and the creation of a new town called Craigavon, irritated Roman Catholics and provoked a mixture of impatience and hostility. In January 1964 the Campaign for Social Justice had been founded, and began campaigning for social reforms, which were far more radical than anything envisaged either by officials or by more enlightened Unionist politicians like O'Neill. Those in power were beginning to recognise the vast field of inequities in Northern Ireland, but were psychologically and politically ill-equipped to keep pace with the pressure coming from the protesters.

The main organisation engaged in protest was the Northern Ireland Civil Rights Association (NICRA). This had come into existence at the time of Lynch becoming Taoiseach, and it publicly declared its programme of action in February

---

[19] In 1971 the IRA destroyed the link-up in an explosion.

Nora Lynch with her youngest son, Jack.
(Courtesy of Liam Ó Tuama)

Jack Lynch, top row, third from left, with his class at St Vincent's Convent which he first attended in 1922. The school register, recording this, is still held at the convent by Sister Aquinas, who was a pupil in the girls' school at the same time as Jack Lynch. (Courtesy of Liam Ó Tuama)

The Shandon area where Jack Lynch grew up. His house is the one with the white chimney at the side of the church. The Cork Butter Market is the overgrown area on the left; the circular Firkin Crane building has been restored. At top right, behind the churchyard, are Skiddy's Almshouses. (Courtesy of W.E. Peard)

The imposing portico of the old Cork Butter Market, once the largest such market in Europe. Jack Lynch and his friends used the pillars as their goalposts for street games of hurling. (Courtesy of W.E. Peard)

St Nick's, the North Parish under sixteen football champions, 1929. *Front row:* J. Sheehan, P. Riordan; *Second row:* J. O'Donoghue, John Lynch, Charlie Lynch, Jack Lynch, W. Lattrell; *Third row:* T. O'Reilly, W. Corkery, L. O'Keeffe, D. Byrne, M.O'Brien, T. Kiely, C. McGrath; *Back row:* A. White, P. Corkery, T. McCarthy, Finbarr Lynch. Three Lynch brothers were on the team. John Lynch was no relation. (Courtesy of Liam Ó Tuama)

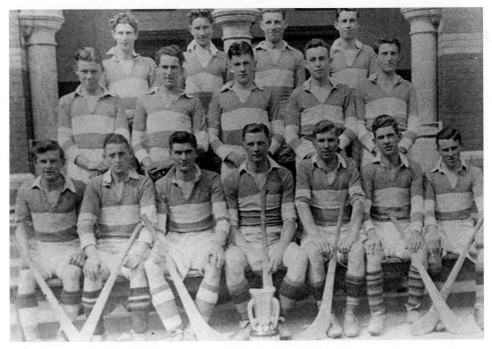

Harty Cup winners, 1936. *Front row:* M. Goggin, P. O'Riordan, J. Reilly, Jack Lynch (Captain), P.J. O'Riordan, P. Callaghan, M. Kidney; *Second row:* D. O'Kelly, M. Flynn, P. Hogan, C. O'Leary, S. O'Leary; *Back row:* M. Cleary, L. O'Neill, C. McMahon, T. Winning. (Courtesy of Liam Ó Tuama)

Jack Lynch, Captain, with the McCarthy Cup, after a victory over Dublin in the All-Ireland final, 1942. The team left the train at Blarney Station, where this photograph was taken, and travelled into Cork through Blackpool in a horse-drawn carriage. (Courtesy of Liam Ó Tuama)

Glen Rovers *versus* Sarsfields, County hurling final, 29th September 1940. Jack Lynch is followed by "Fox" Collins, Danny Matt Dargan, Jim Young, Dave Creedon, Dan Coughlan, Paddy Hogan, Jack Buckley, and the team. (Courtesy of Liam Ó Tuama)

G.A.A. Cork *versus* Tipperary, national league hurling final, Croke Park, 31st October 1948. Jack Lynch kicks the ball over the bar despite losing his hurley. Jim Devitt (Tipperary) comes in to challenge him. (Courtesy of Liam Ó Tuama)

The Cork *versus* Kerry Munster football final, 1943. Jack is lifted on the shoulders of his supporters. (Courtesy of Liam Ó Tuama)

The Cork hurling team which won the 1942 All-Ireland. Jack Lynch, who was Captain, is in the front row, fourth from left. (Irish Press Photo, Courtesy of Liam Ó Tuama)

Cork *versus* Tipperary in the Munster Championship, Limerick, 1949. "Carbery" writing for the *Irish Independent*, described "the old master, Jack Lynch [displaying] a real flash of his superb genius. Ranging upfield as the time was ebbing, he took the law into his own hands. Showing surprising speed, the ball in perfect hopping control, he bore his weaving way through the staggered Tipp. Backs, and fifteen yards out, he let fly with a short, sweet wrist-snap. The net bulged and Cork were one point behind." Another Cork player equalised and the game was a draw. Tipperary won the replay. (Courtesy of Liam Ó Tuama)

One of the first meetings with Máirín, at Glengarriff during a break in training for the All-Ireland football semi-final, 1943. *From left:* Frank Casey, Jack Lynch, Noreen Dillon, Beryl Fagan, Con Prior, Máirín O'Connor, Finbarr Lynch, Sheila Crowley, Paddy O'Donovan. (Courtesy of Liam Ó Tuama)

On the day Jack Lynch was called to the Bar, in 1945. Standing behind Jack and Máirín are, *from left:* Máirín's mother, Mrs O'Connor, Beryl Smith by then married to Brendan Smith, Father Jack's elder brother, Charlie Lynch, Mrs Hoeing, Finbarr Lynch, and Finbarr's wife, Rita. (Courtesy of Liam Ó Tuama)

Jack and Máirín with Jack's brother, Charlie, standing between them. The other priest is Father Hayes. The picture was taken at Jack's sister Eva's house in Redemption Road, Cork, at the end of August 1945. Charlie and Father Hayes had worked in London during the Second World War and had helped victims of the Blitz in Balham, in the Southwark Diocese. (Courtesy of Dan Harvey)

Jack and Máirín on their wedding day, August 10th 1946.
(Courtesy of Liam Ó Tuama)

A rare occasion: the four Lynch brothers together, at a North Mon presentation. Father Charlie is on the left, Finbarr on the right. Theo, standing beside Jack in the centre, was christened Timothy. Using the Irish form of his surname, O'Loinghsigh, led to him being called "T.O." This became Theo. (Courtesy of Dan Harvey)

Seán Lemass, Jack Lynch and Charles Haughey boarding an aircraft at Dublin Airport to fly to London for trade agreement talks in 1965. (Courtesy of *The Irish Times*)

Jack Lynch and Jim Young lead out the Glen and New York teams at Gaelic Park, in New York at the end of September 1966. Jack Lynch was in the United States with Dr T.K. Whitaker, Secretary of the Department of Finance, for talks at the International Monetary Fund. He told Whitaker on that trip that he had decided in favour of going for the leadership of Fianna Fáil which Seán Lemass had suggested to him. (Courtesy of Liam Ó Tuama)

Jack Lynch and Seán Lemass at a meeting of the European Movement, 20th June 1969. (Courtesy of *The Irish Times*)

Jack Lynch, after the Dáil had voted him in as Taoiseach, leaves Leinster House surrounded by a congratulatory crowd on his way to Áras an Uachtaráin to receive his seal of office. (Courtesy of Maxwell Picture Agency Ltd)

Éamon de Valera and Jack Lynch on the occasion of the formation of the 1969 Government. (Courtesy of Maxwell Picture Agency Ltd)

Captain Terence O'Neill, the Northern Ireland Prime Minister, with the Taoiseach, Jack Lynch, at their meeting in Stormont Castle, 7th December 1967. (Courtesy of *The Irish Times*)

Jack Lynch makes a presentation to Fianna Fáil Party Secretary Hetty Behan. Between them are Gus Healy, Jack's long-term running mate in Cork, and Celia Lynch. Máirín Lynch is on the left next to Kit Ahern and David Andrews. It was Hetty Behan who went out to find a shoebox to hold the ballot papers in the leadership election in 1966. (Courtesy of Kit Ahern)

Jack and Máirín Lynch set out on official business. (Courtesy of Maxwell Picture Agency Ltd)

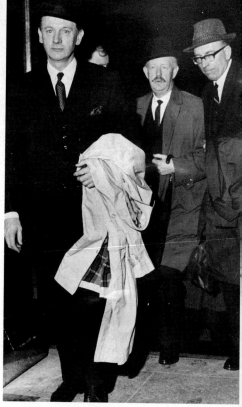

Jack Lynch, followed by J.C.B. MacCarthy, Secretary of the Department of Industry and Commerce, and Dr T.K. Whitaker, Secretary of the Department of Finance, return from talks in London, 30th November 1968. (Courtesy of *The Irish Times*)

Giving Máirín a "birdie" in Buncrana, County Donegal. (Courtesy of Colman Doyle)

Jack Lynch, statesman, *Clockwise, from left:* laughing with Mrs Jacqueline Kennedy at a reception in Dublin Castle, 30th June 1967; before an official lunch at Dublin Castle with U.S. President Richard and Mrs Pat Nixon, 5th October 1970; and being put at ease by Muhammad Ali in Leinster House, 1972. (Courtesy of Lensmen; Associated Press, AP; *The Irish Times*)

1967, followed up in August by a protest march in Dungannon on the issue of housing. The outcome of this event brought out the deeply tribal and prejudiced nature of authority in Northern Ireland, but from NICRA's point of view it was a public relations success of considerable importance, both in confronting injustice and in achieving worldwide attention through television. It encouraged a Civil Rights march in Derry on 5th October that led to a major confrontation with the Royal Ulster Constabulary (RUC). The level of sectarian prejudice, of violent and aggressive behaviour by the Northern Ireland police force, and the political misjudgement by the Home Affairs Minister, William Craig, made of this a turning point, but it was one in which the Republic failed to become engaged in any responsible sense. Jack Lynch must bear blame for this. Brave and heavily outnumbered men and women of the Civil Rights Movement were being beaten with batons in the streets of Derry.

Meanwhile, government Ministers in the south were campaigning for the kind of electoral structure that would make possible in the Republic precisely the kind of arrogance and oppression that was bedevilling the North. That, at least, was how many in the North saw southern indifference. It is also widely felt that it contributed to the heavy defeat of the P.R. referendum in southern Ireland with a 60 per cent vote against in rural areas and 70 per cent against in urban areas.

At the end of November 1968 Terence O'Neill announced a reform programme which promised sweeping changes, and followed this with his "Ulster at the Crossroads" broadcast. Two days later he dismissed Craig. It was too little, and it was too late. Jack Lynch's endorsement of Terence O'Neill was the only proper course open to him, but it could go no further. At that time there was no possibility of exerting any pressure. It would have been counter-productive, and in any case Lynch himself faced problems in the Republic. He was confronting his first general election, and to some extent he was in the hands of a party many members of which had reservations about the Northern Ireland policy adopted by Lemass and taken over by the new leader.

The gut instinct of Fianna Fáil was anything but reformist. If this was a general principle in many domestic aspects of social and moral behaviour, it was even more acutely the case in respect of Northern Ireland. While Lemass and Lynch both espoused a policy of reconciliation, and while both leaders, together with Éamon de Valera, accepted that reunification should be achieved only with the consent of the people of Northern Ireland, this view was by no means universally held. Serving in Government with Lynch were Ministers who had other thoughts about resolving what was known as "the national question", and they focused on the use of force.

Neil Blaney became the key figure within this irredentist rump. He was firmly and irrevocably opposed to Lynch and his policies; he did not believe that Northern Ireland was recoverable as a political entity, nor did he think reform was possible. As a consequence, he began at this time to work to a different agenda. Energetically and on a wide front involving many groups, organisations and individuals in Northern Ireland and the Republic, Blaney sought to disrupt and reverse the politics of consent and agreement which Lynch had been pursuing. Though the policy had its practical origins in Lemass's visit to Captain Terence O'Neill, Northern Ireland's Prime Minister, in January 1965, it went much further back. de Valera had never supported an overtly militarist solution for the North, and no one in Fianna Fáil under his leadership had put forward the kind of thinking which Blaney was now expressing.

His first contentious speech came in the autumn of 1968 and included criticisms of the Civil Rights Movement for not having the reunification of Ireland on its agenda. He attacked at that time the meetings which Lemass and Lynch had held with Terence O'Neill. His views were seen in the South as a challenge to Lynch's leadership. To a considerable extent Blaney's audience during these speeches was essentially south of the Border. North of it he was fundamentally at odds with the leaders of the Civil Rights Movement and also with Nationalist politicians who had participated in the early Civil Rights demonstrations. They had specifically sought support from the South in getting United Kingdom reforms extended to the North, and not in pursuing the United Ireland objective, which was old-style Fianna Fáil politics.

None of this stopped Blaney. He consistently opposed and sought to undermine not only the position occupied by the Government of which he was a part, but also the democratically elected representatives of the nationalist community in Northern Ireland as well as the popular Civil Rights Movement for reform. In fact he dedicated nearly all his time and energy, between the Derry riots of October 1968 and his removal from office, and later from membership of the Fianna Fáil party in 1971, to sustained challenge against Lynch's leadership.

Extraordinary though it may seem, the approach pursued by Blaney was handled with subtlety and skill. He was ostensibly voicing Fianna Fáil policy when he spoke out on the reunification of the country or on the national sovereignty claim, and this made it difficult for Lynch to call him to account. There was some legitimacy in his criticism of the Civil Rights approach. His basis position was *echt* Republican.

Even so, Blaney got what was happening in Northern Ireland quite wrong and it reinforces the conviction that his real political target was Lynch and those who supported him in the Republic. In a speech he made in Derry, for example, in January 1969, he was clearly out of tune with events, his words directed towards Dublin rather than towards Derry, Belfast or the Westminster Government.

As we have seen, a policy of sorts had been drawn up to contend with the relatively low level of violence which the Civil Rights organisations in Northern Ireland, with their all too legitimate demands for fair treatment of the minority, had to face. The first marches, during the month of August a year earlier, had been peaceful. Not so peaceful had been subsequent demonstrations and marches. In due course at Burntollet Bridge, near Claudy, County Derry, in the Civil Rights march that had begun to make its way across Northern Ireland from Belfast to

Derry on New Year's Day 1969, violence of a vicious and unprecedented kind erupted. Protestant extremists, led by Major Ronald Bunting, one of Ian Paisley's close aides, ambushed the Civil Rights marchers, beat them with clubs and stoned them, injuring 300, while a far from impartial RUC looked on.

Even this disgraceful episode was contained within the policy guidelines to which Lynch was working. He had invited the leaders of the Nationalist community in the North to Dublin and had talked with them. He based his thinking on their advice, and that had been sufficient for the first six months of the year. It had carried Lynch, the leader as yet untried by the challenge of a general election, into his summer campaign. Now it was the subject of re-examination.

As part of his platform and as a further gesture of disdain towards the Civil Rights Movement, Neil Blaney in that January 1969 speech decided to call instead for new political initiatives. Some of these were overtly stated – including federal or national councils for Ireland – which would help silence and replace the Civil Rights organisations. He was proposing a Dublin-Belfast axis or a Dublin-London-Belfast federal council. Since the North had just gone through the electrifying spectacle of the brutality at Burntollet directed by the RUC and the B Specials against the People's Democracy four-day march from Belfast to Derry, Blaney's solution was unrealistic. But it was an embarrassment to Lynch, and one that he could not easily silence since it accorded with the dreaded and tedious comprehensiveness of Fianna Fáil's Northern Ireland policy. Both Blaney and Boland were expert in this, and able to quote from a variety of sources. They did so, it often seems, not to further a peaceful resolution of the North's tinderbox situation, but to foment difficulties within their own party, their own Government, and their own part of Ireland.

Blaney got the Civil Rights situation wrong: he also, as a result, got developments within the Unionist Party wrong. On the one hand he found unacceptable the agitation for reform instead of a campaign for reunification ; he found equally unacceptable the reforms that were initiated, then and later, by the British Government and by the Unionists led by Captain Terence O'Neill. Blaney had quite another agenda, aimed at satisfying hard line republicanism within Fianna Fáil and obstructing the principles of consent and agreement espoused by Lynch.

Despite the resignation of Brian Faulkner from the Northern Ireland Government in January 1969, Terence O'Neill did rather better than expected in the Northern Ireland general election which took place on 24th February 1969. To southern dismay, the northern Nationalists, traditionally aligned with Fianna Fáil, were eclipsed by what were effectively Civil Rights candidates, who were to become the Social Democratic and Labour Party of Northern Ireland (SDLP).[20] O'Neill's apparent recovery did not last. Two months later on 28th April, O'Neill

---

[20] Unionists won 39 seats. The Nationalists were reduced to 6 seats, and others took 7. John Hume and Ivan Cooper, at that time identified as Civil Rights candidates, were elected to Stormont.

announced his resignation, and on 1st May was succeeded as Prime Minister by Major James Chichester-Clark.

Lynch, in a characteristically passive piece of role-playing, kept his counsel and waited on developments. He faced his first general election as leader. He knew well enough that in the eyes of the vast majority of people in the South the events in Belfast, Derry and elsewhere were of little significance when set beside the key bread-and-butter issues on which the election would be fought. Part of the preparation for this came in the form of the *Third Programme for Economic and Social Development 1969–1972*, which set the tone for the election debates. What also set the tone was Kevin Boland's Electoral (Amendment) Act, which increased the number of Dáil constituencies from 38 to 42, and effectively redrew constituency boundaries to benefit Fianna Fáil. Boland was a tough operator. A month after introducing the Bill, he abolished Dublin City Council and put control of the city under a commissioner.

*

It could not be said that Jack Lynch's first period as Taoiseach showed him either in firm control of the party, or successfully achieving the targets he had set himself. He had wanted to create a team spirit among his Ministers, to achieve greater cohesion in the Government's operation, and he naturally wished to exert his personal authority. A question mark hangs over the fulfilment of each of these objectives. Yet the picture of a man not in control has been excessively the product of commentary, much of it based on the mistaken interpretation of him as an uncertain and reluctant leader, and at least some of it promulgated by his enemies. The record of his speeches both inside and outside the Dáil and the wide understanding of his ideas and commitments presented a favourable image of him as leader. He was calm, relaxed, thoughtful, and invariably accurate and precise in what he said.

Although he made much of the difficulties of following Lemass, he actually followed him with reasonable ease and confidence. He did have difficulties with colleagues. As Lynch himself said:

> There was another difficulty, during the latter years of the Seán Lemass reign. He had deliberately allowed individual ministers a degree of personal freedom which is unusual in a government. He had frequently spoken of government departments as 'development corporations'. He had also wanted to create the opportunities for ministers to show their individual flair and enterprise prior to the change of leadership which he, almost alone, knew was in the offing before it was generally suspected.[21]

Even under Lemass in the period before the 1965 general election, this approach had led to the development of Fianna Fáil's own brand of corporatism when it

---

[21] Jack Lynch, "My Life and Times" in *Magill* (November 1979), p. 43.

gave birth to the Taca organisation. The effect of Lemass's interpretation of ministerial freedom after 1965 was clearly ill-judged and it grew worse under Lynch. The Constitution does not invest the Taoiseach with much power. He is legally the chairman of a group called the Government in which all real power is, or should be, invested. Any liberal interpretation of the approach adopted by Lemass, of which Lynch writes, creates a diversity of difficulties that would colour Irish politics for a long time to come.

As the party came to the end of its fourth year in office, in the early summer of 1969, with a general election not far off, the team spirit, such as it was, gave cause for concern. It had been made ragged by Neil Blaney's individualist interpretation of republicanism. Lynch's own leadership had been subtly insulted by Haughey, who adopted a style and attitude in the Department of Finance tantamount to an alternative leadership. One shrewd observer of the political scene at the time, Owen Sheehy Skeffington, wrote perceptively of him:

> He has an arrogance which beats the band... He can be very charming, it is true, to those who flatter him, but a deep inner insecurity gives him a low temper-flashpoint, which renders him often petulant and sometimes absurd.[22]

Kevin Boland's position was that Fianna Fáil had a duty to make good in Northern Ireland the deficiency of a Nationalist community that had no commitment to reunification. This effectively meant that another route had to be found which would bypass the objective of reform, the cross-border collaboration of Jack Lynch with Terence O'Neill, and the respect for the principle of consent. There was only one force in Ireland that offered such a route: the IRA.

The organisation, with good reason, was suspicious at this time of any contact, however covert, between itself and Fianna Fáil. The IRA had known where it stood with de Valera and Lemass, and had seen no value in links of any kind. In the case of Jack Lynch, the whole matter was open to various interpretations. Newspaper coverage of Fianna Fáil affairs during the first three years of Lynch's leadership had emphasised the instability of his control. Every expression of independent thought by Blaney was seized on as evidence of uncertainty in the leadership, and there was a degree of speculation about the future which gathered momentum as marches in Northern Ireland became progressively more violent.

Lynch himself sustained a Northern Ireland policy that was consistent and realistic. But inevitably it lacked the drama of any solution and sought a consensus that, in contrast with the fire and brimstone issuing from Blaney and others, seemed to be weak and uncertain. He did in fact maintain the basic Fianna Fáil principle of "the unification of the national territory". This was the result sought by the party, and it always had been. But it was to be achieved "by consent", and

---

[22] *The Irish Times*, 11th May 1970, article entitled "They'll none of them be missed...". It was a commentary following the dismissal of Ministers in the Arms Crisis.

the people of Northern Ireland were a long way from granting that consent.

Lynch's speeches throughout this period were carefully worded and delivered in a tone that sought a peaceful resolution to an increasingly violent conflict. They were listened to, read, analysed, criticised and condemned in a mood of volatile uncertainty. In this there were many strands of irresponsibility, not a few of them having their source within his own Government.

*

Everything hinged on the forthcoming general election. The main players in the heightened atmosphere which seemed to surround the supposed leadership issue – and they included Blaney, his supporter Boland, and Haughey – would be deeply involved in fighting that election. Nothing profitable could be achieved until it was over and so the sequence of events in the first half of 1969 took on a complex character. On 21st May the eighteenth Dáil was dissolved.

Under normal circumstances the performance of Fianna Fáil and its apparent instability and uncertainty of direction would have threatened its electoral prospects. The contradictory views on Northern Ireland were examined in the press in the context of a party leader who did not have unqualified support, and the party had inflicted damage on itself through the attempt to remove proportional representation. This was a defeat as much for Blaney and Boland as for anyone; the hard men, used to winning elections and capable in party management around the country, were discredited. It was an open invitation to Fine Gael and Labour to come together and offer a coalition option. The electorate was expressing a stout defence of the system that favoured partnership.

They did the opposite. Fine Gael saw the point but, with a breathtaking disdain for political opportunity, the Labour Party rejected their offer of electoral co-operation or partnership. Brendan Corish, the Labour Party leader, was a rugged, rural socialist, old-fashioned in his political views and intellectually limited. The senior members of the party included men of considerable talent. Its leading intellectuals were Conor Cruise O'Brien, David Thornley and Justin Keating. The general secretary, Brendan Halligan, was a shrewd enough organiser who had the wit to explore the prospect of a coalition stance with Fine Gael. The same sense of opportunity inspired Garret FitzGerald. He had come up within Fine Gael and had contributed, with Declan Costello, to the reconstruction of its policies. This centred on a document entitled *Towards a Just Society*, which undoubtedly indicated a social democratic way forward. A new view of the way Fine Gael might recapture power was evident in party thinking and acceptable, with reservations, to the party leader, Liam Cosgrave. But despite having a good deal in common with the political thought which then fuelled the energies of the Labour Party, nothing came of it. For some unimaginable set of reasons, Labour thought that Ireland was at a watershed that would lead to a political division of Left and Right. In the event the two parties failed to come together with an electoral pact for the 1969 election, and gave to Jack Lynch the opportunity he needed. This was to concentrate on domestic successes, ignore Northern Ireland, put the mistake of the P.R. referendum firmly behind him, and conduct a campaign in which his undoubted personal appeal throughout the country gave him a distinct advantage over the other two party leaders. He was supported by his wife, Máirín, who went with him on the campaign trail and greatly enjoyed the experience. It covered all parts of the country, beginning in Dublin where he attended election conventions with one in Dublin North Central on 25th May, a Sunday. He commenced the countrywide tour the following Tuesday in Kilkenny and then on to Waterford followed by campaign meetings in Thurles, Nenagh, Mallow and Tralee.

On the Saturday night Lynch's party were in Letterkenny, in North Donegal. This was Blaney's territory and he was very much in control. At the end of the speeches he ushered the platform party into a side room away from the crowded hall. Máirín wanted to meet the local people and she insisted on doing so. Blaney was not at all pleased at this nor was she too happy with his approach. It seemed he either misread the appeal the party leader and his wife were having around the country, or deliberately wanted to obstruct the impact.

Jack Lynch went on through Ballina and Roscommon, two volatile constituencies at that time, and then on into Meath and Offaly for election meetings in Navan and Tullamore. After that he went to Athlone and then across to the West and Castlebar. On Friday, 13th June, at the end of the second week, he made an election broadcast. Throughout the country the reception he received was warm and people were supportive. The disastrous P.R. campaign should have helped the opposition parties yet, in the circumstances, it failed to work.

> He went on to Galway on the night of the broadcast, and then to Ennis and Limerick, and then back to Wicklow. The final election rally in Dublin was on the following Monday, and then he went down to Cork for a final rally there. In a note of regret he said: 'It has not been possible for me, on this occasion, because of my countrywide tour, to spend as much time as I would have wished among my own people here in Cork.'[23]

Lynch took a hard line at the end of the campaign. He said:

> We have been witnessing a contest between Fine Gael and Labour, not for Government – since neither stands a chance of that – but for Opposition. At least both parties have now got the message loud and clear that the Irish people have reserved special places for them on the Opposition benches and that it is there the people intend to keep them. . . . The result of the general election was most satisfactory. The campaign was a fine example of the democratic process in action and the result testifies to the political maturity and sound judgement of the Irish people.[24]

---

[23] I am indebted to the archivist of the Boole Library, Cork University, for the material for this tour which is in their collection of Lynch Papers.

[24] *Ibid.*

Lynch enjoyed the advantage of a sense of national well-being. Haughey, in a series of social changes in the Budget – which were later treated as far-sighted – including concern for the less well-off, had prepared favourable conditions for the campaign. In effect he had delivered a populist instrument deliberately suited to the election.

The combination had proved successful. Of the many political issues that faced Lynch, none stood out as particularly burdensome or intractable. The decade that was drawing to a close had been one of unprecedented national satisfaction. There had been steady growth, and the economy was sound. A good deal of thought and work had gone into Ireland's trading position. Inevitable dependence on membership of the EEC was the conclusion.

The confidence was reinforced by other factors. One of these was television. The Irish channel, Radio Telefís Éireann, opened at the beginning of the decade. By 1969 it had transformed social and intellectual life, and had fundamentally changed traditional values. The dominance of the Catholic Church had been challenged, sometimes in frivolous ways, but in the broader sense undermining for ever the exclusive role it had enjoyed in respect of personal morality and cultural control. A new media force was now responsible for the presentation of culture and morality. It had, in turn, changed perceptions about how politics and politicians were to be seen. It was exploited more effectively at first by the talent within the two opposition parties, but it also helped towards public understanding of a middle-of-the-road, accessible political charm in Lynch himself.

Winning a convincing victory in the summer of 1969 changed the view of Lynch as a compromise leader. It also changed the idea that Fianna Fáil needed to rely too heavily on the party machine that Blaney controlled, or the razzmatazz which the director of elections, Charles Haughey, brought to the campaign trail. They and others within the party were too Fianna Fáil. Lynch, in contrast, reached out to the Irish people in a way that transcended political labelling. A political balance in Fianna Fáil's favour had been confirmed yet again. de Valera's general election victory in 1957 had been followed by two terms under Lemass – 1961 and 1965 – and now in 1969 another leader of the party had comfortably held at bay the divided strengths of the two main opposition parties. He was much more firmly in charge, and he had confirmed yet again that Fianna Fáil, two leaders on from de Valera, had exorcised the towering ghosts of the past.

When the Dáil resumed on 2nd July, Lynch made minimal changes to his Government. Frank Aiken, who retired to the back benches, was replaced as Tánaiste by Erskine Childers, Lynch's most senior colleague. Patrick Hillery moved from Labour to External Affairs and Pádraig Faulkner from Lands to Education. But the main appointments were renewed, with Charles Haughey returning to Finance, George Colley to Industry and Commerce and the Gaeltacht, Neil Blaney to Agriculture and Fisheries and Kevin Boland to Local Government, with the addition of Social Welfare.

CHAPTER SIX

Jack Lynch and the Northern Ireland Crisis

Jack Lynch formed his Government on 2nd July 1969. He had won a comfortable majority and could look forward to a full term in office and the exercise of an authority earned by electoral achievement. The election had brought Fianna Fáil together. Quite deliberately, there had been silence from Neil Blaney on Northern Ireland, and Lynch himself had avoided the subject during the campaign. Relative calm in Northern Ireland itself had helped to relegate it as an issue to the margins of political debate. James Chichester-Clark, who had become the Northern Ireland Prime Minister on 1st May, was given an uncontentious honeymoon period of ten weeks.

But Northern Ireland lives by its political calendar, and the relative political calm of May and June is as predictable as the turmoil which comes with the marching season. On 12th July, the anniversary of the Battle of the Boyne, there were Orange Order marches in Northern Ireland, and rioting broke out in Derry, Dungiven and Lurgan. On both sides there was shooting, and two people were wounded by police. Then on 14th July, in Dungiven, the first death resulting from the Civil Rights campaigning occurred. It was an unfortunate by-product of the confrontations, rather than the result of deliberate police brutality. An elderly farmer, who was an onlooker, was struck in a mêlée between opposing groups outside the Orange Hall. This incident aggravated the difficult security situation. Sectarian clashes followed in Derry and Belfast and there were serious riots in Belfast at the beginning of August.

Chichester-Clark, an urbane and limited man with a background of Eton and the Guards, was faced with a crisis which very rapidly involved the British Home Secretary, Jim Callaghan, and the Minister of Defence, Denis Healey. The British Army presence at the time was small and was under General Sir Ian Freeland. Though put on alert at the time of the earlier riots, it was not anticipated that it would be deployed on the streets. The main security force remained the RUC, despite the Catholic communities deep distrust of them.

The main focus of concern was the Apprentice Boys' march in Derry on 12th August. The confrontations and the violence were widely signalled before the event. Chichester-Clark had the option of banning the march, but if he exercised it and the Apprentice Boys defied the ban, there could have been a general breakdown of law and order. This reasoning represented the public stance of the Stormont Government. The Nationalist people in Derry had been warned and threatened with Unionist, Orange Order and RUC "reprisals" for what had happened in the riots in July, as well as those which followed the Burntollet ambush on 4th January 1969 when 300 people were injured. Events had exposed in graphic detail, and on a worldwide scale through television coverage, the brutality and oppression of the Northern Ireland security forces. They were unrestrained by any British Army presence on the ground, despite garrisoned forces in the North. The Nationalists in Derry were determined now to defend the Bogside at all costs and to this end prepared petrol bombs and put up barricades. These were in place on the morning of the march.

The violence that followed, even in the shadow of events in January, April, July, and earlier in Belfast in August, was unprecedented. Beginning in Derry, it spread elsewhere, and became vicious and sustained in Belfast. On 14th August 300 British troops were deployed in Derry, and by the end of that week the British Army had taken control of security in both cities.

Lynch was thrown into a sudden and immense crisis. He called the first of a series of emergency government meetings for the morning of 13th August. He was confronted by Ministers with widely different views on what should be done. Some of them were highly critical of him and of what they regarded as a Northern Ireland policy that had been rendered irrelevant by the events of the previous day. Lynch was not so sure, but reacted in favour of the harder line that was proposed.

Though essentially this was a government crisis, Lynch felt that it was also one that impinged directly and forcefully on himself in respect of the policy for the North that he had consistently espoused and delivered. Fundamentally, he believed in what he had been saying over the previous twelve months. In principle, nothing had changed. But a sharper edge was needed, among other things, in order to assuage the violent reaction within his own Government and the Fianna Fáil Party. What followed would dominate his life for the next two years, turning into a formidable challenge to his leadership.

The reverberations have lasted over thirty years. There were deep divisions then; they remain today and are reflected in continuing arguments and debates. Furthermore, despite the release of a great deal of documentation, very little has been added to our understanding. Many of the questions raised at that time will never be answered.

*

The narrative in the Republic of Ireland is in itself remarkable. Though the response was ostensibly to the situation in Derry, it very rapidly deteriorated into confusion, disagreement and recrimination. "Let's fight among ourselves!" might well have been the designating instinct. This visceral reaction was combined with an atmosphere of dispute about where to start. The principles on which the

Fianna Fáil party had been founded, some of which had been worn out and in all practical terms abandoned, were seen by certain Ministers as in need of dusting off and reconsidering as part of the Government's response. Other Ministers were confused by what was going on, relieved that it was a hundred miles away, and focused on what advantage might be obtained out of this. Some saw it as the beginning of the end of the Lynch era.

What Lynch himself faced, at the government meeting on the day following the Apprentice Boys' march and the subsequent Derry riots, was in reality a multi-tiered challenge to his leadership, his policies, and the personnel who were advising him. It did not fully emerge on that occasion, but was made clear to him by the end of the week.

Government documents suggest that the senior civil servants advising Jack Lynch and other Ministers, advice which came to the Cabinet on 13th August and on subsequent days on which the Government met, were in favour of restraint generally. This is confirmed by Dr T.K. Whitaker whose advice Jack Lynch sought privately that week and who subsequently became a significant figure in the evolution of policy. The Civil Service view was that Jack Lynch could be manoeuvred into a position where he was taking greater responsibility for events in Northern Ireland without having any control over those events. This was relevant in particular over the choice between seeking for a United Nations peacekeeping force for Northern Ireland as opposed to greater direct British involvement in keeping the peace through the deployment of the British Army. The latter course, if the Republic of Ireland became more directly involved, was full of risk. No one could predict what the reaction in the different communities in Northern Ireland would be to the British soldiers taking over from the RUC. No one could predict how this reaction would be coloured by direct Irish Government intervention. To be party to such a development without exercising any control over it was regarded by the reasonably well-informed officials advising the Government as foolhardy.

Yet members of Lynch's Government at the time were contemplating far more hawkish options and far more direct and provocative interventions. It was almost pre-emptive of this dangerous line of thought that the Government decided to press upon the British Government the need for a United Nations peacekeeping force to be sent to Northern Ireland. It was not anticipated that the advice would be followed. There were troops already in place to back up the civil power and more could be rapidly deployed, as in fact they were. In contrast, United Nations agreement, even if Britain conceded to the Irish "request", together with the creation and deployment of such a force, would take weeks, perhaps even months. The fact that government action was taken immediately on this, while the actual meeting continued, is evidence of the pre-emptive purpose, designed to head off the far greater risk of seeking an inter-government meeting during the days of crisis.

At that government meeting a consensus did prevail. It recognised what the political and practical limitations were. The main danger of interventionist thinking was that it would involve the Government accepting responsibility, but at the same time having no direct control or involvement in Northern affairs.

The civil service advice at the time reflected and expanded on government policy as enunciated by Jack Lynch. The case, often made, that Lynch, during the Cabinet meetings that took place in that week of crisis, was somehow manoeuvred into adopting a new and harsher policy on Northern Ireland and towards the British Government, led by Harold Wilson, does not stand up.

The policy that was followed was, however, very much at odds with the view taken by Neil Blaney, which he also had forcefully and publicly expressed on a number of occasions, and which now motivated his contributions to government thinking. Tacitly, or overtly, Blaney was supported by other Ministers.

In facing this situation Jack Lynch had a further difficult judgement to make. The supposed hardening of the Government's attitude on Northern Ireland – much more a matter of words than action – and its expression in the statement which Jack Lynch later made, was used by his opponents as evidence of their supremacy. The impact on the public was quite significant: people *believed* there had been a change of direction.

Again, it was not the case. What the opponents appeared to have achieved was precisely the embarrassment that the senior civil servants feared. It seems probable that this, despite its blatant foolishness recognised by Lynch and others, was the real intention of some of them. In other words, Jack Lynch knew he was confronted by men in his own administration who quite conceivably wanted him to make the very mistakes that senior civil service advisers had identified as those which would put the administration most at risk.

Ministerial pressure on Lynch, about which Ministers later became boastful, was to adopt a harder line towards the British. It was clearly consistent with what Neil Blaney had been saying publicly. He was supported around the Cabinet table, though for different reasons. Boland would not have been adverse to direct intervention by the Irish Army. Quite who in government knew what Haughey believed is unclear; but they were opposed to Lynch continuing as leader of Fianna Fáil and as Taoiseach. The crisis presented Haughey and Blayney in particular with an opportunity to make a concerted effort towards destabilising his leadership.

Jack Lynch clearly recognised the possibility of this disgraceful motive being part of the developing crisis. He knew that in the volatile circumstances prevailing at that precise time in Northern Ireland he was more vulnerable to their threat to his authority than ever before. His judgement on how to proceed had to accommodate the possibility that they were giving expression to a genuine set of perceptions about how government policy on Northern Ireland should proceed in the light of events. He also had to absorb the high level of instability deriving from press, radio and television reporting and comment. But behind it all experience had now taught him that the hidden jockeying for power within Fianna Fáil was never far from the minds of senior Ministers in the Government.

To a very significant extent Jack Lynch's experiences during that week of crisis in August 1969 shaped his judgement and this particular week overshadowed events until the spring of the following year.

The main pressure within the Government was in favour of a public expression of toughness towards the British and strong support for the minority communities in Northern Ireland. It came principally from Neil Blaney, supported by Kevin Boland. Charles Haughey was of the same mind but not as vocal. These three were supported in different degrees by Brian Lenihan, Micheál Ó Móráin, Jim Gibbons and, possibly, Seán Flanagan. They were variously motivated. Boland gives a brief and pithy account of the disposition of government members: "The minority was Blaney, myself and Haughey with support from Gibbons and with Moran not opposed but obsessed with the over-riding need to guard against 'subversives'." Those in favour of Lynch's approach are listed as Colley, Hillery and Childers. "This group was typified by Lenihan, who cheerfully and appropriately described himself as the X in 'oxo' with one leg on each side of the fence."[1] It was a description that came to fit Lenihan throughout his political career.

Those who backed Lynch were Erskine Childers, Patrick Hillery, Joseph Brennan, George Colley, Pádraig Faulkner and Patrick Lalor. Boland[2] described as "a small minority" those who were opposed to Lynch, but actually the numbers were more evenly balanced. However, the fragmentation represented a serious problem and, fortunately, Lynch had a clear grasp of the implications of this. He had long since clarified his own thoughts on Northern Ireland, had spoken frequently on the subject, and was clear on the basic principle of consent. Never before had he been confronted around the government table with the kind of argument and disagreement which now emerged. It was in no sense the time for a reconsideration of Ireland's historic conflict with Britain, and how it bore upon the events of the day. It was certainly not the occasion for exploitation. Astonished though he was by the arguments that were being made, he had to acknowledge the legitimacy of reaching agreement. In the final analysis, government decision-making depended on this, and he had to judge where the centre of gravity was. He was helped, of course, by reasonably accurate police intelligence and by the far less extensive military intelligence. Nonetheless, he and other government Ministers were seriously thrown, particularly by the knowing approach adopted by Blaney, whose supposed first-hand knowledge, often embroidered and exaggerated, was nevertheless a persuasive enough insight to sway others. Lynch was disposed to discount it somewhat, but this did not mean that he could persuade other Ministers to do the same. In the heightened atmosphere of violence renewed on an unprecedented scale, he recognised that events could unfold day by day to his political disadvantage. Above all, he recognised that he needed to hold the centre ground.

The men he had to watch turned out to be Blaney, Haughey and Boland. But

---

[1] Kevin Boland, *Up Dev!* (published by the author, Dublin, 1977), p. 11.
[2] *Ibid.*

in the first instance Blaney was the one most overtly opposed to Lynch's policies. In different degrees and with different emphases, these men disapproved of the policy of conciliation towards the authorities in Northern Ireland, and the reliance on Britain to control security and to reform Northern Ireland's social and democratic structures. They had not favoured Lynch's meeting with Terence O'Neill. They did not want him to achieve a parallel relationship with Chichester-Clark.

Blaney, a "machine-man" in politics generally, saw the need for Fianna Fáil to have a greater say in Northern Ireland affairs and to be directly involved there. In his view this was not going to happen through government co-operation at prime ministerial level. Nor would it be achieved through talks with members of the Unionist Government. In Blaney's eyes political vacuums had been created, a situation achieved by Civil Rights Movement marches and demonstrations of which he did not approve. Part of his objection was that the movement was definitely not campaigning for a united Ireland. But beyond that, the very concept of "civil rights" was alien to Blaney's view of politics and of political power.

Kevin Boland was of the same view, and later recorded of this time: "We considered the establishment of Fianna Fáil on the other side of the Border and had almost decided that this might have to be done." This view was not widely canvassed in the party at the time. Nevertheless, Blaney and Boland had a considerable degree of influence and were widely in touch with the grass roots. In the increasingly aggressive and militant atmosphere of the time, this included the more republican wing of Fianna Fáil.

Their position was logical, if perverse. If events continued to run out of control as they were doing, with the pace of progress being set by issues of "civil rights", this would adversely affect Fianna Fáil in the future both north and south of the Border. Fianna Fáil was anything but a party of tolerance and of rights. It sought power and control, and parts of it were firmly in the hands of individuals whose concern for democracy was at best questionable and whose belief in militancy and the use of force was well developed.

Haughey's position was rather different. Being more opportunistic and less inspired by issues of principle or ideology, he had by now discovered to his cost that the Lynch leadership of the party was by no means an interim event. Lynch's removal would require action rather than patience. It was no longer a matter of time. If the use of force, on the other side of the Border, was a means to the end Haughey cherished – of replacing Jack Lynch – then those means would be espoused.

The alternative to a Fianna Fáil push into Northern Ireland – which was in truth unrealistic – was the sponsorship of an alternative such as the IRA. Initial approaches, before the 1969 general election, were treated with grave suspicion by the organisation and nothing came of them. But they did set the tone for interventionist thinking, and this now surfaced as part of the fragmented and disorganised response by the Government to the Battle of the Bogside in August.

The Republic of Ireland Government was trying to respond to a range of intractable problems on which all too little time and thought had been spent. Lynch had managed to win a general election with hardly a mention of the North and its fundamental problems of inequality, prejudice and suppression. Now, in dealing with the sudden eruption of violence fuelled by suppressed hatred and bigotry, Lynch found himself confronting a crisis of leadership. Within it, every member of the Fianna Fáil party, every deputy and senator in the Dáil, leaders of the community, commentators, the police and the army had to assess themselves and their role in a new light. Parts of the island of Ireland were aflame, riots were sustained for days on end, barricades went up, petrol bombs were prepared and thrown, and the RUC and the auxiliary police force, the B Specials, were engaging in acts of terrorism directed against the Catholic community.

In practical terms the options were very limited. A government statement, worded in the strongest terms, was a first requirement. The second was some form of aid. The Government debated whether this should be military, medical, diplomatic, financial, or a programme of public relations agitation designed to focus world interest on Northern Ireland, and on the inequalities there, for which Britain was largely responsible. At no stage was there any question of making arms available to individuals or groups on the other side of the Border.

Military intervention was rapidly ruled out. Army strengths were down, as some of the best troops had already been committed for United Nations service in Cyprus. In any case, without agreement from the British, an incursion would have been an absurd and futile act of aggression, particularly since no negotiations had broken down. Any singling out of one trouble spot – and the idea of sending the Army to Derry was discussed and ruled out – would have provoked pogroms elsewhere, most notably in Belfast, where military aid would have been out of the question. It was in fact deemed out of the question everywhere.

The truth was that, despite living right beside the problem, the Irish Government was more surprised than the British and far less intelligent in its reaction. The British may be blamed for allowing themselves to be overtaken by events, but the military and other interventions on which they engaged worked. The preliminary ideas expressed around the government table on 13th August were not well informed and, at times, not logical. There was in fact an intelligence vacuum. Furthermore, relations were vitiated by division and in some cases by an impotent and emotional rage.

There were clearly other possibilities, the most sensible being to prepare accommodation for people whose homes, property and lives had been attacked or were threatened, and who were terrified of a further increase in the violence. It was decided that army camps and other places of refuge in the South would be prepared for use and that field hospitals, organised and manned by military personnel, would be set up.

The immediate decision, made and implemented during the government meeting, was to ask the Irish ambassador in London to request a United Nations force in Northern Ireland. This was followed by the diplomatic initiative of sending Patrick Hillery, Minister for External Affairs, to London to advise the British

Government of the need for this UN peacekeeping force. The same message was to be delivered to U Thant, the United Nations Secretary General in New York.

The first reaction of the Government was summarised and made public in a statement which Lynch delivered on radio and television that evening. It was hard-hitting and critical, but its essential points were not inconsistent with his Northern Ireland policy. There had supposedly been a process of drafting at the government table, with the original departmental draft being strengthened and then having the sentence at the beginning of the first paragraph to read "The Government of Ireland can no longer stand idly by". For want of better evidence of their determination to act on behalf of the minority in the North, the word "idly" became a symbol of the difference between the hardliners in the Government and the majority who supported Lynch.

The statement was an effective summary of that first government meeting. It was the Republic's response to the crisis of worsening Northern Ireland violence. The text, as delivered by Lynch, read:

> The Irish Government can no longer stand by and see innocent people injured and perhaps worse. It is obvious that the RUC is no longer accepted as an impartial police force. Neither would the employment of British troops be acceptable nor would they be likely to restore peaceful conditions, certainly not in the long term. The Irish Government have, therefore, requested the British Government to apply immediately to the United Nations for the urgent dispatch of a Peace-Keeping Force to the Six Counties of Northern Ireland and have instructed the Permanent Representative to the United Nations to inform the Secretary General of this request. We have also asked the British Government to see to it that police attacks on the people of Derry should cease immediately.
>
> Very many people have been injured and some of them seriously. We know that many of these do not wish to be treated in Six County hospitals. We have, therefore, directed the Irish Army authorities to have field hospitals established in County Donegal adjacent to Derry and at other points along the Border where they may be necessary.
>
> Recognising, however, that the re-unification of the national territory can provide the only permanent solution for the problem, it is our intention to request the British Government to enter into early negotiations with the Irish Government to review the present constitutional position of the Six Counties of Northern Ireland.
>
> These measures which I have outlined to you seem to the Government to be those most immediately and urgently necessary.
>
> All men and women of goodwill will hope and pray that the present deplorable and distressing situation will not further deteriorate but that it will soon be ended firstly by the granting of full equality of citizenship to every man and woman in the Six Counties area regardless of class, creed or political persuasion and, eventually, by the restoration of the historic unity of our country.

The statement ended up being Jack Lynch's, and he edited it and softened it by such excisions as the word "idly" and by the insertion of "eventually" in the last sentence. He knew that the diplomatic missions to the British Government and his own Government's stated concern would produce an effective British reaction, which it did. He knew equally well not to exacerbate the situation. The Republic's potential for action, on the Border, in the North, with Britain or internationally, was very limited.

What he really feared, however, were the reactions within the Government, within his own party and within the IRA. He was well informed on the last. He knew that the IRA was active in trouble spots in Northern Ireland and was seeking to exploit the situation. Their primary purpose, reunification by the removal from Ireland of the British "presence", however defined, had been largely set aside during the 1960s in favour of socialist ideals. Though the organisation was still unitary, there were growing divisions and a tendency now to revert to the use of subversive military force. The Department of Justice, and notably its secretary, Peter Berry, was well informed about the organisation and fearful of its capacities, and Lynch was aware of this.

His most critical problem was located very close indeed, around the table at which the government members met and from where they exercised power. Constitutionally, they were sovereign and he was their chairman and their "voice". His leadership and his dominance were negotiable matters not legally underpinned, as in the British and other systems. In personality, he may have enjoyed a marginal pre-eminence over the rest of them, but in the end agreement was the basis for all decisions.

The three who were politically the strongest members of the Cabinet were ranged against him. Four other men were no more than camp followers. Three of these were heavy drinkers: Lenihan, Flanagan and Ó Móráin. The fourth, Gibbons, la newcomer to Government, was unsure of himself, and comparatively easily influenced by others. Lenihan, extremely bright but lacking in judgement, had been caught up in the world of Taca and mohair suits. He was not using the party to his own ends, and never did, but not being clearly motivated by anything he followed the group that made him welcome. Flanagan was probably motivated by the supposed interests and political views within his Mayo constituency. In due course these four were all to desert the republican wing within the Government, but at the outset of the crisis Lynch judged them as being, on balance, against conciliation.

In summary, the situation was more evenly balanced than has been generally the view. This made it constitutionally threatening if critical issues came to decisions by voting. Erskine Childers, who had a poor opinion of Haughey and of Blaney, was staunchly behind Lynch; so, too, were Patrick Hillery, Joseph Brennan, George Colley, Pádraig Faulkner and Patrick Lalor. In the circumstances, Lynch could expect to hold the line he had established at that first crisis government meeting, but he was alert to the vulnerability of his own position as leader.

The sequence of events in Northern Ireland is reasonably straightforward. It was immediately clear that the Chichester-Clark Government could not control the situation. British troops were on the streets of Derry within two days of the Apprentice Boys' march. Three hundred men of the Prince of Wales' Own Regiment were deployed on the streets of Derry by 5.15 p.m. on Thursday, 14th August. By the end of the week British troops were patrolling on the Falls Road and in the Ardoyne in Belfast; they were also out in other towns. Within a week of the Derry riots the British Government was in effective control. On 19th August General Sir Ian Freeland took authority for the B Specials and three days later they were ordered to hand in their arms. Highly important British government reports, on which subsequent reforms were based, followed rapidly. The Cameron Commission's Report on Disturbances in Northern Ireland appeared on 12th September. It found the Stormont Government at fault for Catholic grievances. It also found RUC intransigence and bias to blame for many of the disturbances. A month later the Hunt Committee recommended the disbanding of the B Specials, the reform of the RUC and the creation of two special constabularies, one under British Army control, the other a police reserve. The B Specials were in fact disbanded on 30th April 1970. By the end of that year the majority of the reforms sought by the Civil Rights Movement had either been the subject of legislation or had become part of British government policy.

Incipient riots and street violence were of course to continue. It is important, in the light of the circumstances that Lynch faced from August 1969 up to the Fianna Fáil Árd Fheis in 1971, to recognise that the principal reforms in Northern Ireland were rapidly implemented and that many of his troubles came from nearer home.

The residual fear was palpable. Expectations of a repeat performance in 1970 of what had happened in 1969 were real enough, and this fuelled the fears and foreboding in the Republic just as much as it did in the North. But the situation, although tense, and even though the North saw a number of deaths from shooting during riots, was effectively under control.

*

The two narratives for the two parts of Ireland, not just for this period but for years to come, have remarkably little in common. The fundamental paradox for anyone considering this period is how little developments in the Republic had to do with real events in Northern Ireland, and how little Northern Ireland considered the Republic as having any relevance at all – except as an irritant. Jack Lynch had a battle on his hands and he recognised that fact from the government meeting on 13th August. Dealing with Britain over Northern Ireland was only part of it. In the initial phase the statement that the Irish Government "can no longer stand by and see innocent people injured and perhaps worse" had an immediate impact, with the dispatch of British troops to Derry. Then the RUC and the B Specials, geared up to go into the Bogside and inflict further terror, were replaced by soldiers whose initial impact was to create a kind of euphoria throughout the

Catholic communities. The action, however, had a decidedly unhappy outcome in Belfast, where vicious and fatal riots took place on the night of 14th August and for some days following.

Following the government meeting of Wednesday, 13th August, there were meetings each day up to and including Saturday. On Thursday it was decided that the Minister for External Affairs would seek a meeting with the British Minister at the Foreign Office to press Ireland's case for UN involvement. Ambassadors around the world were to be instructed to inform governments to which they were accredited of the situation in Northern Ireland and there was to be a similar approach to Security Council members. The Minister for Defence was instructed to arrange adequate military defence for the Irish Army Field Hospitals. Most significantly, it was decided that Garda Síochána intelligence – in other words, the Special Branch – would extend its intelligence coverage in Northern Ireland; there was no mention of military intelligence.

It was also at this government meeting that a committee of some significance for Jack Lynch was authorised. This, though of lower profile, involved the Secretaries of the Departments of External Affairs, Defence, and Local Government – not Finance – and they were to "keep the situation under continuous review and advise the Taoiseach on the matter".[3]

The government meeting on the morning of Friday, 15th August began at 11.30 a.m. and lasted until 1.40 p.m. Lynch was troubled at the increased level of rioting and by the deaths of five adults and a child the previous night. Patrick Hillery had flown to London after the government meeting held on the previous Wednesday, but his proposals for a United Nations peacekeeping operation in Northern Ireland had been rejected by the Wilson Government.

Lynch knew he was in for a difficult time. Earlier that morning he rang Dr T.K. Whitaker, former Secretary of the Department of Finance and now Governor of the Central Bank. Whitaker, who was born in Rostrevor, County Down, was privately an adviser to Lynch on Northern Ireland and had helped in writing speeches. Lynch lacked an informed voice on the North; not someone who could tell him what was going on – no one could do that in a set of circumstances that were changing hourly – but someone who could advise him how the Republic could best deal with the North, and what the informed and considered view was. He wanted to understand the perspective of northern opinion on the southern Government free of the hysteria and fear of the immediate set of circumstances, and stripped also of the political motivation of groups and individuals coming south in order to get help.

Whitaker was in part the architect of Lynch's policy, which was largely responsible for a major change in Fianna Fáil thinking towards the principle of consent. He responded with a clear argument advising restraint and the blocking of any acts that might be construed as aggressive. He was very guarded about action along the Border; this was an emotional structure of forbidding height in

---

[3] See Government Minutes in the National Archives.

the minds and hearts of Irish men and women, far more obstructive psychologically than on the ground, where it was principally a territory for smuggling. Ill-considered action there that could be construed as threatening would be counterproductive, in Whitaker's view. This, in turn, would have an adverse effect on the treatment of the minority community in Northern Ireland wherever it was vulnerable. Any overtly threatening actions or, indeed, speeches would simply exacerbate the situation, reducing the Irish Government's impact in the future. What Lynch had been doing – what he was doing now – was right in Whitaker's view, and he advised Lynch that he needed to persuade those who were wavering within the Government of the correctness of his approach.

Thus armed, a beleaguered Taoiseach faced the Government on that Friday while the smoke of burnt-out fires lingered over Belfast, where families mourned their dead, and where evil forces considered how to regroup and wreak further havoc. The decision was made to mobilise the Front Line Reserve in readiness for a joint British-Irish military force should there be agreement on such an initiative. No such initiative was taken.

On the diplomatic front the Wilson Government's rebuff of Hillery meant recourse to the United Nations. There was little hope of success internationally; Britain, in the Security Council, had a veto on UN intervention, and clearly this would be used. Militarily, the only argument that carried any weight was for the Irish Army to be prepared and ready if the British requested help from the Dublin Government. No other intervention was acceptable and even the most republican Minister, in public, recognised that fact.

It was also acknowledged that the Civil Rights Movement, once capable of working on a province-wide basis, was now becoming the victim of violence and fear, and was being challenged in a much more local way by the Defence Associations and in the background by the IRA. The full impact of the British Army presence in Northern Ireland, which within a week would be comprehensive, and which in the early stages had been welcomed by the communities the soldiers had come to protect, was not apparent to that morning's government meeting.

On Saturday, 16th August the Government had to deal with the meeting which had been held between the Minister for External Affairs and Lord Chalfont, Minister for Foreign and Commonwealth Affairs. The British reaction to Irish approaches, on this and subsequent occasions, was not co-operative, and led the Government to intensify its actions at the United Nations. Hillery was to circulate a document on "The Situation in Northern Ireland" and ensure that the issue of the North was tabled on the agenda for the next meeting of the UN General Assembly. It was decided that Jack Lynch would attend that session.

As a result, the ill-fated Government Sub-Committee for the Relief of Distress in Northern Ireland, the seedbed for later catastrophe, was formed. Its composition was both organic and fortuitous. Three Ministers who came from Border constituencies were on it: Neil Blaney and Joe Brennan (both held Donegal seats) and Pádraig Faulkner (Louth). The fourth member was Charles Haughey, who claimed strong Northern Ireland connections, and who as Minister for Finance, was the person responsible for the committee's funding of £100,000. Its brief was contained in the words: "for the relief of distress." Constitutionally, it was answerable to the Government and, of course, its doings were to be reported back to that Government.

Haughey would later claim in his evidence before the October 1970 Arms Trial that the committee had been "given instructions" to develop the widest possible contacts with people in Northern Ireland. They were "to try to inform ourselves as much as possible on events, political and other developments, within the Six County area." Various other so-called "briefs" were invented or imagined for the committee. These included that it was "to deal with the whole problem of the North", that its scope was general, embracing all eventualities and that, effectively, it could define its own terms. None of this was true. One member of the committee, Pádraig Faulkner, recalls its brief as being simply to keep the Northern Ireland situation under review, a fact confirmed by Cabinet minutes.[4] Yet the committee only met once and never reported anything at all back to the Government. At the end of that meeting the date was decided for a second meeting to be held in the Department of Finance. Brennan and Faulkner, who were both loyal to Lynch and supported his policy on the North, turned up. The other two members did not. Effectively, Brennan and Faulkner were disengaged from then on and played no part in any of its supposed actions. The work that was subsequently done in the name of the committee was then carried on exclusively by Haughey and Blaney. They also exercised exclusive control over the funds. More significantly, other funds attracted from private sources, either to the Fianna Fáil party or to "the committee" were added to the resources under this two-man control.[5]

As Faulkner understood it, the money "could not be spent on arms under any circumstances". This view was in part based on the fact of Red Cross involvement, announced by the Government on the day the committee was set up, 16th August. Faulkner regarded this as a form of guarantee. But much more conclusively, it would have been totally against government policy as adumbrated then and later by Lynch. Any government statements at that time, including those that referred to aid for those in the North who were under attack, were statements about government policy and not about the actions or responsibilities of the committee, for which, effectively, there was "no blank cheque, there was no unfettered discretion". But it was Haughey, as Minister for Finance, who was designated in the press statement as the member of the committee who would "have early

---

[4] See Cabinet Minutes in the National Archives.
[5] A full account of both government funding and private contributions for the relief of distress in Northern Ireland, much of it channelled through the Irish Red Cross, has yet to be written. Government documents in the National Archives relating to this August period record a cheque from the Catholic Archbishop of Dublin, Dr John Charles McQuaid, for £1,000 which the Taoiseach received and passed to the Irish Red Cross. As will be seen, Haughey gave instructions to the Irish Red Cross for the dispersal of funds. Other sources suggest that private contributions were substantial.

consultations with the chairman of the Red Cross".[6] This led to the Red Cross being used without its knowledge as the first route for funding the IRA in Northern Ireland.

The other decision made at that government meeting in the light of Hillery's lack of success with the British Government was to mobilise a team of press and public relations representatives to travel to different parts of the world, "putting Ireland's case". This is a euphemistic description. The real purpose was to raise questions about the British position on the North.

The other very significant event at that government meeting was that Kevin Boland resigned. He did so abruptly, verbally declaring his position, and then got up, took his papers with him and left the meeting well before it had completed its business. He returned to his office in the Custom House, where he cleared his desk, and then went home. He did so because of the Government's failure to initiate any actions involving the Irish Army directed at the protection of northern Nationalists. What he specifically wanted was the recall of the United Nations contingent in Cyprus, 500 men strong, and the mobilisation of the "second line reserve". This of course was not done, then or later. After his departure the Government decided not to accept or process his resignation. Instead, Blaney and Haughey tried to persuade him to change his mind.

Understandably, Lynch's position was extremely difficult. The stated policy, which was dominated by the concept of legal or constitutional change in Northern Ireland being achieved *only* through consent and by peaceful means, had been agreed and remained central to all government action. He had one senior Minister openly opposed, another who had been making speeches against his policy, and still others – Gibbons, Ó Móráin, Haughey – who either supported Blaney or were opposed to his leadership for reasons of their own self-interest. Despite the evident unsuitability of Boland remaining in the Government, when he was so directly opposed to its policy, keeping him there was seen by Lynch as necessary at the time.

The situation in Northern Ireland was unpredictable and volatile. The politicians in the Republic were sympathetic to the northern minority but bewildered as to what should be done. This induced an emotional atmosphere undermining good judgement and allowing for diverse expression, often of militancy. The policy of Lynch's Government precluded overt action and his principal preoccupation was, quite properly, security. He didn't know which Ministers he could trust, or which of them was trying to undermine his authority,

---

[6] The chairperson was in fact a woman, Mrs Leslie de Barra. Though he denied it at his trial, Haughey used the Red Cross organisation as cover for the transfer of money from the Red Cross account, in the Bank of Ireland in College Green, eventually to one in Clones, County Monaghan. It was from this account that cash withdrawals were made over which the Red Cross had no control. The Red Cross was precluded from operating in Northern Ireland by its own charter, but it was not prevented from operating within the Republic. Whatever its "charter" position, it was nevertheless used as the first money route.

or why. His alleged indecisiveness was the subject of vocal criticism at the time. Yet Lynch reiterated to the Government the essential decisions which followed the agreed policy. These were: no Irish troops would be deployed in Northern Ireland, the "second line reserve" would not be mobilised, requests for arms from groups and individuals in the North would be refused, and people from Northern Ireland would not be trained in the Republic in the use of firearms. Initially, some civil defence training was offered, but it, too, was stopped.

Fortunately for Lynch, the violence in Northern Ireland calmed down and politics reverted to a war of words. The stand-offs and the rioting continued over the following weekend and the barricades in Derry and Belfast were kept in place. The British Army presence was generally welcomed, and to a large extent defused the tense and fearful atmosphere. The Government also welcomed the new security force as being preferable to the RUC and the B Specials, even though they made a public declaration against the deployment of British troops. Evidence of the calming down is to be found in the records of government meetings. On Thursday, 21st August Northern Ireland was still on the agenda, but no new decisions were made. By the time the Government met next, on the last Friday in August, Northern Ireland was no longer on the agenda as far as decisions were concerned. At the meeting of 9th September it was decided to replace Jack Lynch with Paddy Hillery for the address on Northern Ireland to be given before the UN General Assembly.[7]

Divisions within the Government were effectively concealed from the Irish public. Attempts by Blaney and Haughey to persuade Boland to withdraw his resignation failed at first. Seán MacEntee's assistance was invoked. That, too, failed. Then de Valera asked Boland to see him and pointed out that the crisis which his resignation might cause could result in a Fine Gael-led Government. Boland was persuaded. He saw the danger of "a serious reverse for the national position". But in retrospect he later admitted: "In this I was wrong. A Fine Gael Government would probably have been as bad but it certainly couldn't have been worse."[8]

Lynch now engaged in two strategies. The first involved the construction of an effective and updated policy with respect to the North that went beyond the broad principles and dealt with the practicalities of the British Government's stated position. This excluded the Republic of Ireland from involvement at any level in Northern Ireland affairs. On 19th August Harold Wilson's Government issued a declaration that Northern Ireland was a matter for domestic jurisdiction and that the Border was "not an issue". The stated authority for the British position was the Ireland Act of 1949 which maintained Northern Ireland as part of the United Kingdom.

Lynch replied two days later. He asserted that the Ireland Act had been undermined by the transfer of security from Stormont to Westminster and that

---

[7] Government Minutes in the National Archives.
[8] Kevin Boland, *Up Dev!* (published by the author, Dublin, 1977), p. 13.

this opened up the constitutional position. The situation also encouraged from Lynch a further request for United Nations involvement, though he anticipated that this would be turned down. More for domestic consumption than for any Anglo-Irish reason, he expressed in strong terms the rights of the Irish people and of the Irish Government over Northern Ireland:

> The claim of the Irish nation to control the totality of Ireland has been asserted over centuries by successive generations of Irish men and women and it is one which will never be renounced.[9]

Lynch was taking out insurance against the possibility, then still quite strong, that matters would continue to deteriorate. He was also rallying his own party behind him, and giving no hostages to his opponents within the Government. There was, in addition, the problem of the IRA. In the wake of the riots in Derry and Belfast in mid-August, Cathal Goulding, IRA Chief of Staff, issued a statement on 18th August saying that the organisation was putting its men on full alert and had already sent units into Northern Ireland.

Lynch was skilful in handling his own conduct at this time. If one remembers his earlier performances under stress, going back to the tackling of sporting challenges in his youth, a consistent manner of dealing with problems emerges. As a sportsman and member of a team the relevant timing is generally the length of a match. Lynch made an early success in sport by judging his capacities against opponents and making sure he timed and paced his performance in order to win. As a captain, in the various leagues, and then in Munster and All-Ireland competitions, he worked to a different time-scale, but the objectives were the same. He came to understand the nature of captaincy, the requirements of leadership, and the complexities of getting the best out of sporting colleagues.

In all his time in politics Lynch paced himself well, making few mistakes, giving no hostages to fortune, and building a reputation for integrity and competence, even occasionally for excellence. However, in one close friend's opinion he was at heart reactive rather than innovative as a ministerial figure. In the previous chapter the foresight, subtlety and skill which he brought to the Fianna Fáil leadership contest is a powerful contradiction of received opinion that he was uncertain and dilatory. In fact he measured and assessed the party as neither of his predecessors had done, because they did not think it necessary. But times had changed. Lynch faced a different order of morality in power. In his case the need was already evident within the party in the early 1960s, and his prescriptions for it were only just sufficient for the deviousness which would emerge during his first period as leader.

He performed extraordinarily well in the 1969 general election, given the P.R. referendum disaster that preceded it. During three years as leader his course had been difficult, but at the end of the crisis events of August 1969 he had

---

[9] Government Information Service Statement, 21st August.

demonstrated a mettle that was impressive, even if it was elusive and cautious as well. He still held to the fundamental principle that he had espoused on becoming leader, which was to keep the Government together and mould a united team out of it. He knew that his standing in the country through any future vicissitudes would depend on maintaining the sense of being leader of a united group of Ministers, however much this aspiration was threatened by some of them. Instinct told him that his troubles were only beginning, and told him also that his powers were limited. He was the creature of a democracy that could be destabilised. He was vulnerable to people who ignored the law and ignored their constitutional duties. Just how serious a threat this could prove to be would be demonstrated in the months ahead in that summer of 1969.

CHAPTER SEVEN

"This autumn of poisoned cups"

– Tom Mac Intyre

Jack Lynch believed that the government meetings during this week of crisis, 12th to 18th August, had achieved a reasonable consensus on Northern Ireland policy. He had no cause to believe otherwise. Sensible proposals had been put forward to deal with unprecedented circumstances in another jurisdiction. These proposals recognised that the authority of the British Government, in terms of what the Republic of Ireland might do, was against intervention from Dublin. The scope was therefore very limited. Lynch knew there were members of his Government who took a more republican view than himself, the leading and most outspoken of these being Neil Blaney. But at the government table the collective view transcended individual opinion. By Thursday, 14th August, according to Eoin Neeson, head of the Government Information Bureau: "Government Policy had been decided." He added, "In fact, the Government was in more or less continuous session from then on."[1]

Practical decisions had been made and there had been general recognition of the limitations under which the Government was operating. It would not deploy troops nor engage directly on Northern Ireland territory. It would not hand out guns to those coming from Northern Ireland who requested such armoury. The emotional case for action was persuasive in its way, but, if taken, all normal political and diplomatic relationships would rapidly break down. During that week the British Government had made very clear how it intended to proceed. This included blocking the Government in Dublin from direct involvement in Northern Ireland, and also from international action at the United Nations and elsewhere. Apart from informing other governments around the world through the team of press and public relations "ambassadors", there was nothing concrete that could be done in the short term to shape or change British policy.

The character of this policy was consistent with the situation within the British Government at the time. With a general election only months ahead of him, Harold Wilson had shown considerable reluctance about becoming directly involved when the serious rioting broke out in Derry. He left control in the hands

---

[1] Note to the Taoiseach, 1st December 1970, outlining the chronology of events during the second week in August 1969.

of his Home Secretary, Jim Callaghan, and was satisfied with the immediate response of sending in British troops.

Lynch was unhappy about this from the start. In the initial stages the deployment of troops clearly worked. The soldiers were well received in Catholic areas. Their presence meant that the RUC and the B Specials were withdrawn; but it also meant a suspension of ordinary life in the North and the abnormal dominance of a security solution carried with it many problems. Lynch immediately identified the obvious one: "Once they became part of the political geography of Northern Ireland, a pre-emptory withdrawal of the troops would have caused even further chaos."[2] He expressed the view that the deployment of troops would not "be acceptable nor would they be likely to restore peaceful conditions, certainly not in the long term".[3] This became the basis for the Government's demand for a United Nations peacekeeping force. The British Army presence nullified this, but it also allowed Britain to ignore Dublin's appeal for a review of "the present constitutional position of the Six Counties of Northern Ireland". Such a review was simply not going to be part of Harold Wilson's rather low-key response on the North. This approach was politically sound from his point of view. He was coming to the end of his term in office and would soon be facing a general election. He did not want to enter territory which represented a potential minefield.

Lynch's other concern about British troops in Northern Ireland and their capacity to impede political progress related to what was likely to happen within his own Government. Consistency over Northern Ireland policy would wear thin in a stalemate particularly when the honeymoon period for the British troops came to an end, as surely it would and did.

There was a third problem: the IRA. The private diaries of the Secretary of the Department of Justice, Peter Berry, are obsessively concerned with the IRA and what he calls "the infiltration of communists". It was an obvious concern internationally. Not only was the Cold War very much in people's minds; fear of communism had inspired United States action in its worst foreign war by far, the Vietnam campaign, which was then beginning to run out of control. But the fear of communism in Ireland was largely of a spurious nature and, though Berry himself was genuinely concerned about the spread of communist ideology, the politicians (particularly those in Fianna Fáil) had for long seen it as of use mainly for electoral purposes. The "Red Scare" was invoked as a slur on socialism and radicalism generally and was turned against Labour and other parties of the Left, including Clann na Poblachta, at election time. But it was hardly a driving force for consistent oppression or persecution. In May 1969, before the election, Berry had in fact handed to Minister Ó Móráin an up-to-date portfolio on "over 60 organisations of a subversive character with IRA or communist affiliations".[4]

---

2 Jack Lynch, "My Life and Times" in *Magill* (November 1979), p. 44.
3 Statement made on RTÉ, 13th August 1969.
4 "The Peter Berry Papers", *Magill* (June 1980), pp. 50–52.

Ó Móráin had responded by using the "Red Scare" himself. Other Ministers did the same during the 1969 general election campaign. Communists were seen as having infiltrated the IRA as well, and this, combined with a militant campaign in Northern Ireland, was the seedbed of the fear generated by the speech made by the IRA Chief of Staff, Cathal Goulding, on 18th August.

The fear was focused in the wrong direction. Goulding's obsessive Marxism had no real relevance to events in Northern Ireland and the speech itself was motivated by the IRA leader's recognition that the organisation would rapidly become irrelevant if it did not find a practical answer to violence on the streets in Northern Ireland. Marxist republicanism did not have such an answer. Its philosophies might recognise the social problems that were urgently in need of reform but did not comprehend the sectarian divide, the bigotry and the division of urban society in the North into ghettos. Doctrinaire Marxism had blinded many within that organisation to what was happening on the ground, and the Goulding speech was an acknowledgement of this and an attempt to turn the situation around. It was already too late. Neither the IRA in Dublin, led by Goulding, nor the Belfast leadership at the time of the riots had handled them with sufficient conviction or courage. A change of leadership was imminent and, although Fianna Fáil would seek to be part of the development within the organisation, the grasp of even those like Blaney who were supposedly close to events in the North was quite marginal. Already, through the establishment of the Central Citizens' Defence Committee on 16th August by Jim Sullivan, who was second in command of the IRA in Belfast, the alternative structure to the Dublin-dominated "Official" IRA was in place.

Berry's intelligence on the IRA was detailed and in general reliable. The day after the Goulding speech, he received a report at his home from the head of the Special Branch describing a meeting between the IRA Chief of Staff and a government Minister. It suggested that there had been a deal between the two men. The IRA would call off all violence within the Republic in return for "a free hand" in operating a cross-Border campaign directed at Northern Ireland. This undertaking was categorically contradicted in Lynch's public statements, particularly that of 19th August. Not surprisingly, this had thrown the IRA Army Council into confusion. They hardly expected public support, but in the aftermath of the August violence in Derry and Belfast they were responding to the collective cry for help from northern Nationalists and felt they had prepared the way for some kind of tacit endorsement.

Berry's own report to his Minister on security matters generally was taken before the government meeting of 20th August. Ó Móráin read it out. The reaction caused him to tell Berry "that was the last time he would bring anything like that to the notice of all members of the Government".[5] Clearly, the Minister was given a hard time for what seemed irrelevant in the circumstances of the crisis. He appeared to be presenting anti-IRA intelligence, combined with the "Red

---

[5] "The Peter Berry Papers", above, n.4, p. 51.

Scare", as ongoing security concerns. He told Berry that, in future, he would bring such departmental security reports directly to the Taoiseach.

Ó Móráin said to Berry that no Minister had met Cathal Goulding. "He then went on to say that Charlie Haughey had mentioned that he had been asked to meet some fellow from the IRA but that he had not paid heed to what was said, that it was not of any consequence."[6] One can see Haughey's gesture of dismissal and hear the voice disparaging the very idea of such an encounter having any importance, but conceding that it had taken place. Berry added two and two together and came to an immediate conclusion. Haughey had indeed offered the deal to Goulding and knew from the Ó Móráin report that he had been identified by the Special Branch. He had responded by making light of the encounter and by not identifying in his turn the person he had met. In this way he passed it off as unimportant. This was a ploy that later would become habitual and even characteristic in Haughey's responses to embarrassing or accusatory questions.

Haughey was moving very rapidly. Even earlier, following the 15th August government meeting, he had told Eoin Neeson, the head of the Government Information Bureau, that Séamus Brady, a journalist who wrote speeches for Neil Blaney, was to be employed by the bureau "at a fee of £200 a month". Brady was to become part of the Blaney-Haughey team for Northern Ireland.

*

From this point, two distinct policies on Northern Ireland developed side by side. One was public, and expressed consistently and fairly regularly through speeches and statements by Jack Lynch. This policy, while not inconsistent with that previously stated, was refined by Lynch in the light of events in August 1969. He expressed it and other Ministers, except in very general terms, kept off the subject. Haughey hardly spoke on Northern Ireland. Even Blaney became less vociferous, though when the reasons for this emerge they will be seen as sinister. For both Blaney and Haughey now became engaged in another policy for Northern Ireland. It had no mandate from Fianna Fáil and involved their own personal interpretation of how things should be represented. It was covert, conspiratorial, and in direct conflict with agreed government policy. When it suited them, they represented it as coming "from Government". Yet nothing – no minute, no instruction, no discussion – had ever given them the right to do this.

All government members shared a common and overriding interest in intelligence. The first period of crisis, up to the climactic events of mid-August, had cruelly exposed the inadequacy of knowledge about Northern Ireland. Lynch's determination to rectify this included a number of measures, among them the stepping up of army and Garda intelligence and, at the level of his own public statements, the increased involvement of Dr T.K. Whitaker as a private personal adviser and speech-writer. Whitaker was responsible, for example, for the speech

---

[6] "The Peter Berry Papers", above, n.4, p. 52.

in which Lynch expressed in a clear and concise form the principle of consent and agreement within the whole of Ireland:

> It will remain our most earnest aim and hope to win the consent of the majority of the people in the Six Counties to means by which North and South can come together in a re-united and sovereign Ireland earning international respect for both the fairness and efficiency with which it is administered and for its contribution to world peace and progress.[7]

But the search for better intelligence also made him and others in the Government vulnerable to misinformation *and to deliberate exclusion from full information*. This was to become a major failing within the Government.

In public, whenever the two divergent policies became entangled, or there was a confrontation, Lynch's views prevailed. Yet behind the scenes, in the management of a number of issues, including the relief of distress, but inevitably embracing security and intelligence as well, it was not so clear-cut. This was because of the transfer of responsibility for certain aspects of policy related to the North to the government Sub-Committee for the Relief of Distress in Northern Ireland. In Pádraig Faulkner's judgement, the committee's more general responsibility was to "keep the Northern Ireland situation under review".[8]

In any normal sense this committee did not work from the start. Pádraig Faulkner and Joe Brennan were dropped after the committee's first and only meeting. The "shell" of it was kept on, but Haughey and Blaney now ran it for their own purposes, using it as some kind of "cover" and as a "badge" of their authority. They did not really need it. Both men demonstrated in their general behaviour the bold assurance of bullies, and they carried a great deal of political weight. It would be a strong-minded civil servant, legal officer of the State, or military figure to challenge the basis on which orders and decisions were now being made. Charles Murray, the Secretary of the Department of Finance, who had succeeded Whitaker, told Berry of the prevailing atmosphere in dealing with Haughey. Murray, understandably concerned, given his position as the figure legally responsible for public funds, nevertheless had learnt to be circumspect.

> He had been uneasy about the way that the Grant-in-aid for Northern Ireland Relief was being disposed of and went on to say that if he had raised a ruckus he would have been thrown out of the room by the Minister ('You know what the bloody man is like', or words near that). I interjected that on an occasion the same Minister [Haughey] had literally thrown a file at me and I had walked out of his room, leaving the papers on the floor.[9]

---

[7] Speech given by Jack Lynch in Tralee, 20th September 1969. The speech was a pivotal statement of government policy and was indeed seen as such by his Ministers, including Paddy Hillery, who described it as "the most important speech during the whole period". See Stephen Collins, *The Power Game* (O'Brien Press, Dublin, 2000), p. 67.
[8] Pádraig Faulkner to the author, Spring, 2001.
[9] "The Peter Berry Papers" in *Magill* (June 1980), p. 67.

Haughey, for example, took a fairly immediate and leading part in directing the intelligence activities of Colonel Michael Hefferon, head of army intelligence, and Captain James Kelly, who was the officer responsible for Northern Ireland military intelligence. How it emerged that military intelligence for Northern Ireland became a matter for these three men, with the later direct involvement of Blaney as well, has been and remains a mystery. Some of the practical detail is outlined below but what is puzzling is the absence of any convincing intelligence structure in the Irish Army at the time. Irish military intelligence had been outstanding on previous occasions in the country's history. This was most notably so during the early years of the State and during the Second World War especially, when a major and highly secret contribution to Allied intelligence emanated from Irish army intelligence. In the period after the War and up to the 1960s the Department of Defence was bureaucratised and became starved of funding. As troubles in Northern Ireland worsened, in the late 1960s, there does not appear to have been any coherent or considered examination of the country's needs. What was done seemed at best *ad hoc*.

Haughey was involved in one aspect of the press and publicity drive, namely Séamus Brady's mixture of intelligence-gathering and propaganda in Northern Ireland. Haughey was also beginning to hand out money. Well before the payment of £500 to help fund the Bailieborough meeting,[10] money was given to one of the relief centres, in County Monaghan, where refugees from violence in Northern Ireland, or those whose homes had been burnt out, were accommodated before being moved south. It is by no means clear where the money came from, then or later. Private subscriptions, also designed to help relief work in the North, came in from a variety of sources, including Fianna Fáil supporters. Haughey's position made him the natural recipient, but no accounting has survived.

Part of the intense interest in the information-gathering process was focused on the relief centres. The Irish Army, which nominally controlled them, reported back to the Government, and Lynch himself received some security briefing. At this stage he kept in touch with both police and military intelligence. However, it seems clear that a separate parallel information operation was organised through Colonel Hefferon and Captain Kelly, with the channel of reporting uncertain, though mainly going back to Haughey and to Blaney. Haughey had the supposed legitimacy of being the central figure of the government sub-committee and now, in respect of Captain James Kelly and Colonel Michael Hefferon, was the main source for decisions and for money.

Confusion of a high order prevailed. This resulted from a combination of the interrogation of people coming south, the transmission of publicity and propaganda material north, the distribution of money for intelligence personnel and the funding

---

[10] Bailieborough is a town in County Cavan. A meeting there in October 1969, hosted by an army intelligence officer, has been widely regarded as "the genesis of the plan to import of arms". Captain James Kelly so describes it. See James Kelly, *The Thimble Riggers* (published by the author, Dublin, 1999), p. 20.

of the Monaghan office. The further movement of cash elsewhere had no effective co-ordination. The circumstances in Northern Ireland may have been chaotic, but there was no justification for elements within the Government in the Republic aggravating the situation. Public perception of the destabilised situation was reinforced by newspaper, radio and television coverage which dealt with, among other things, details of the personal experiences of people from the North. In fact, after the August riots had been brought under control and with the arrival of the British Army, the situation began to calm down considerably. The announcement of the measures decided on at the mid-August government meetings had helped in this; but the real progress was a product of fairer security on the streets and the fact that the marching season was coming to an end.

*

According to Peter Berry, there had been intelligence reports from the middle of September 1969 in which "the name of Captain James Kelly cropped up again and again as consorting with known members of the IRA". Berry also recorded allegations that "he [Kelly] was so forthcoming in advocating the use of arms that doubts were entertained by his listeners as to whether he was, in fact, an intelligence officer".[11]

Captain Kelly was acting in a chain of command which ostensibly ran back through his immediate superior, Colonel Hefferon, head of army intelligence, to the Chief of Staff, then to the Minister for Defence, and lastly to the Government. But that was hardly how Kelly saw it, nor was that how it was structured. At an early stage Haughey and Blaney had intruded into this normal chain of reporting and of command. Using the dubious authority of a government sub-committee that was presented as being "in charge" of intelligence and security matters, but in fact was no longer in existence, the two men largely took over the direction of operations of what in effect was a tiny and isolated army intelligence service. They made it part of their wider activity. This was focused on political aims in Northern Ireland and in the Republic. They did not report to their government colleagues. Sometimes acting together, sometimes independently of each other, the two Ministers appear to have diverted the activities and reporting functions of both Hefferon and Kelly. As Kelly later made clear, he saw the four members of the government sub-committee as people whom he should keep informed on the situation in Northern Ireland; however, he met neither Joe Brennan nor Pádraig Faulkner. Of these four it was in fact to Blaney and to Haughey that he reported. In turn, they checked with him on the background of people coming from Northern Ireland to see them in Dublin.[12]

---

[11] "The Peter Berry Papers" in *Magill* (June 1980), p. 52.
[12] In Kelly's evidence at the Arms Trial (13th October 1970) quoted in Tom Mac Intyre, *Through the Bridewell Gate: A Diary of the Dublin Arms Trial* (Faber and Faber, London, 1971), p. 137.

Captain James Kelly's position as the representative of military intelligence on the ground in Northern Ireland makes little sense. By his own admission, he visited the North only three times, the visits being of less than a week's duration.[13] The first visit, which began on 11th August, was when he was on leave from his post as an intelligence officer at Army HQ in Dublin. He travelled on that day to Belfast and then on to Derry. He stayed to see the riots – "The Battle of the Bogside", as it came to be called – and then travelled to Belfast where he witnessed the more serious riots on the Falls Road. He was there with the MP Paddy Kennedy when Jack Lynch made his statement on radio and television. He returned to Dublin on the afternoon of 14th August and later recorded in his autobiography:

> ... although technically on leave, I reported immediately to my superior officer, the Director of Intelligence, Colonel Michael Hefferon. He instructed me to develop further the various contacts I had established in Belfast and Derry and to concentrate on Northern Ireland affairs for the foreseeable future.[14]

In the second week of September 1969 Kelly made his second and final visit to Belfast. A week later he wrote:

> I was in the Derry area and, once again, it was evident that the Nationalists there looked to the South for assistance. I reported on my various meetings to the Director of Intelligence and, on his instructions, I did not enter Northern Ireland again during my army service.[15]

Kelly's intelligence-gathering, from then on, was carried out within the Republic of Ireland.

Captain Kelly appears to have had no liaison with Special Branch intelligence. He says nothing of being briefed either by his Minister or his superior officer. His views, where he expressed them in his autobiography or in his intelligence reports, are very general and very political; moreover, they seem to be inspired by information gleaned only from the nationalist side in Northern Ireland. He felt that the radical Marxist Sinn Féin ideology which then prevailed was of no value and that it was being changed. In his first intelligence report to Colonel Hefferon, written on 23rd August, he proposed the following:

> It would seem to be now necessary to harness all opinion in the State in a concerted drive towards achieving the aim of reunification. Unfortunately, this would mean accepting the possibility of armed action of some sort as the ultimate solution.[16]

---

[13] James Kelly, *The Thimble Riggers* (published by the author, Dublin, 1999), pp. 6–13.

[14] *Ibid.*, p. 11.

[15] *Ibid.*, p. 13.

[16] See Justin O'Brien, *The Arms Trial* (Gill & Macmillan, Dublin, 2000), p. 58. They are footnoted as "military intelligence documents in the author's possession". Additionally, James Kelly was interviewed by the author.

He also suggested that the Government should "co-operate with the IRA and extreme republicanism generally".[17] Justin O'Brien suggests in his book *The Arms Trial* that this report demonstrates that Captain Kelly was "acutely aware of how the volatile situation in the north could threaten the stability of the Southern state". O'Brien further suggests that Captain Kelly could not have "remained in place if his analysis were out of kilter with at least some powerful figures in Dublin".[18]

What is not clear is the value of Kelly's generalised intelligence reporting which, even if it fitted in with Blaney's frequently declared views, was totally at variance with government policy. With an agreed and declared opposition to the use of force or of arms in any form whatever, the relevance of reporting that recommended "armed action... as the ultimate solution" has to be questioned.

On that second visit to Belfast, in September, Captain James Kelly met John Kelly, who was to be a fellow defendant in the Arms Trial in the autumn of the following year. They were introduced in the house of Gerry Fitt, a Labour politician who later became the first leader of the Social, Democratic and Labour Party. James Kelly describes John Kelly as coming from "a staunch Belfast Republican family and having been imprisoned for six years for his involvement in the 1956 IRA campaign in Northern Ireland."[19] With the renewed troubles, John Kelly had become involved in the Citizens' Defence Committees and by that September meeting with James Kelly he was the Central Defence Committee organiser for Northern Ireland.[20] John Kelly and his brother, Billy, were involved together in Defence Committee work. They were leading figures, too, in the wing of the IRA opposed to Marxist politics. James Kelly reportedly said:

> The Kellys [John and Billy] and their friends have no time for PD [People's Democracy] and for the new Sinn Féin policy in the South and arrangements are underway to re-establish control by pure republicanism which is concerned solely with a 32-county Ireland. In this connection they are willing to co-operate with the IRA in the South and would like to make arrangements with various people whom they see as Republican first and not true Sinn Féin socialists. In fact they see Sinn Féin politics as having disrupted the whole IRA/Republican movement.[21]

Whatever the intelligence value of the reports containing these and other global observations on the thinking of unspecified groups in Northern Ireland, they are a reflection, although perhaps more naively expressed, of Neil Blaney's political views. Since there had been a prolonged and very public debate about the issues

---

[17] Justin O'Brien, *The Arms Trial* (Gill & Macmillan, Dublin, 2000), p. 58.

[18] This is true. The "powerful figures" were Blaney and Haughey.

[19] Kelly, above, n.13, p. 13.

[20] *Ibid.*

[21] O'Brien, above, n.17, p. 60. The quotation is footnoted as "military intelligence documents in the author's possession".

and the differences raised by Blaney in his disagreements with Lynch, it was odd that James Kelly should have continued to pursue a line in his intelligence-gathering and reporting which was quite clearly not the Government's. It raises questions about the nature of the direction he received from Colonel Hefferon about these activities. It also raises questions about why there were no checks on this relatively junior army officer, who was below field rank. He evidently believed that he had instructions to determine vast generalisations about the direction of State policy in relation to a part of Ireland that was suffering a crisis of unparalleled proportions.[22]

Two senior government Ministers, Blaney and Haughey, were engaged in an extraordinary operation. Its ostensible focus was relief of distress. It included in addition political observation, liaison work with subversive organisations and with Citizens' Defence Committees, meetings with Northern Ireland politicians and journalists in the pay of the Government Information Bureau. Moreover, the lines on which this was being done were undoubtedly at odds with the publicly stated policies of the Government.

*

Of course, the watchers were being watched. Peter Berry's Special Branch, a far more refined and experienced intelligence-gathering operation than that run by Colonel Hefferon, was watching and reporting on Captain Kelly as he pursued his work through Northern Ireland contacts and continued to gather information.

There was no comparison between the two intelligence services. Special Branch intelligence, and that of the Gardaí generally, were of a high order. Checks and cross-checks were run on all serious intelligence information, and the system had a proven worth dating back many years. They were under the firm control of an objective and very experienced man in Berry, who made his years of experience and judgement available to the State. In Berry's eyes, Special Branch vigilance in its surveillance was fully justified.

Initially, wild decisions were made. Gardaí were approached with a request to "turn the blind eye to the movement of men and materials (weapons and explosives)".[23] Fort Dunree, an army camp in Donegal, was opened with the intention of it being used for the training of men from the North, particularly Derry, in small arms. Lynch saw the danger of this kind of thing escalating and when Berry, in the absence of his Minister, reported to Lynch, he simply replied: "No fraternisation." Fort Dunree was immediately closed down, on Lynch's orders.

Then came the Bailieborough meeting of 4th October 1969. Later identified

---

[22] For comparison, see the summarised intelligence report given to Lynch a year later, on 27th July 1970, see below, pp. 143–144.
[23] "The Peter Berry Papers" in *Magill* (June 1980), p. 52.

as the meeting that was "the genesis of the plan to import arms",[24] this encounter in a small town in County Cavan was of considerable significance. Bailieborough was the birthplace of Captain Kelly. The Commercial Hotel, in the town's main street, was owned by Vincent Kelly, another of the Captain's brothers, and this was where the meeting took place. It was between members of the Central Citizens' Defence Committee, and representative of defence committees throughout Northern Ireland. Captain Kelly believed and claimed that he was acting as a liaison between the people at the meeting and the Irish Government. He was also there to offer funding and to assume the role of arbiter over the sanctioning and distribution of money agreed by the Government. He has discounted the more lurid reports of the meeting subsequently made to Jack Lynch.[25]

Special Branch officers were well informed and their reports, covering most of what was happening, were going directly to the Secretary of the Department of Justice despite his serious ill-health at that time. He was suffering from an aortic clot and had endured several seizures. Berry went for treatment into Mount Carmel Private Hospital on 27th September. In spite of this, he had no intention of letting security matters pass from his hands and transferred control to his hospital rooms. He was given a suite with ground floor access, where he received sensitive reports and was visited by the Garda Commissioner, Michael Wymes, and Chief Superintendent John Fleming, head of the Special Branch.

It was in Mount Carmel Hospital on 4th October that Berry received a report of a meeting that had been held between Captain Kelly and the IRA Chief of Staff, Cathal Goulding. He recorded in his diary that Captain Kelly "had set up a meeting for that weekend in Bailieborough with persons from both sides of the Border with a known history in the IRA".[26] Berry tried phoning his own Minister and the Taoiseach without success, and then he tried Charles Haughey. Haughey travelled immediately to the hospital and was given details of the Bailieborough meeting and the meeting with Goulding. Haughey was, according to Berry, "quite inquisitive" about what Berry knew of Goulding. What Haughey did not tell Berry was that he had been in direct contact with both Colonel Hefferon and Captain Kelly. The two men had visited him at his home in Kinsealy the previous day, when he had given them £500 to cover the expenses of the weekend meeting in Bailieborough.

Berry did not know of Haughey's direct involvement in "the genesis of the plan to import arms" until the Committee of Public Accounts' investigation into

---

[24] "The Peter Berry Papers" in *Magill* (June 1980), p. 53. Berry is quoting from Captain James Kelly's testimony to the Committee of Public Accounts. James Kelly concurs in this description. The phrase he uses is "a meeting which was the genesis of a later attempted importation of arms." See *The Thimble Riggers*, above, n.13, p. 20.

[25] For Captain James Kelly's account of the Bailieborough meeting see *The Thimble Riggers*, pp. 18–20.

[26] "The Peter Berry Papers" in Magill magazine, June 1980, p. 52.

the "disappearance" of the distress fund in January 1971. Nor could this advance of money itself be construed as a direct involvement or involvement at all in arms dealing. He did not know of the *suspicion* of Haughey's involvement until the end of the year. Still less did Lynch know. In all that Berry said at this time to his own Minister, to his staff, and to Jack Lynch when the Taoiseach visited him later in the month, he could not report on *any ministerial involvement*. Nor could he report on a plan as such.

During the first weekend in October the Commercial Hotel, and indeed the streets of Bailieborough, had been thick with security personnel from the Army, the Gardaí, and, quite probably, British intelligence as well. It had also bristled with men from the IRA. The organisation was already beginning to move towards the split. This would eventually lead to the setting up of the "Official" and the "Provisional" wings. At that stage it was more of a geographic division, north and south, with all the emphasis in Bailieborough on representation from northern defence committees. Captain Kelly judged that the meeting, which had quite a sizeable attendance from Derry and Belfast, had no one from the Dublin IRA. At the same time, nobody could be sure about loyalties in the prevailing atmosphere.

Captain Kelly was also at pains to reassure the people from the North who attended the meeting that Fort Dunree would reopen in due course and that the arms training by the Irish Army would resume. His intelligence "cover" was that of the sympathetic army officer. The Irish Army seemed, at face value, to be the only organisation actively concerned with the welfare of people in the North. This was in line with government policy. Concern over welfare was a particularly high profile aspect of that policy, since, from Lynch down, the presence of the Irish Army represented a clear demonstration of the Republic's desire to help. It was assumed that whatever undertakings Captain Kelly might give represented an extension of the general instructions given to the Army by the Government. It does seem, however, a long way from true intelligence work.

Reports reached Berry on other worrying security matters, and it was not until 16th October that he became alarmed enough by further information about Bailieborough to make contact with the Taoiseach's office and ask for a meeting. Lynch called to Mount Carmel Hospital the next day. In the circumstances, with Berry surrounded by nurses and doctors, and with a tube through his nostril to his stomach, the encounter was brief and unsatisfactory. Berry should never have called it. He had nothing to report that was not already the subject of stringent ordinances that had existed at the time of the Fort Dunree training and subsequent close-down.

Unfortunately, Berry's diary entry for 17th October, as well as being confused as a result of his medical treatment, is largely *post factum*. He filled in the greater part of the entry at a much later date (probably in 1971, or even later), quoting extensive documentary and other support for what he had said. The picture he gave to Lynch was bizarre enough:

I am quite certain that I told him of Captain Kelly's prominent part in the

Bailieborough meeting with known members of the IRA, of his possession of a wad of money, of his standing drinks and of the sum of money – £50,000 – that would be made available for the purchase of arms.[27]

Lynch was incredulous about this sum of money. Berry named possible Taca sources. Lynch reportedly said that such party supporters "didn't give it up easily". Berry later added to the entry his own view that he had given to Jack Lynch:

> ... information of a most serious kind in relation to a plot to import arms and that he avoided making any more than a cursory inquiry. Indeed, I formed the impression from time to time that he was consulting me to find out how much I did not know and that he was not thankful to me for bringing awkward facts to his notice.[28]

The "awkward facts" known at that time were very few. The critical one – covering the involvement of members of the Government – had not been discovered. Berry, after a lifetime of intense and dedicated service to the security of the State, had summoned the head of the Government for a meeting that was catastrophically unsuccessful in that it conveyed no substantial information for the head of the Government. If what had happened mattered it was for the security forces and the relevant Ministers to address. What Lynch was told was either unsupported by the necessary intelligence or was imperfectly explained. Lynch nevertheless mentioned the meeting to James Gibbons, Minister for Defence, who asked Hefferon about it, referring to the more bizarre fact of Captain Kelly "waving a wad of notes around and promising money".[29] In describing these events in his book about the Arms Trials, Mac Intyre used the phrase "this autumn of poisoned cups". It is an apt description of the whole period from August 1969 to May 1970.[30]

The Bailieborough meeting, later to assume significance as a pivotal moment, does not conform to the later view nor have the importance that Berry gave it in 1971. Rather, the episode can be viewed today as an embryonic intelligence operation watched with great scepticism and some indulgence by the serious professionals in the Special Branch. It seemed to involve centrally a junior army officer whose reported behaviour was giving cause for alarm. Lynch appears to have seen it like that. Quite properly, he was prepared to leave the matter in the hands of the formidable head of the State's police and intelligence services, together with the Defence Minister. The real story was happening elsewhere and remained unreported.

The distribution of money, from coffers that Haughey either controlled or

---

[27] "The Peter Berry Papers" in *Magill* (June 1980), p. 54.

[28] *Ibid.*

[29] *Ibid.*

[30] Tom Mac Intyre, *Through the Bridewell Gate: A Diary of the Dublin Arms Trial* (Faber and Faber, London, 1971), p. 139.

manipulated, went on through the autumn and winter of 1969–1970. It was the single most significant factor in the reorganisation of IRA power and influence throughout Ireland. This went on against a background of an improving situation in Northern Ireland, with the British Army confronting Protestant paramilitary organisations, seizing arms and ammunition, and arresting those in possession of them.

*

Meanwhile, Lynch's position was paying off. The policies he had adopted were in line with the increasingly regularised circumstances in the North, with the British Army taking down the barricades, policing the borderlines between warring communities, and adopting a far more even-handed approach. This was a matter of encouragement for the Government and for Lynch personally.

The situation in the Republic was reassuring as well, but falsely so. On the surface there was the return to more balanced relations between Ireland and the United Kingdom on the issue of Northern Ireland. The return to comparatively normal circumstances within Northern Ireland was the direct result of the deployment of the British Army. This was widely recognised by the politicians and by the leaders of human rights organisations. Nevertheless, during this whole period there existed an elaborate and complicated plot orchestrated by Haughey and Blaney. It is the backdrop to all that happened from mid-1969 until early 1971, when the Fianna Fáil Árd Fheis saw the end of the challenge to Lynch's leadership. Its first major focus, when elements in the plot emerged in intelligence reports, was the Bailieborough meeting. But it was conceived earlier than that. It then surfaced in subsequent controversies up to and including the dismissal of the two Ministers in May 1970. Lynch's knowledge of events and his reaction to them are important to our understanding of his character. The events themselves played a major part in his life then and later, but above all there loomed the two figures who allowed their opposition to him and to his policies distort their duties to the State and their obligations as members of the Government, ultimately compromising their honesty and integrity.

The first thing to be said about Blaney and Haughey, in respect of this eight-month period from mid-August 1969 to early May 1970, is that the two were not particularly close, had differing objectives, at times acted independently, and were suspicious of one another. Haughey had no time for Blaney and did not respect him as a Minister. On one occasion, as Minister for Finance in the period before the 1969 general election, he referred to some public outburst by Blaney. His view was that Lynch should have got rid of him much earlier on account of his divergent views on the North.[31] But this was in no sense the reason for the rivalry and suspicion. Haughey in 1969 still believed that Lynch was an interim

---

[31] Confidential Public Service source.

figure, and that his departure might be precipitated by events in Northern Ireland. If this happened, it would be in circumstances favourable to Blaney becoming leader of Fianna Fáil. Haughey needed to prevent this, and it required his close involvement in the same activities that Blaney was engaged in, though Blaney was driven by republican ideology. Haughey, in contrast, took the republican cloak and wore it much more privately than Blaney, in order to pace his rival and make sure nothing was done that would undermine his own position.

A similarly devious and complicated approach was adopted to the sequence of events which were set in place during the autumn of 1969. Haughey and Blaney were effectively controlling a range of people and activities, including intelligence, propaganda, publicity, press, and funds for a variety of causes in Northern Ireland, and for that matter in the Republic. The central purpose was simple and extremely dangerous. It was, first of all, to split off the Dublin IRA and Cathal Goulding (its Chief of Staff) from the IRA in Northern Ireland. Then, secondly, it was to shift control within the IRA in Northern Ireland from the Marxists of the 1960s to men who were known to be loyal to Blaney and, to a lesser extent, to Haughey. They were anything but Marxist radicals, but they were shrewd in the business of infiltration and subversion. Their targets were numerous and among them was the Central Citizens' Defence Committee of Belfast. Then there were the local Civil Rights Committees in Northern Ireland, which were the constituent groups of the Northern Ireland Civil Rights Association. But with the growth of violence they had increasingly become local defence organisations, and had attracted a new and different kind of membership, more interested in militant defence and more open to involving those in the Republic who were supportive of defending the minority with arms. They were more than ready to listen to the messages coming from Haughey and Blaney. It was said by one commentator that the Irish government sub-committee's "plan" to penetrate such organisations "cut like a knife through butter".

The argument was strongly put that the local organisations were not getting satisfactory representation on the Northern Ireland Civil Rights Association (NICRA). To remedy this, local committees began to register as affiliates, thus increasing control over NICRA.

A parallel programme of publicity and propaganda publications emerged through pamphlets and periodicals mainly written by Séamus Brady, and including such titles as *Terror in Northern Ireland*, *Eye-Witness in Northern Ireland*, and the news-sheet *The North*.[32] There was also a mobile independent radio station.

The penetration strategy was backed up by money. It was distributed, as was discussed at Bailieborough, largely to the Central Citizens' Defence Committee structure; effectively, as the autumn wore on, this meant the emerging Provisional IRA. The IRA organisation had become factional. Control from the Dublin HQ was being steadily diminished, as was Goulding's authority.

---

[32] Not to be confused with *The Voice of the North*, a later publication. Two issues of *The North* appeared.

It was Captain Kelly's practice to give assurances to the different factions that the aid would continue, despite differences over the uses to which the money was put. In all of this Captain Kelly acted in pursuit of what he believed was government policy. Those members of the IRA involved at the time regarded Kelly as sincere in what he did, and believed that he was motivated by a strategy that emanated from the Government. To them he was, in effect, the main liaison figure. The fact that he had control over the money was more than adequate proof of this. It was clearly at odds with government policy that this strategy seemed to be backed with a directive about possible Irish Army incursions, and to have as its Northern Ireland objective the breakdown of law and order. Yet the confusion was so great and there were so many conflicting views and statements that it carried sufficient conviction to help the power shift from Dublin to Belfast. At certain stages during this period even Berry suspected that hidden government strategies were being considered and pursued.

As early as the final week of September 1969, the men who would become the leaders of the Provisional IRA were being schooled in the conditions for funding their takeover in Northern Ireland. These conditions were the breaking of the link with the Dublin IRA and the removal of left-wing radicals from key positions in the organisation. Charles Haughey's younger brother, Pádraic or "Jock" Haughey, was one of those who carried fresh funds to Northern Ireland's new IRA coffers.

*

Lynch had been concerned at the plan to train people from the North, particularly from Derry, in the use of small arms. This had been authorised by Gibbons and was carried out on army property. Suspended for a time, this activity was renewed towards the end of the year. Strictly, it did not allow trainees to travel with arms in the State. As a result, a group from Derry, presumably travelling home from a training session and carrying arms at the end of that year, but in fact found by the Gardaí in a disused house near the Donegal border, was arrested and brought to Mountjoy Prison late in December. Berry reported the matter to his Minister, who consulted with Lynch. The Taoiseach took a tough line and ordered them to be charged.

They were to be charged in accordance with Lynch's strongly expressed views on how the illegal possession of arms in the State was to be addressed. Haughey heard of this and rang Berry, calling the decision "stupid". Berry thought the men would be discharged by the court, but not if they took the traditional IRA line of "not recognising the court". Haughey told Berry that he would fix this.

The court appearance would prove to be generally embarrassing, yet it conformed with the strict security attitude Lynch had taken. However, embarrassment was not the first concern of Haughey or Blaney. Neither was Lynch's dilemma. The main difficulty for both Ministers was how to get the men out of prison and out of the jurisdiction. There was a danger that their extensive activities in Northern Ireland could be exposed.

Blaney intervened with the Department of Justice. Using his position on the government sub-committee and his considerable forcefulness of personality, he arranged a visit to Mountjoy Prison in order to brief the men. Like Berry, he knew there was a prosecution strategy to organise their release from the charges. Lynch, having made the gesture against threatened physical force, saw the potential embarrassment of custodial sentencing. But it was necessary for the men held in Mountjoy to co-operate. They were to follow a particular line in court. Blaney, who visited and advised them, had created more confusion than clarity. The Secretary of the Department of Justice sent one of his own staff in to tell the men to recognise the court and to "plead guilty to the lesser charges that would be preferred". No "hardware" would be produced and "a lenient outcome could be anticipated from such non-contentious proceedings".[33] This happened, and the men did not return to Mountjoy.

The episode had significance for all concerned. It revealed Lynch in a tough light on a specific issue involving arms and winning approval for that, but at the same time avoiding a doctrinaire response. It also showed a direct involvement by two senior Ministers, Blaney and Haughey, in the affairs of the police, the Department of Justice and the courts. This revealed to the Secretary of that Department a level of conflict within the Government that connected alarmingly with other security information concerning arms. This indicated that, at the very least, Haughey and Blaney were directly involved in the acquisition and movement of arms which were intended for the IRA.

Berry's recall of the detail is uncertain. Owing to his illness, he did not adequately absorb the significance of the facts when first alerted – nor did he want to. Neither did anyone else. The distinct impression, as facts began to come in linking members of the Government with arms importation, is one of denial. This intelligence began in late October. Berry told the Garda Commissioner, Michael Wymes, that the Ministers' names should not be *recorded* in security reports until further checks had been made. This approach was endorsed by Berry's own Minister. Berry could not believe that Haughey would have become involved in arms importation on the IRA's behalf or else he believed, as he later told Lynch, that it had been authorised but was "top secret".

As a result of his illness, Berry remained at home during these critical revelations, directing security affairs from there. When it was confirmed by the Special Branch on 10th December 1969 that the two Ministers appeared to be engaged in the importation of arms, no one knew what to do. Berry contacted the Garda Commissioner and suggested that he should make a formal report to the Minister for Justice. The Minister knew already. A meeting took place between Wymes, Superintendent Fleming, the head of the Special Branch, and the Minister

---

[33] From a confidential Public Service source.

for Justice, Ó Móráin. None of them was prepared to act, nor was any memorandum kept of the meeting.[34] The Minister, who was operating in an alcoholic haze for much of the time, did not have the capacity to confront the appalling vista of two very powerful colleagues being exposed to charges of serious illegalities. Andy Ward, Berry's deputy in the Department of Justice who later succeeded him, attended the meeting and reported on it to Berry. It seems that Superintendent Fleming's inability to give detailed information on Charles Haughey's brother, Pádraic, was used to raise doubts about the general validity of the information put before the meeting.

Wymes, according to Berry, owed his promotion in the Garda Síochána to Haughey, who, as Minister for Justice, had supported his promotion to Assistant Commissioner of the police over the heads of nineteen other more senior candidates in 1963.[35] Berry was finding it difficult to believe what was now emerging. Here was a former political boss, whose strengths in the Department he had so much admired, and whom he had consulted in the early stages, apparently involved in a conspiracy. In the circumstances, as Berry recorded:

> [I]t would have been only natural that Mr Wymes should hope against hope – as I did myself – that the police information was not true in relation to Mr Haughey, or that at least whatever he was doing was government policy.[36]

Nothing was done. In mid-January Berry talked with the Commissioner about going *again* to their own Minister, but Wymes argued that the initiative lay with Ó Móráin. Berry then took it upon himself to talk with his Minister. Berry said that the matter should be reported to the Taoiseach. Ó Móráin "hesitated to be the harbinger of such bad news".[37] There were many polite references at this time in Berry's diary to his Minister's "ill-health" and his inability to function, either in the Department or in the management of his solicitor's practice in Castlebar. Ó Móráin did talk with the Minister for Defence, Jim Gibbons, who checked with Colonel Hefferon. The Colonel dismissed as "pure poppycock" even the Bailieborough involvement of Captain Kelly. When Berry raised this with the Special Branch, the reply added to the general atmosphere of disbelief and bewilderment: "Christ, Hefferon must be in the swim, too."[38] It was the view of key figures in the Department of Justice at the time that Colonel Hefferon

---

[34] See "The Peter Berry Papers" in *Magill* (June 1980), pp. 54–55.

[35] Wymes was subsequently made Commissioner when Brian Lenihan was Minister for Justice. Lenihan was not in favour of the most senior police appointment going to Wymes, but Haughey helped to push it through at Cabinet. See "The Peter Berry Papers, *ibid.*, p. 55.

[36] *Ibid.*, p. 55.

[37] *Ibid.*, p. 58.

[38] *Ibid.*

was reporting very little to his superior, the Chief of Staff. He was running the army intelligence operation at his own discretion.

An atmosphere of denial, supported by a certain degree of fear, all of it relatively easy to understand, prevented anyone from doing anything. The Minister for Justice, the Minister for Defence, the head of one Department, the head of army intelligence in the other, the Commissioner for Police, and even the head of the Special Branch, Superintendent John Fleming, were all frozen. In the midst of this inaction, Fleming was promoted to Chief Superintendent.

*

Jack Lynch did not know. He has been criticised over a period of thirty years for inaction and vacillation, yet the enormity of what was going on was kept hidden from him. His action in setting up the government sub-committee, at the time a kind of sop to the more outspoken republicans among his Ministers, had ceased to have serious relevance because the situation in Northern Ireland, to everyone's relief in late 1969 and into 1970, had settled down. It was a relatively peaceful time. The logic of what Haughey and Blaney were doing, in a covert way, made no sense. But what they had started could not easily be stopped.

In February 1970 there were at least two importations of arms through Dublin Airport. In early April Garda Richard Fallon was shot during a Saor Éire bank raid. This small, far-Left extreme republican organisation or splinter-group was responsible for "a series of ideologically-inspired bank raids"[39] in 1970, which included the taking of a £14,000 payroll in Strabane, County Tyrone.

Then, out of the blue, on 13th April, Jack Lynch phoned Peter Berry; he was looking for Micheál Ó Móráin. In the Minister's absence, he summoned Berry to his Department that evening to give him a report on the IRA and the situation in Northern Ireland. In the interim, Berry's Minister, Micheál Ó Móráin, appeared and Berry told him that he would have to raise the information about Haughey and Blaney being involved in arms importation.

When Berry gave Lynch an account, which by this stage dated back four months, of the involvement of two of his Ministers in illegal activities, Lynch "seemed to be genuinely surprised".[40] Berry had limited information with him at the meeting and was astonished that Ó Móráin had apparently told Lynch nothing.

Five days later, on Friday, 17th April, word came from the Department of Transport and Power to the Department of Justice that a chartered cargo plane was due at Dublin Airport and Captain James Kelly's name was associated with the consignment. It consisted of 6.8 tons of arms and ammunition, listed as being for the use of the Army and the Gardaí. Berry was adamant that the cargo be

---

[39] See Patrick Bishop and Eamonn Mallie, *The Provisional IRA* (Heinemann, London, 1987), p. 131.

[40] "The Peter Berry Papers" in *Magill* (June 1980), p. 60.

allowed in and then seized. It was a high-risk approach. He also had to make security provisions at four other airports in case the flight was diverted. He believed that the strategy would prevent the IRA from trying again and would also drain their resources. In fact, their "resources" were coming from the State.

The cargo was due on Sunday, 19th April. Haughey, who had become aware that Berry knew of the cargo's imminent arrival, rang Berry on Saturday to clear its passage through the airport. Berry refused. He did, however, answer a question raised by Haughey that was crucial from his perspective. Haughey asked: "Does the man from Mayo know?"

Berry told Haughey that Ó Móráin *did* know, but it was a lie. Haughey, by asking the question, had revealed that this was not a government-sponsored importation but the work of a "caucus". All intelligence and police work depends on spotting when people say the wrong thing, have the wrong reaction, or ask the wrong question. Haughey had slipped up. Berry knew that what was happening was unknown to other Ministers and unknown to the Taoiseach. The reports going back to December, which had so stultified all the people in the line of action, were confirmed.

Berry then did a surprising thing. He contacted President de Valera. Without telling him the nature of the "matters of national concern", he asked de Valera if his responsibility ended with informing his own Minister or whether he should take the details to the Government that had appointed him.

"You have a clear duty to Government. You should speak to the Taoiseach," replied the President.[41]

*

Jack Lynch returned to Dublin from Cork late on the Sunday night, and Berry saw him the next day, shortly after noon, giving him a police report and telling him about the events of the Friday, Saturday and Sunday. Lynch saw Berry again the following day to hear his explanation of the delay in coming to the head of the Government. To Lynch's intense fury, Berry confessed that he had thought that by raising the issues he would be "intruding on a secret government mission". A week later, Lynch told Berry:

> When you said last Tuesday that you thought that the Government might be secretly involved I saw *red*. I was not able to speak to you, I was so furious.[42]

There is a footnote to that momentous day that gives an insight into Lynch's mind. On Monday he had been faced with a crisis deepening beyond any point he could have imagined. His energies had become focused upon two Ministers

---

[41] "The Peter Berry Papers" in *Magill* (June 1980), pp. 61–62.
[42] *Ibid.*, p. 62.

and the betrayal of their responsibilities to the Government. They were acting in breach of their oath of office and clearly against the Constitution. Despite all this turmoil, Lynch found time to sit down and hand-write a short letter on an entirely different matter. It was to Dr Martin O'Donoghue, asking him to call. "I would like a meeting with you which would last about twenty to thirty minutes." It reinforces the calm and judgemental approach Lynch had to a crisis over which many people could easily have panicked. The meeting took place later that week. It began an association which lasted until the end of Lynch's life and led to O'Donoghue becoming closely involved with the party and with politics, successfully standing for the Dáil and in due course serving as a member of a Lynch Government. O'Donoghue's name was given to Lynch by Dr T.K. Whitaker.

Much has been made of two crucial dates: 13th April, when Berry told Lynch of the involvement of two of his Ministers "in supplying arms to the IRA"; and 20th April, when he gave the Taoiseach the full details of the attempted importation through Dublin Airport. When this information, covering what happened between those two dates, is filled in, the fundamental difference between the information in the first encounter and that in the second will be readily evident. For months, all senior security personnel, including Berry, had been aware of a general plan to aid the IRA financially, and to provide them with arms. There had indeed been deliveries of arms consignments to Dublin Airport. But the final linking up of Haughey with the shipment and the revelation that the whole business was extraneous to the Government fell into place only on the weekend of the intended landing of the arms. Lynch's statement on this matter is not in doubt. He only knew on 20th April. However, what happened from then on is more puzzling.

*

The danger itself had been avoided. Berry's "ring of steel" around the airport had paid off. Lynch had time to absorb the enormity of what was facing him. He was surrounded by political desolation. Two of the most powerful Ministers in his Government were directly abusing government authority and engaging in a serious and highly dangerous conspiracy. Unknown to the Government, they had been so engaged for months. A third Minister, Ó Móráin, was in a state of physical and mental breakdown as a result of alcoholism. His Minister for Defence had been destabilised to the point of not having reported on critical intelligence work, which instead had been directed to the service of the conspirators in the Government. At least one other senior Minister, Boland, would almost certainly have sided with Blaney, and the Taoiseach could not be sure of the loyalty of a couple or more Ministers. It had the makings of an All-Ireland final in terms of who did what and when. Timing and judgement were more important than courage and confrontation. Above all, Lynch was not going to be hurried into an open confrontation at the government table. Such an approach could easily delay but not resolve matters. Things had gone too far for that. It could go woefully wrong if the numbers supporting him did not add up. At the same time, Lynch knew he could no longer face the danger of disaffection. He had to carefully time the removal of the conspirators.

Lynch was not lacking in courage. He was still, however, lacking in certainty. He had serious doubts about ministerial loyalty and was relying on eccentric sources of information. He could easily find himself wrong-footed if Berry's known mood of near hysteria about security, combined with the Minister for Justice's physical and intellectual collapse, turned out to constitute a terrible set of misjudgements. In his heart he must have known that Berry had brought him incontrovertible facts which, essentially, represented treason.

Lynch needed to run a series of tests, rather more serious in their implications than the tests he had run at the time of the leadership change in 1966. The cohesive team he had hoped for then and had worked for since was in a state of fragmentation. He did not know its shape.

He had the choice of confronting the crisis within the Government or of confronting it outside that framework. After all, members of his team had become profoundly unreliable and unpredictable. His rights, and the Government's rights, were clearly defined in the Constitution. The Taoiseach could hire or fire Ministers; apart from that, his role was one of chairmanship. If he opened up a decision-making process within the team of men at the cabinet table, there was no predicting which way it might go. It was clear to him that Ministers such as Gibbons and Ó Móráin were both unreliable and intimidated by colleagues. If it turned out that other, more marginal, supporters of the more republican line formed up with the culprits, then he would be facing a situation in which he might be forced to resign or would have no alternative but to seek a dissolution. By initiating a debate, he would have weakened and even pre-empted his potential choice of straightforward dismissals. Lynch was, at the very least, unsure of where he stood with men such as Seán Flanagan and Brian Lenihan. With Boland, who was a strong and fearless figure with determined republican views, Lynch knew exactly where he stood, but it did not help him in terms of relying on any clear-cut decision in his favour.

The choice he made was to confront Blaney and Haughey with the evidence against them. Before seeing them on 29th April, he had a meeting with Berry, who recorded how troubled Lynch was, walking up and down the room, muttering to himself.

> I heard him say 'What will I do? What will I do?' and, thinking that he was addressing me, I said: 'Well, if I were you, I'd sack the pair of them and I would tell the British immediately, making a virtue of necessity, as the British are bound to know, anyway, all that is going on.'[43]

Lynch reacted angrily. Peter Berry, who had a personal interest in all this and a position to protect in very threatening circumstances, appears to have

---

[43] "The Peter Berry Papers" in *Magill* (June 1980), p. 63.

misunderstood what was going on. He thought Lynch could just act along the lines he had advised and became fearful at what seemed to be a lapse in the Taoiseach's courage and judgement. In asking himself "What will I do?" Lynch was exploring the more difficult options, not a simple way forward.

Lynch saw Blaney in his office and told him that the information he already had to hand justified asking for his resignation. Blaney refused to resign. Lynch allowed him to reflect on his position. He then went to the Mater Hospital, where Haughey had been taken following an accident. Lynch requested Haughey's resignation; Haughey responded by asking for time to reflect. This was granted, though both men knew the choice was the stark one between departing voluntarily or being sacked. Lynch knew there was no turning back. He could postpone the ultimate sanction, which involved going to the President, and did indeed postpone it, but the idea that the future of the two Ministers was somehow still in the balance is a misunderstanding both of Lynch and of the position he faced as Taoiseach. The only option, if he did not push for the removal of Blaney and Haughey, was his own resignation.

He saw Berry again the next day. Berry felt particularly vulnerable, having been the first person to confront Haughey over the attempted importation at Dublin Airport. Lynch, according to Berry, told him "the matter was ended; there would be no repetition". Berry took it to mean that Haughey would remain as Minister for Finance and was seriously worried at Lynch's rather hollow promise, as Berry saw it, when Lynch assured him: "I will protect you." Berry concluded his account with the words: "I felt a very sorry man returning to my department where I told the tale to my usual colleagues."[44]

Lynch was still piecing information together, though now it was being gathered for the justification of the actions he had contemplated and had already set in motion. He summoned the Garda Commissioner, the Head of the Special Branch and the new Head of army intelligence, Colonel Patrick Delaney, who had replaced Colonel Hefferon on the latter officer's retirement. He also brought in Colm Condon, the Attorney General, to advise on the legal implications of matters at this stage. Lynch still had to move very carefully.

He did not give information in return; he had become too cautious for that. This reflected badly in the minds of two key figures, Berry and Chief Superintendent Fleming. Fleming was puzzled at not being asked questions at the meeting in Lynch's house on the evening of 30th April and decided to call on Berry afterwards. Lynch also phoned Berry, but apparently without grasping Berry's and Fleming's fears over developments. Berry recorded in his diary for that day, though it was obviously written at a later point: "As a result of the misstatements already recorded, with more to follow, I lost respect for the Taoiseach's credibility."[45]

On 1st May Captain James Kelly was arrested. He sought a private meeting

---

[44] "The Peter Berry Papers" in *Magill* (June 1980), p. 63.
[45] *Ibid.*, p. 65.

with his Minister but this was refused, though the Minister saw him in the company of others. Kelly then made a statement. The close rapport between him and Gibbons was noted by Fleming, who assumed that the Minister for Defence knew of the attempt to import arms. Lynch had seen other men serving in intelligence and agreed to a meeting with Kelly, who was keen to see the Taoiseach. But the two had entirely different views as to what this might achieve. Kelly sought to justify his position and hasten his release. Lynch wanted the naming of names, including his two Ministers and full details of what Kelly knew about the arms importation. The encounter was brief and unproductive.

There was a government meeting on that same day. Lynch informed those present about the attempted importation of arms and that he had reason to believe that two Ministers were involved. The men in question had denied this and, for the present, the matter was closed. Lynch did not invite debate, nor was there any. A Minister who attended that meeting described the event:

> When Lynch came in to the Government meeting, and before the start of business, he said: 'I have something to say. Information has come to me of an attempt to bring in arms. It has been suggested to me that two members of the Government were involved, Neil Blaney and Charles Haughey. I have spoken with them, and they have denied all knowledge. I have accepted their assurances that they are not involved...'
> Blaney was present for this, and remained silent. Haughey was in hospital. The meeting then dealt with various issues, one of which involved the Department of Agriculture, and during it the meeting was given what amounted to a lengthy 'lecture' from Neil Blaney on the shortage of money for farmers.[46]

According to this account, there was discussion among government members immediately after the conclusion of the meeting and absolute astonishment at what Lynch had said. One close group of colleagues in Government at that time consisted of Paddy Lalor, George Colley and Pádraig Faulkner. Colley claimed that they discussed the looming crisis in a mood of disbelief.[47]

Blaney was not sure where he stood, but Boland was reasonably certain that the danger of dismissal was past. He went to see Haughey in the Mater Hospital.

At 8.45 a.m. on the morning of 4th May Jack Lynch went to Mount Carmel Hospital to request Ó Móráin's resignation. The Minister for Justice agreed to give it in writing that afternoon. Leaving the private hospital, Lynch said to Berry: "He will go quietly."

Some time on the following day, the leader of the Opposition, Liam Cosgrave, was given an anonymous note indicating that there had been an illegal attempt to import arms and naming the men involved. This reinforced earlier information that had come to Cosgrave from Phillip McMahon, formerly a detective in the

---

[46] From an interview with Paddy Lalor, July 2000.
[47] Interview with the author, June and July 1979.

Special Branch, and one of the most highly regarded intelligence officers the State had ever employed.[48] His contacts within the IRA were particularly good. The information had been in Cosgrave's hands for some days and had been made known to Ned Murphy, political correspondent of the *Sunday Independent*. He in turn had told his editor, Hector Legge, but Legge, protecting what he thought was the national interest, decided not to publish its contents. Cosgrave now went to Lynch and showed him the note. Lynch informed him that he was going to dismiss the two named Ministers, but not the third, Gibbons.

There is a view that the note was passed to Cosgrave as a result, directly or indirectly, of Lynch's actions at the time. The extent to which he anticipated what might happen and indeed intended to happen is open to question. It is probable that Lynch did intend the final pass in the game to come from the leader of the Opposition, thus sealing all uncertainties and allowing his position to become that of a man who was forced to dismiss two powerful government Ministers. The timing of the first leak coincided with the conspiracy to import arms becoming a reality, albeit one that was aborted. When the first leak produced nothing, there was a second. It would have been consistent with Lynch's way of operating and his shrewd judgement of the difficulties surrounding his own position to act thus.

The rationale behind what happened is straightforward enough. Berry's own sense of outrage and fear, in the face of Lynch's apparent refusal to dismiss, was misguided but real. It was echoed at the top levels of the Garda Síochána. There may have been dismay at the prospect of a hush-up of what had been going on, particularly in the Special Branch, which had been so persistent and so effective in revealing ministerial involvement in the importation of arms. But no hush-up had been attempted. There was no convincing reason why the men concerned, trained to silence and surveillance anyhow, should have leaked information about illegal acts which were already blocked or aborted. Their instinct would have been to wait. The leaks reinforced the dismissals and strengthened Lynch's hand. They did not stop any further criminal activities. Various attempts were made at the time, and have been made since, to trace the supposed Garda source of the leak, but without success.

One thing is certain: Peter Berry was wrong in thinking that it had come from a particular member of the Government who "was incapable of resisting temptation to air his knowledge".[49] Berry himself would not have leaked anything

---

[48] Phillip McMahon was an outstanding Special Branch officer who became its head and was Chief Superintendent when he retired. He had established a number of high-level informers within the IRA dating back to the campaign in the 1950s but still relevant and valuable as sources until 1971. Uniquely in the force, McMahon's service was extended and though further extensions were refused he established a special relationship within State security after his retirement. He was close to Jack Lynch. Before Jack and Máirín bought their Rathgar home, they had a flat in the house owned by the McMahons.

[49] "The Peter Berry Papers" in *Magill* (July 1980), p. 65.

to anyone, but he must have been relieved when it happened, precipitating the final moves in the crisis.

Lynch had now to deal definitively with Blaney and Haughey. On the same Tuesday evening, 5th May, at 9.45 p.m. precisely, Blaney received a note requesting him to go to the Taoiseach's office. At the time he was presiding at a meeting of the Fianna Fáil party's organisation committee. Boland and Paudge Brennan, a Parliamentary Secretary and supporter of Blaney's, were both present. Blaney passed the note over and said: "What did I tell you? This is it. Will you take the chair?" Boland did so and adjourned the meeting. When Blaney returned, it was to tell them that Lynch had asked for his resignation. Blaney had wanted time to reflect until the following morning, but Lynch had refused this request. Boland's view was the more constitutional one:

> I still think that when a Taoiseach asks for the resignation of a member of his Government he should get it straight away whether his reasons for requesting it are reasonable or not.[50]

He understood at the time that Haughey had also sought a period for reflection on Lynch's request for his resignation. Blaney left to visit the Mater and Boland gave his opinion that both Ministers were wrong in not meeting Lynch's request right away. He wrote out his own letter of resignation there and then.

*

Charles Haughey and Neil Blaney were dismissed on Wednesday, 6th May. Kevin Boland resigned from the Government. Ó Móráin had already resigned. Desmond O'Malley was appointed Minister for Justice. Effectively, the crisis was over, although the debate about it would create a new and quite different crisis of public confidence and a degree of unprecedented disbelief. But the Government had survived and would survive. Effectively, Lynch had won the battle. His public position was assured, in spite of his having been the subject of a huge amount of criticism – for weakness, vacillation, uncertainty, lack of courage and poor judgement. The arguments over these charges have continued ever since, but the essential achievement which came to so dramatic a conclusion during the early hours of 6th May was convincingly and irreversibly in his favour. In all important respects, Jack Lynch was totally in command.

---

[50] Kevin Boland, *Up Dev* (published by the author, Dublin, 1977), p. 75.

CHAPTER EIGHT

"The arena of politics, impure and unsimple"

– Sir John Peck

The crisis was over.[1] The most momentous political event in the State's history had been successfully negotiated and settled by Jack Lynch. He had survived a plot within his own Government to subvert the State and he had made an unprecedented move against two senior government Ministers. He had given them the option of resigning or being fired. In the end they were both dismissed. The public now witnessed their humiliation.

He had successfully come through a sequence of events that could have developed into a coup against himself. This was the real danger, and it was a danger *inside* the Government. It was Lynch's judgement, and his alone, that could deal with this. He did not know conclusively which members of the Government he could trust. His hold on events, even his leadership, had been and was being contested by others. Blaney and Boland may have been the most outspoken of his critics, but looking round among the others he could not tell where their ultimate loyalties lay. What he did know was that the potential division was evenly balanced. This was a very dangerous numbers game, indeed, if it had to be played out around the government table. Wisely, he held off from this course of action throughout the period of uncertainty and growing crisis. By not bringing the matter to the surface, and above all by not debating it within the Government, he maintained a tacit control over events. He did this by reserving to himself the right, uniquely his, to hire and fire. But exercising the right needed powerful logic behind it. For it to work he had to move alone, his actions had to remain tacit, and his timing needed to be impeccable.

Deliberately since the previous August, Lynch had placed the potential for confrontation at arm's length. He did this by the creation of the Government Sub-Committee for the Relief of Distress in Northern Ireland. It was clear long before August 1969 that his attempts since becoming leader "to create a team spirit among the Government ministers, to impose a greater cohesion on the

---

[1] A second, quite different, crisis arose late in the year, following the acquittals in the Arms Trial. For the present, despite the collective political uproar that went on for days, the actual crisis threatening the Government and the Taoiseach was effectively settled by the time Lynch announced the two dismissals and the resignations.

operation of the Government as a whole and to exert my personal authority"[2] had failed. Faced with a growing crisis which no one fully understood, his Government had rapidly become divided. There were two key, powerful figures in it who opposed his leadership in any shape or form, and were prepared to use whatever issue arose in order to challenge that leadership. Blaney had a vestige of merit in his opposition, in that he knew the North better than Lynch and genuinely believed that his remedies for it, which were militant and republican, offered the correct solution. However, he showed a callous disregard for the collective responsibility of the Government which the Irish Constitution required. Haughey's opposition was more nakedly opportunist. Jealously, he eyed Blaney's credentials. Covertly, he bypassed them, engaging in activities which proved futile and damaging.

Lynch was aware of the disdain with which they had regarded him during the first three years of his leadership of the party. He felt, wrongly, that the winning of the 1969 general election might change things. It certainly began the process of removing the perception of his being a temporary or interim leader within both the party and the Government. When the crisis broke in mid-August 1969, Lynch had few illusions about where he stood.

One of the difficulties he had recognised from the very beginning of his leadership was that the mantle of de Valera and Lemass was not transferable in its entirety. They had enjoyed the unique authority of being heroes before they were politicians. They carried their heroic stature, grounded in revolution and the making of Ireland's independence, into the business of democratic politics. The aura it gave to them – and indeed to other men of their generation, like Seán MacEntee and Frank Aiken, including the parents of some of his opponents in government – was not a possibility for the next generation. Lynch himself was conscious of this:

> I also found it difficult to visualise myself assuming the mantle of the likes of Éamon de Valera and Seán Lemass. They were both towering figures in my mind and the thought that I could adequately fill their place seemed to me the height of presumption.[3]

It undoubtedly was. The best he could hope for was being *primus inter pares*[4] and even that was hard to achieve.

Most significantly of all, he recognised the constitutional dilemma. He was secure as Taoiseach until such time as he lost the confidence and support of the Dáil. But power resided in the Government. He was its chairman and its "voice", but the idea that he was in control was not a legal reality. Nor did it have any

---

[2] "My Life and Times" in *Magill* (November 1979), p. 43.

[3] *Ibid.*, p. 42.

[4] "First among equals". This was the constitutional position. Apart from the right to hire and fire, and to decide when to seek the dissolution of the Dáil, a Taoiseach has no powers over his colleagues in government.

meaning constitutionally. His predecessors had exercised a moral authority that had been impressive and had imposed rigorous standards of behaviour on Fianna Fáil. Around Lynch in the 1960s a different, tribal psychology had developed. Within the party it was reinforced by arrogance and a level of moral turpitude that drew from George Colley the criticism that "some people in high places appear to have low standards".[5] Strictly speaking, the party was more democratic. Lynch would have seemed draconian had he dismissed Blaney for expressing views on Northern Ireland that were different from his own. It needed more than that to justify firing a senior figure from his government position. So long as he was sure of the support of the Government his own position was secure. This was his reasoning. But if that security was shaken or undermined, as in fact was happening periodically, his own position could in certain circumstances become untenable.

From August 1969 this potential, which would render Lynch vulnerable, was a distinct possibility. One of the reasons for his acceptance of the government sub-committee, that was subsequently so widely questioned and condemned, was that setting it up served an important purpose in the difficult circumstances that emerged at that time. It put the issue of the relief of distress in Northern Ireland at one remove. Debate over detail was placed outside the Government. The issue of arms had already been decided. None would be given to Northern Ireland Nationalists; no arms would be sent across the Border. The committee was a very imperfect mechanism but there was a rather cruel realism behind it.

Lynch was no longer sure of any of his colleagues. He could not, and did not, confide in them. For years afterwards, in the unending debate about what he knew or did not know, what he should have done and how he should have done it, there has been little recognition of the acute dangers he was facing. The State and its Government were vulnerable and the choices that were open to him as the country's leader contained options that were fraught with danger. In the end, in dealing with the crisis, he transcended the confrontation within government, and exercised his own judgement and his unique constitutional role in deciding on its membership. He then made that decision the central political issue, and no one could argue with it. In dismissing Haughey and Blaney, and in gaining the very considerable bonus of Boland's resignation, he resolved the crisis in terms that were carved in stone.

*

No one believed that the crisis had in any way been resolved on the morning of Wednesday, 6th May. For the media, for politicians, for a majority of the

---

[5] Speech in Galway, May 1967, to an Ógra Fianna Fáil conference (the party's youth organisation). Colley always denied that it referred to Haughey. At the time it contributed to a changed approach by Lynch, who terminated the Taca organisation and brought in a new fund-raiser, Des Hanafin.

Government and the vast majority of the Fianna Fáil party, the crisis was only beginning. In a more general sense, this was true. Considerable damage was inflicted on the standing of the Government and on respect for the security forces. The country was cruelly exposed. The reputations of Ministers and of Lynch himself had also been severely damaged. Northern Ireland policy was badly battered. Nevertheless, the real crisis had been settled and there was no going back from the dramatic dismissals.

There were huge questions unanswered about what would happen next. The reaction of the Fianna Fáil party was a matter of great concern. The way the Dáil would handle things was also open to the widest possible speculation. Northern Ireland and international reaction was unpredictable except in terms of the shock effect that a scandal involving illegal arms importation might have. Even so, in the real sense of an irreversible conclusion and response *to* action threatening the State, Lynch, as Taoiseach, made resolute decisions, thereby removing uncertainty.

From the morning of Wednesday, 6th May Lynch had a Government and a public service either loyal to himself, or silenced in their reservations. He had implicit trust in the main security services. He had a commanding position in the Dáil. He faced uncertainty over his voting strength when Boland resigned his ministerial position, though Boland's own judgement was to stick with Fianna Fáil and not to assist in bringing in an alternative administration.

From Lynch's point of view the advantage of being rid of a powerful and outspoken opponent manifestly outweighed the possible undermining of his majority. Boland acted with personal integrity throughout, and successively resigned his membership of the Fianna Fáil parliamentary party, and then the party altogether, finally completing his exodus when he gave up his seat. Others were less principled and stayed within the party for the time being.

Not surprisingly, when Lynch came into the Dáil that morning he looked drawn and haggard. Paddy Hillery maintains that Lynch lost half a stone in the period leading up to the dismissals.[6] He knew he was in for a hard time and that it could go on for hours, days and, possibly, weeks. In fact, the reverberations went on for decades and still, long after his death, are not over. The re-running of the narrative, the motives and the judgements, has become a form of political sport even within the generations unborn at the time.

The actual statement which made public the affair was issued at 2.50 a.m. on the Wednesday morning:

> I have requested the resignations as members of the Government of Mr Neil T. Blaney, Minister for Agriculture and Fisheries, and Mr Charles J. Haughey, Minister for Finance, because I am satisfied that they do not subscribe fully to Government policy in relation to the present situation in the Six Counties as stated by me at the Fianna Fáil Árd Fheis in January last. Caoimhín Ó Beoláin [Kevin Boland], Minister for Local Government

---

6 Interview with the author, August 2001.

135

and Social Welfare, has tendered his resignation as a member of the Government and I propose to advise the President to accept it. A special meeting of Fianna Fáil deputies will take place at Leinster House at 6 p.m. today to consider the position that has arisen.

In view of the fact that Lynch had orchestrated the purging of his Government on his own sole authority within the Constitution, it is important to deal with matters in this context rather than in the context of the situation in the Dáil. There are differences of emphasis and language between what he said publicly outside the Dáil chamber, and the answers he gave inside it. But the critical issue of arms was not mentioned in the first announcement. The reason given was non-concurrence with Northern Ireland policy. The source for that policy was deliberately chosen, linking Lynch and his decision with the sovereignty within Fianna Fáil of its annual conference. The critical event of the day was the parliamentary party meeting at 6 p.m. that evening.

Lynch had obtained prior opposition agreement to an adjournment until after that meeting and the need for this became clear when Lynch told the Dáil that he had not received the resignations requested more than ten hours earlier. "The constitutional position is that I am entitled to act on my request."[7]

The two opposition parties acted independently. The Fine Gael leader had enjoyed privileged information about the crisis. He had attempted to leak this to the press and had then taken the details to Lynch in order to confront him with his supposed inaction. Brendan Corish was in a different position. After the Dáil had met and adjourned, at 11.30 a.m., he called a meeting of the Labour parliamentary party to debate what should be done in the crisis. The party decided to vest authority in Corish himself and to allow him discretion to act as he saw fit. He decided to go and see Lynch. At the meeting Corish expressed concern for Lynch's position and told him that the Labour Party would support him and the elected Government, whatever he decided to do. Sitting face-to-face with Lynch, he expected some reaction; but Lynch, apart from nodding his acknowledgement of what Corish had said, remained totally silent and gave him no answer at all.[8]

Not surprisingly, Corish was bewildered by this reaction. Looked at from Lynch's point of view, however, the silence was essential. If in advance of the meeting of the Fianna Fáil parliamentary party, at which Lynch was going to have to confront backbenchers with what he had done, there had been the slightest indication of agreed opposition support for the Government, it could have seriously prejudiced his position. The legal and constitutional definition on which Lynch was relying could not be diluted by political intervention, however altruistic.

---

[7] *Dáil Debates* Vol. 246, Col. 631.

[8] The source of this information is an interview with Brendan Halligan, general secretary of the Labour Party at the time and a close colleague and adviser to the Labour leader. He claims that Corish's determination to come to a pre-election agreement with Fine Gael dated from that morning. Also, Corish became convinced that Ireland needed some kind of "privy council" approach in the event of national crisis.

Furthermore, he had no knowledge of how far he could trust Corish. The altruism was there; but no one could be sure, least of all the man under the most intense pressure in the encounter.

It was important to Lynch to sustain the "constitutional position" in which he had invoked his right to dismiss; and he was determined to exclude all other matter from debate or argument. Time was spent during that day working out the detail within the Government. When the party meeting took place that evening, a motion was put to it endorsing the absolute right of the Taoiseach to hire and fire Ministers. No one could take issue with this. For those who might have done so, and who had worked during the day towards widening the discussion, there was the problem that they had failed to get Haughey's support. Their option for extending the debate would work only if they were all solidly behind it. Haughey, as so often happened in moments of crisis, became indecisive and pulled back. He was perplexed by the problems of choice and did not want to be part of a team of rebels. He was frightened of the implications of a confrontation on republicanism and, indeed, of any kind. Lynch, absolutely sure of his ground, obtained unanimous support for his actions. Even his opponents accepted the humiliation of dismissal; the main hurdle of the day was cleared.

Again, Lynch issued a carefully worded statement of exactly what had happened:

> At the special meeting of the Fianna Fáil party, held at Leinster House, the party unanimously endorsed a motion by the Taoiseach that the party approves such nominations as he would make to replace the members of the Government whose appointments had been terminated. Each of the three former Ministers, deputies Neil Blaney, Kevin Boland and Charles J. Haughey, and the former Parliamentary Secretary, deputy Paudge Brennan, expressed unreservedly his loyalty to the Fianna Fáil party and the Taoiseach.

Taking the earlier resignation of Micheál Ó Móráin into account, the political casualty list had risen to five. The statement was a sign that Lynch had won, that the crisis was over, and that he would go on to win the Dáil divisions. Going into the resumed debate in the Dáil that night, Lynch knew he had the necessary votes to survive whenever the discussions in the chamber concluded, and whatever further matter they brought to light.

*

In the Dáil he did what he had done with Fianna Fáil at the party meeting: he confined the debate. This time it was limited to a simple motion seeking approval for the appointment of Desmond O'Malley as Minister for Justice. He said he was open to a wider debate later in the week, but in the immediate aftermath of the dismissals he wanted to restrict the Dáil to what could be described as tackling the central problem, namely the State's security which had gone so sadly wrong.

It would be a mistake to read too much into this. Clearly, Lynch had to debate an issue relevant to the circumstance of a sequence of resignations or dismissals, and the earlier resignation of Ó Móráin had created a vacancy of proven importance in the critical area of security, making it the first priority. But for Lynch it was a watershed. He had been profoundly let down by Ó Móráin and he was now choosing a young and completely untried newcomer to the Dáil, Desmond O'Malley. He was placing his trust, mainly on instinct, in a man who in due course would come closer to him than any other politician and do so with the utmost integrity. Ó Móráin's performance in Justice had been a disaster and to his mistakes and inertia could be traced many of the difficulties which Lynch had to clear up.

Lynch was very brief, his speech lasting barely five minutes. He did not confine himself to the motion. He spoke now of the attempt to import arms and the involvement of two Ministers. He told the House of seeking their resignations from the Government a week earlier, of their failure to comply, of their sustained refusal, and of his own decision to have them dismissed. "I did so on the basis that I was convinced that not even the slightest suspicion should attach to any member of the Government in a matter of this nature."[9]

It would be wrong to say that Lynch enjoyed himself during this aftermath of the crisis. Yet he played each moment as though making a critical run or a crucial stroke in a game of hurling. There is something both deadly and laconic in the way he handled himself. He dealt with the two opposition parties almost indulgently. They were uncertain about what to do, and divided in the demands they were trying to make on Lynch about how to proceed. They had no agreed strategy on how to debate the issues because they did not really know what the issues were. By each statement Lynch led them forward. They could debate when they wanted and for as long as they wanted. All he asked was that the motion for debate concern itself with the logical outcome of what he had done. By this, instead of having a messy and emotive discussion based on a motion of confidence in the Government, the wording concerned new appointments.

The other strategically important decision that Lynch made at the time concerned the future. It hardly attracted attention with so many other things on the minds of deputies, but, in what was demonstrably generous to a fault, he singled out Ó Móráin as being quite a different case. Despite the fact that Ó Móráin had caused a good deal of the trouble by being almost entirely derelict in his ministerial duties, he was described by Lynch as someone who was not involved in "the matter with which I now propose to deal". Boland was not involved either, but was clearly opposed to Lynch's Northern Ireland policy and was therefore in a different category.

What Lynch now outlined, in what was the kernel of his speech, was the illegal nature of what had been done. Without being specific, he now linked the attempted importation of arms to the decision to go ahead with the dismissals. It

---

[9] *Dáil Debates* Vol. 246, Col. 643.

was not, therefore, failure to comply with government policy only, but the fact that Lynch "had information which purported to connect them with an alleged attempt to unlawfully import arms".[10] It was on the basis of this that their resignations were sought. "Each of them denied he instigated in any way the attempted importation of arms."[11]

In the careful language that was Lynch's hallmark, he gave the sequence of events while at the same time explaining the order of his actions. He could not easily dismiss any individual on suspicion of a series of illegal acts that would require the courts to prove or disprove. He could more easily dismiss a member of his administration on the issue of lack of full agreement with government policy. He had created circumstances where the victims of his purge had to agree with its constitutional legitimacy. They could not make any argument, nor deny his right.

There was an admirable calm and patience in the way Lynch explained this under extremely testing circumstances and at the end of the longest week in his life. It was a truthful account of the final stage of a crisis that went back much further than was generally thought. When opposition leader Liam Cosgrave rose to speak, he gave a very simplified version of his own part in the story. The implication was that his action bringing knowledge of the attempted importation to the Taoiseach had precipitated the move against Blaney and Haughey. There was no advantage to Lynch in contradicting this. Indeed, quite the reverse. Cosgrave's part in their downfall made Blaney's and Haughey's position more isolated, and their room for manoeuvre more restricted. It reinforced public astonishment and dismay at what had been going on, and it helped to create a climate of sympathy for the inevitably violent reactions there would be to the criminal charges that would have to follow.

The myth of Cosgrave being the hero of the Arms Crisis was the first to be established that night. It was simple politics designed to reinforce calls on the Government to resign. Cosgrave pointed to a failure on Lynch's part to deal with the matter and this, too, became part of the True Story of the Cross Lynch Bore. In fact, Cosgrave had handled the information in anything but a straightforward manner. He had known from two sources of the attempted importation of arms. In the first instance he sought the help of his press contact in Independent Newspapers, Ned Murphy, who was political correspondent of the *Sunday Independent*. Cosgrave knew and trusted him, and gave him the details, thinking this action would bring the facts out indirectly. Murphy wrote a version of the story and had it on the desk of his editor, Hector Legge, on the night of Thursday, 30th April, but Legge decided not to publish.

This threw the matter back to Cosgrave. It gave him enough knowledge to allow him to challenge Lynch when announcing the resignation of Ó Móráin.

---

[10] *Dáil Debates* Vol. 246, Col. 642.
[11] *Ibid.*

"Can the Taoiseach say if this is the only ministerial resignation we can expect?" Lynch replied rhetorically on that occasion. "I do not know what the deputy is referring to." Cosgrave tried to spell it out: "Is it only the tip of the iceberg?"[12]

The second myth, that Lynch did not know Cosgrave had the details, reinforced the first. But the possibility of it being true seems remote. It is far more likely that Lynch was puzzled that Cosgrave took so long to arrive at the appropriate course of action, which he did only under advice from colleagues on his Front Bench.

Others in the debate praised Liam Cosgrave, including Conor Cruise O'Brien, who claimed that Blaney and Haughey would not have been exposed and dismissed without Cosgrave's intervention. O'Brien quite correctly blamed Fianna Fáil for the damage that had been done to Ireland, and in particular for the polarisation in the North. Not many other speakers in the debate focused on Northern Ireland, however. The main interest was on the dismissed men, with Tom O'Higgins, who was later to become Chief Justice, raising the issue of criminal charges.

There was no prospect of an election. Lynch had a comfortable margin when the vote was taken in the early hours of Saturday morning, 72 to 65. But Corish, leader of the Labour Party, was probably accurate enough when he put, in voting terms, the actual situation within Fianna Fáil, which was 65 in support of Lynch and 10 against. Five of those ten had been "outed"; others would follow.

Though the Opposition saw no prospect of an election, Lynch's sobering skill and his masterly handling of an unprecedented set of circumstances, brought them to their senses in respect of the future and encouraged them to prepare for that eventuality. A year earlier they had suffered an embarrassing setback in the general election primarily because the two parties had failed to reach any kind of electoral agreement. The common ground needed for this was now emerging in terms of a loose and at first slightly fumbling solidarity between Fine Gael and Labour.

Lynch was concerned with sorting out his own party and his Government. The confirmation in office of Desmond O'Malley on Thursday, 7th May was followed by the presentation to the Dáil of the names of three new Ministers. Bobby Molloy was to be appointed to the Department of Local Government. Jeremiah Cronin was to be Minister for Defence. Gerard Collins was nominated as Minister for Post and Telegraphs. George Colley took over Haughey's job at the Department of Finance. James Gibbons moved to Agriculture. Joseph Brennan, the Donegal deputy who had been on the ill-fated sub-committee, took Social Welfare in addition to Labour.

This restructuring of his Government, as Lynch had agreed with the opposition parties, was the formal purpose of the thirty-five hours of continuous debate, on the Friday and Saturday of that week in which 69 deputies spoke. The opposition

---

[12] *Dáil Debates* Vol. 246, Col. 519.

parties had 53 speakers. Of the Fianna Fáil party, these included Neil Blaney and Kevin Boland, both of whom gave long and detailed explanations of their positions. A statement was issued on behalf of Charles Haughey who was still in hospital.

*

Jack Lynch could afford to look with indulgence upon the multifaceted opposition diagnosis of the crisis. Much as they might call for the Government's resignation and for the election of an alternative administration untainted by men who had engaged in illegal acts, there was no possibility of this happening. His security ensured by the solid support of Fianna Fáil for what he had done, Lynch turned towards his real focus of interest. This was nearer home. The most important contributions to the debate, as far as he was concerned, were those of Blaney and Boland.

The views that they represented were prevalent in the party and, indeed, were reflected quite widely in the country. Theirs was an alternative approach that had plenty of logic behind it, however dangerous or ill-advised in current circumstances. With all that lay ahead of Lynch, in terms of legal action to follow up the suspicions he had voiced in respect of arms importation, the strength of his opponents was a reality of power politics.

To begin with, it must have come as some relief when Haughey, reacting to his dismissal, signalled a clear divide between himself and the other two former Ministers. He denied everything. He claimed from his bed in the Mater Hospital, through his solicitor, that he needed to look at the evidence. He included in his statement his full acceptance of the Taoiseach's right to dismiss him: "I now categorically state that at no time have I taken part in any illegal importation or attempted importation of arms to this country."

In a curious remark made by the Fine Gael deputy, Gerald L'Estrange, in the subsequent debate, Haughey is said to have gone into the Department of Finance, despite his state of health, to remove his private papers. Apart from that brief visit – clearly of a vital kind in terms of what documents might have been there – Haughey adopted an aloof attitude to the events in the crisis. This astonished Boland.

Haughey gave no indication of his own opinion on how the Northern Ireland crisis could be resolved, nor did he indicate what his beliefs were about the future development of a policy that might help towards ending violence. In contrast, both Boland and Blaney sought to explain their actions and past speeches in a policy context which approved of the direct involvement of the Republic in Northern Ireland affairs and the use of force in certain circumstances.

Boland, while he accepted Lynch's right to have people of his own choosing in his Government, gave an account of the reasons for his resignation. These included an absolute rejection of the alleged surveillance and security measures used against his government colleagues. What had happened was "highly objectionable not to mention undemocratic and a violation of human rights... intolerable... inconsistent with the dignity of a free man".[13]

Blaney's position was compelling for a different set of reasons. He had refused to resign in the end, forcing Lynch to seek the President's dismissal of him, because:

> I believed that, by so doing, in view of the extremely delicate situation in the Six Counties, I would be aiding, perhaps causing, something that would result in some explosion about which we might be very sorry in the future.[14]

Since by most of his actions during the previous eight months Blaney had deliberately raised the possibility of explosions across Northern Ireland, as had Haughey, this had an unconscious irony that intensified the criticism from the opposition benches of his role in the crisis. But from Lynch's point of view, Blaney's apologia was worrying. Lynch's political judgement transcended the immediate debate and looked towards the future. It was early May. The marching season was still weeks away. No one could predict how long the generally benign impact of the British Army would prevail, or if there would be a Protestant backlash following the humiliating disbanding of the B Specials and the imposition on the RUC of a role inferior to that of the British Army.

Blaney, who generally talked in a circumlocutory style that was quite hard to analyse, did deliver himself of a very direct remark indeed. This was when, following a further resignation by Boland, this time from the Fianna Fáil National Executive, Blaney said: "It isn't over yet." Nor was it, by a long chalk.

A different crisis, but with the same basic motivation, the same personnel and the same broad ideological differences, was brewing. The ingredients for it came to the surface in the course of the Dáil debates on 8th and 9th May and through the speeches of Lynch's two main opponents in the continued absence of Haughey.

Not alone were they at odds with other speeches from within the Fianna Fáil party, they were totally opposed to the growing opposition conviction that guns provided no answer at all. It was a conviction that had gained virtually unanimous support within the two opposition parties, but only with the passage of time. In the previous summer, at the time of the August riots, deputies from all parties in the Dáil had subscribed, at least verbally, to the idea of force being used for defence in the North. Lynch was sanguine enough about the present, but had an open mind on the future, which could easily become more difficult for himself.

He might have wished for opposition speakers to be perhaps a little more restrained in condemning Blaney's form of republicanism. When Blaney spelled it out, it did have a certain logic; he did not favour violence or the use of force in order to bring about reunification. Blaney never had. Guns from the Republic in

---

[13] *Dáil Debates* Vol. 246, Col. 744.
[14] *Ibid.*, Col. 868.

Northern Ireland, however they made their way there, had as their limited objective the defence of Nationalist people. He referred to them as "our people". He then repeated, in its fuller version, restoring to it the word "idly", the phrase from Lynch's August 1969 address to the Irish people: "We in this part of Ireland cannot stand idly by in these circumstances."

Like Boland, Blaney remained remarkably cool and in command of himself within Leinster House during this whole period. He calmly put forward the central issues behind his interpretation of Northern Ireland policy. They were based on the belief that the root cause of Ireland's problems lay in the British presence on the island of Ireland, and until this could be resolved there would be no solution.

Lynch knew that there was a prospect of renewed violence in Northern Ireland. It was in his interest to attend carefully to the arguments mooted by his enemies.

*

On Wednesday 27th May Captain James Kelly, John Kelly and Albert Luykx, a Belgian businessman and friend of Blaney's, were arrested and charged with conspiracy to import arms. The next day Charles Haughey and Neil Blaney were arrested and charged with the same offence. On Lynch's initiative, Kevin Boland was expelled from the Fianna Fáil party on Thursday, 4th June. Boland had accused Lynch of felon-setting and had sought his removal from the leadership of Fianna Fáil and of the Government. The voting was 60 to 11. New names among those supporting Boland included Flor Crowley, from west Cork, Lorcan Allen from Wexford, Des Foley and Seán Sherwin. Later Boland resigned from the National Executive and his father, Gerry, one of the party's founding fathers and a vice-president and trustee, also resigned from his positions.

In the British general election in June Edward Heath defeated Harold Wilson. The change of Government, which brought to power a party formally known as "The Conservative and Unionist Party", was to have dramatic impact on events in Northern Ireland. Far from it producing the anticipated support for Unionism, Heath significantly shifted the ground in favour of a more even-handed approach, greater intervention, and the first moves towards power-sharing.

In the Dublin District Court on Thursday, 2nd July 1970 the charges against Neil Blaney were dropped. The other defendants were returned for trial.

With the Dáil in recess and the central issue of the alleged importation of arms a *sub judice* matter, and therefore outside the scope of public debate, the summer became a fallow period. Behind the scenes the loopholes in the system and the obvious security shortcomings that had been laid bare by events were addressed. The tone of Captain Kelly's intelligence reporting reflected the heightened emotional atmosphere engendered by events in Northern Ireland and should not be judged too harshly. However, after the trauma of dismissals, resignations and the bringing of charges, broader and more focused intelligence, outlining the general circumstances in Northern Ireland, came to the Taoiseach. One such report, furnished on 27th July 1970, is worth summarising. This two-page document gave Lynch material based on "Information from usually reliable sources".[15]

This report showed that British Army strength stood at 9,200 and that the Ulster Defence Regiment had 3,348 men on call (2,774 of them Protestants, 574 Catholics). The report stated that former members of the Ulster Special Constabulary (the B Specials) were trying to set up "Rifle Clubs" but were being refused. It was the view of the two sides in Northern Ireland, according to the report, that the Army in the Republic was not "a relevant factor". "Both IRA Groups", according to the report, felt they came off badly against the British Army. Furthermore, the People's Democracy was becoming more militant.

The report dealt comprehensively with all aspects of life in the North. Stormont was regarded as stronger after the careful control of Orange parades during that month of July. "Major Chichester Clarke is tired of the whole business," Lynch was told in the report. Brian Faulkner was seen as "the likely successor", though he was "still not in favour with the Right Wing". Trade in Northern Ireland was also reported as very bad. People were avoiding central Belfast shops which, as a consequence, were not stocking up.

The troubles in the North were reasonably contained. There was rioting in June, and 550 extra British troops were drafted in. There was rioting again in July, when arms and ammunition were found. Much of the violence resulted from IRA snipers firing on the troops. This led to the deterioration of the good relations between the Army and Catholic areas in the city that had prevailed during the early months of British Army security control. There was a speed-up in the judicial process to cope with the growing number of arrests and remand prisoners after the rioting and other troubles.[16]

In August there was renewed rioting in both Derry and Belfast; rubber bullets were used for the first time in both cities. Nevertheless, the savage tribal violence of August 1969 was not repeated. The decision to go ahead with the prosecutions of the four defendants in the Republic, though not debated as a consequence of being *sub judice*, seemed justified and was awaited with considerable anticipation.

On Tuesday, 22nd September the first of two Arms Trials opened. It was alleged that an attempt to import 500 pistols and 180,000 rounds of ammunition between 1st March and 24th April 1970 had been made by the accused. In the course of heated argument over testimony affecting Albert Luykx, who played a small role in the alleged conspiracy, his counsel accused the judge, Aindrias Ó Caoimh, of unfairness in his conduct of the trial. Ó Caoimh felt he had no choice but to discharge the jury in the face of this criticism of his fairness, and a new trial was fixed. This opened on Tuesday, 6th October and lasted for fourteen days.

*

---

[15] Intelligence report to the Taoiseach, marked TOP SECRET, in the National Archives 2001/8/9.

[16] *Ibid.*

All four defendants pleaded not guilty. The defence offered on behalf of three of them – Captain James Kelly, John Kelly and Albert Luykx – was not to dispute the events but to claim that they had the sanction of the Minister for Defence, Jim Gibbons. Their actions were therefore legal. It could not be proved that there was a formal sanction, however. Rather, the defendants' contention was that it was *implicit* that Gibbons had authorised the importation. Nor was there any proof that the consignment of arms had been ordered or paid for by the Department of Defence, routed into the country in the normal way, or in any other formal detail treated as the legal property of the State. In the end, it was simply the word of the accused that they *thought* it had all been organised in accordance with government policy.

Attempts were made to strengthen this defence by getting Haughey to tell the truth. According to journalist Vincent Browne, there was one occasion when Captain Kelly tried this:

> There was one meeting between Captain Kelly and Mr Haughey in the pre-trial period. This occurred in the Ormond Hotel, near the Four Courts, following one of the remand sessions. There Captain Kelly said in front of Mr Haughey's lawyers that he believed the best line of defence was to tell the truth. There was no response from the other side.[17]

Boland was reported to have taken grave exception to Haughey's refusal to tell the truth. He had been informed by Haughey in some detail of the intended importation of the arms and realised that the defence by Captain Kelly and the others was seriously undermined. But Haughey rejected the case made to him by Boland.

Haughey, then, taking a fundamentally different position from that of the other three defendants, denied any involvement in and all knowledge of the attempted importation. This had been Blaney's defence also; his position had raised questions for the defence teams in the run-up to the trial about whether he should be called as a witness. Despite there being no possible case against him, he remained a central figure. Blaney had been responsible for the involvement of Albert Luykx and probably of John Kelly as well; during much of the period, it had been to Blaney that Captain Kelly had made his intelligence reports, under the misapprehension that Blaney was in charge of government policy on this aspect of Northern Ireland affairs. During the Dáil debate in May, Blaney's speech had represented a very selective denial. Though his role was small, Blaney's protégé, Albert Luykx, in opening up the dealings with the German arms dealer, Otto Schleuter, was crucial and implicated Blaney.

From Lynch's point of view, any analysis of the circumstances of the crisis had to take into account the supposed or actual relationship throughout between his senior Ministers. The line dividing them was, at certain points, thin. True,

---

[17] Vincent Browne, "The Misconduct of the Arms Trial" in *Magill* (July 1980), p. 18.

there was only negligible evidence overall against Blaney, which led to the charges being dropped. It was the clear evidence against Haughey, that he was directly involved in the attempted importation, that was most compelling. Boland was not linked at all with the attempted importation of arms. He had apparently been gratuitously informed of the intended importation and assumed that the rumours of it were common knowledge, but he also made the point: "It is only fair to say that I felt sure this importation would not be agreed to by the Taoiseach."[18] Nevertheless, the positions of all three of them had to be taken into account and this must form the basis for all judgement of Lynch's handling of the affair.

This is particularly relevant in the context of the conversation between Haughey and Peter Berry, on Saturday, 18th April, which formed a significant part of the evidence at the trial. Haughey had to answer for a real cargo, the existence of which was endorsed by the pleadings of the three other defendants. The record demonstrates his direct, hands-on involvement. The fact that no such intelligence involved Blaney in activities to which he contributed forcefully at the time indicates how slender the overall case was. When three of four people involved explain what they did in terms of its legality, the eventuality rather releases the fourth from the particular charge of conspiracy. Haughey had masterminded a scheme that had been exposed. In a skilful fashion, he slipped from the law's clutches and went free. Guilty of criminal intent, he had duped his supposed fellow conspirators just as he had duped his government colleagues and his own party leader.

Both Haughey and Blaney had known from an early stage in their involvement in Northern Ireland affairs of the possibility of Special Branch surveillance. As early as August 1969 this Garda intelligence had identified Haughey in a secret meeting with Cathal Goulding. This made both Haughey and Blaney extremely cautious. In the ensuing eight months, despite intelligence reports linking them together, and reports that connected Captain James Kelly and John Kelly to Blaney as much as to Haughey, it appears that control of the importation was left to Haughey. His fingerprints are on it, not those of Blaney. If the evidence had been sufficient to bring charges against the second Minister, a rather different verdict might have been achieved.

The charge of conspiracy, always difficult to sustain in any circumstances, was a clumsy vehicle for dealing with four men so differently inspired in what they were charged with having done. It was made infinitely more difficult by the presence of the key witness for the State, Jim Gibbons. His evidence was crucial in two ways that conflicted. The prosecution needed him to prove that Haughey was knowingly involved in a plot to bring in a consignment of arms and ammunition. This meant that Gibbons had to know as well. But he had to know only at a late stage in the operation. If it proved otherwise then his knowledge was in conflict with his handling of his own intelligence officer, Captain Kelly. This would affect the remaining defendants.

---

[18] Kevin Boland, *Up Dev* (published by the author, Dublin, 1977), p. 72.

At this level alone, Gibbons was likely to be quite easily confused. Yet on the critical issue, that of the knowledge both men shared in respect of the consignment of arms coming into Dublin Airport, there was no basic disagreement. Gibbons referred to the conversation with Haughey, probably some time on Friday, 17th April, when the Department of Transport and Power informed the Department of Justice of the incoming charter flight containing arms and ammunition "for the use of the Garda and the Army". Berry's strategy of letting the arms in, at first disapproved of by his Minister, may have precipitated the circumstances in which Gibbons, referring to Department of Transport and Power knowledge of the consignment, told Haughey "the dogs in the street are barking it". Haughey undertook to put it off for a month and Gibbons told him: "For God's sake, stop it altogether."[19]

Haughey confirmed that this meeting with Gibbons had taken place. He did not dispute that the attempted importation of "a certain consignment", whatever it was, had been called off. He denied knowledge of its content, and he reinforced the circumstantial innocence of this defence by puzzling over the concern of so many people, among them Berry, about this particular importation. Admitting the meeting but denying the rest was in keeping with his worries over intelligence about physical encounters. He had learnt from the Cathal Goulding meeting that such events were noticed and recorded. So he acknowledged that this one with Gibbons had taken place. But he denied the conversation. The content of this conversation was the issue on which Judge Henchy said that one or the other of them was lying. He said the same in respect of conflict between Haughey's evidence and that of Berry.

*

The performance and general character of all the defendants and of many of the witnesses have been the subject of much comment and detailed analysis over the years. A significant contribution came in 1980, when Vincent Browne published substantial extracts from Peter Berry's diaries in *Magill* magazine, together with detailed articles based on these documents and other information that had come to light at the time. The diaries, more properly described as "The Peter Berry Papers", since he added to and annotated the original daily entries, are so far the main authoritative contemporary source, and were significant enough, at the time, to provoke a special debate in the Dáil. They have been greatly reinforced in recent years by papers released to the National Archives from various State sources, and by papers released in the United Kingdom under the 30-year rule. More recently, Justin O'Brien published a detailed account, entitled *The Arms Trial*, which includes extracts from Captain James Kelly's intelligence reports from August and September 1969. Captain James Kelly himself has published

---

[19] Tom Mac Intyre, *Through the Bridewell Gate* (Faber and Faber, London, 1971), *passim*, but in particular, pp. 33 and 200.

two related books, *Orders for the Captain* and, more recently, *The Thimble Riggers*.[20]

In respect of Jack Lynch, the reports sent to London at the time of the trial by the British Ambassador in Ireland, Sir John Peck, are of some significance. These reports followed his periodic but quite regular meetings with Lynch. The first occasion recorded by Peck, on which Lynch spoke with him about the trial and about Gibbons's performance as a witness, occurred while the trial was still going on:

> Mr Lynch, before he went to New York and while the trial was still in progress, told me privately that he was furious with Mr Gibbons for his performance as a witness, and that he seemed to be getting into an impossible position. I thought it was very likely that his resignation would be ready to be put in the Taoiseach's hands when he returned.[21]

The ambassador did not report on this until later, Tuesday, 10th November. Peck, evidently uncertain about how to explain Lynch's apparent ambivalence over Gibbons, makes the point that his reasons for supporting rather than sacking Gibbons suggested that "his judgement in doing so must be, by any objective standards, debatable…":

> For poor Mr Gibbons was the anti-star of the trial; from his evidence it is hard to avoid drawing a number of inferences, all unflattering: he seems to have been foolish to the point of idiocy…
>
> Mr Lynch has retained Mr Gibbons in his Government and given him his full backing. He is a severe political embarrassment and he still has hanging over him the unrefuted charge of misleading the Dáil when he said on the 8th of May that any attempt to import arms took place 'without his knowledge and consent'. The judicial process is ended, and the affair passes back into the arena of politics, impure and unsimple."[22]

The essential detail on Gibbons reported in rather dismissive terms to the British Foreign Secretary, Alec Douglas Home, by Peck may present a rather abject portrait of ineptitude. It does not, however, suggest that Gibbons perjured himself. It becomes clearer in later parts of the correspondence that Lynch's attitude to Gibbons was far more complicated. Peck pointed out that the actions of Haughey and Blaney represented "an open declaration of political war… and a bid for personal power in Fianna Fáil". Privately Lynch may have been scathing in his comments on the performance of Gibbons as a witness but publicly, once Lynch had got through the challenge to his leadership that followed the verdict in the Arms Trial, he was forced to take a different position.

---

[20] For details of these and other publications see the Bibliography.
[21] *The Irish Times*, 20th April 2001, p. 5. The documents were released in the Public Record Office in London the previous day under the 30-year rule.
[22] *Ibid.*

The full story of Gibbons's role will never be told. He was crucial then. The story of his part in events became important again in April 2001 when James Kelly discovered in the National Archives a transcript of the original statement made by Colonel Michael Hefferon, bearing annotations by Peter Berry, Secretary of the Department of Justice. It seemed, from these comments, that Berry had indicated material in the statement of a supposedly explosive kind implicating Gibbons. Kelly, who had suffered for thirty years as a result of the Arms Trial prosecution, took this as evidence of "doctoring" of the statement by the removal of crucial material implicating Gibbons. The document was also stamped and initialled as having been "seen" by the newly appointed Minister for Justice, Desmond O'Malley. With Berry long since dead and Gibbons also dead, the focus was turned on O'Malley. Demands were made that he should explain why the Secretary of his Department had apparently advised deletions and possibly implemented them as well. O'Malley had problems remembering the episode at all and was further embarrassed by not remembering another document he had endorsed claiming State privilege over a file containing this statement and other documents connected with the trial.

What seemed like a strong case for a State conspiracy to ensure that Gibbons would not be drawn into giving evidence of knowledge of the importation fell apart under closer examination. It transpired that the corrections were made elsewhere and by other people. But it certainly emphasised continuing public interest and concern in the issues surrounding the original prosecutions, the trial itself, and the verdict.

Undoubtedly, the reputations of the men concerned were damaged forever; some deservedly so, others in the tide of betrayals, lies and prevarication. In the course of sorting out the truth from the distortions, O'Malley made absolutely clear his belief that Gibbons did not perjure himself. Others, too, have confirmed this in the strongest terms. The case is really one of a very uncertain man in the context of the August 1969 riots. He was under Blaney's influence. Like many others in Fianna Fáil, he was unclear about the solution required. Being Minister for Defence put him in a central role for which he was ill-equipped and lodged him between a number of conflicting forces. There was the cloak of the government sub-committee and there were two devious Ministers who were dangerous in their planning and not averse to creating a mythic set of rules and objectives. Then there was his own orthodox army staff structure that had allowed to creep into its intelligence system a curiously unmonitored and *louche* parade of personal interpretations of how to report, whom to report to, and what to say. It is hardly startling that Gibbons floundered, but it would be very surprising indeed if evidence emerged confirming him as someone engaged in conspiracy.

*

Mr Justice Séamus Henchy began his summing up in the trial on the morning of 23rd October, telling the jury to disregard the political impact of their decision and the possibility that there might be further prosecutions. He said that the charges had been correctly brought. Not alone was the Attorney General justified in the prosecution he had instituted, but "I even go so far as to express the opinion that he would be unjustified in not bringing it".

The law had clearly been broken and the jury's judgement depended heavily on conflict of evidence involving Haughey. There were fundamental differences between Haughey and Gibbons about one critical conversation in which, Gibbons claimed, Haughey had offered to put off the importation for a month. A second serious conflict of evidence occurred between Haughey and Berry, again over a conversation related to the telephone exchange between the two men on Saturday, 18th April in which Haughey asked: "Does the man from Mayo know?"

However, the problem facing the jury was greatly complicated by the fact that three of the four defendants did not dispute the main facts in the case. What was alleged to have taken place did actually take place and was regarded by Captain James Kelly, John Kelly and Albert Luykx as being within the law. If the jury decided that their pleadings were in some way justified, or that there was sufficient doubt about the instructions which had come from the State, then a verdict of not guilty became understandable, even if it did not conform with the real circumstances. Haughey's acquittal would follow automatically, whether or not the jury believed his testimony. They could not acquit three defendants and find the fourth guilty. The conspiracy with which the four were charged had never really been a sustainable prosecution.

The jury took two hours to reach a verdict of not guilty. The court erupted. Wild scenes of jubilation followed, with Haughey moving centre-stage and delivering himself of a direct challenge to Lynch, though one that was couched in faintly veiled language: "I think those who are responsible for this debacle have no alternative but to take the honourable course that is open to them."

There were similar expressions of political challenge against Jack Lynch. For a time his position as leader was under serious threat, rendered more volatile by the nakedly republican nature of the anger. Haughey, who purported not to know during the proceedings what was in the consignment that he was trying to bring in through Dublin Airport, suddenly espoused as close friends those who did know, and who intended the arms for the IRA under the cloak of the Citizens' Defence Committees. Haughey's sense of triumph in the euphoria of acquittal had him making ill-judged statements about the enormous reaction and support for him throughout the country. Perhaps the least prudent of his remarks was to claim: "In all my time in politics and in public life I have never met a finer person than John Kelly."[23]

Ó Móráin, the Minister for Justice, who had been obliged by Lynch to resign

---

[23] John Kelly was a member of the IRA. He was imprisoned for involvement in the 1956 IRA campaign. He was one of the men responsible for moving the organisation away from the Marxism espoused under Cathal Goulding. For further details see James Kelly, *The Thimble Riggers* (published by the author, Dublin, 1999), *passim*.

just before the main crisis broke in May, now emerged from the hospital treatment and convalescence to which his alcoholism had consigned him. He threw his weight behind the men who had been acquitted. In a lengthy Sunday newspaper interview he called for an immediate change of government. There was no need, he said to his interviewer, John Murdoch, to wait for the annual conference. He also came out very strongly in favour of a change in party leadership, although he declined openly to oppose Lynch:

> There is no use denying there is a leadership crisis in our party, not alone on this issue but on other matters too. This is something which a general election cannot solve. This crisis must be solved within the ranks of our own party.[24]

Murdoch observed: "there is a clear inference that he is not a Lynch man." Ó Móráin was also asked the question: "Would you like to see Mr Blaney, Mr Haughey, Mr Boland and maybe yourself back in office?" He replied:

> I would like to see these men back. They are all good men and Mr Haughey in particular is a man of outstanding ability. Our party can ill afford to lose these three leaders. They have proved to be leaders of our party and of the country in good times and in bad and the amount of support they have and the respect they have is very high indeed.

Ó Móráin, who had been protected carefully by Lynch at the time of the other sackings in May, was a significant voice to emerge from a neutral position within Fianna Fáil. He reflected the brief and frightening possibility, encouraged by the verdict, of an open challenge for the leadership of Fianna Fáil. Haughey had laid it on the line, though in slightly ambivalent language, and the positions of a small number were known. What was not clear, since it had been given no recent expression, was the mood within the party.

On that Sunday the same newspaper published an interview with Jim Gibbons in which both the interviewer and the photographer were described as being taken by surprise that no resignation was forthcoming. This had been widely predicted after the trial by political commentators. They were even more surprised at Gibbons's confidence. He is described as showing no signs of strain, but of being his usual self, pausing and thinking carefully before answering. This had not been the case with the four accused, nor had it seemed to have been so with Ó Móráin.

---

[24] *The Sunday Press*, 25th October 1970, p. 3. The virtually full-page interview with John Murdoch echoed remarks that Haughey had made about party questions on economic policy. This was in a state of crisis, overlooked at the time because of the Arms Trial, but involving strict anti-inflationary measures opposed by the trade union movement as well as by the Opposition. Ó Móráin also gave a lawyer's view of the importance of Colonel Hefferon's evidence. John Murdoch described Ó Móráin as "one of the most extensive civil and criminal lawyers in the west of Ireland, with headquarters in Castlebar".

"For me Jack Lynch is Taoiseach," Gibbons said, "and that is that. The organisation throughout the country – and I am very familiar with it – is solidly behind the Taoiseach." Though admitting there was a crisis, he went on to say: "I have every confidence that we can weather it."

Lynch was in New York addressing the General Assembly of the United Nations in a speech that again outlined his policies on Northern Ireland, his belief in consent, and his view that the Republic of Ireland and Britain should act as joint guarantors of the minority in the North.

News of the verdict was brought to him immediately. Seán Donlon, from the Department of Foreign Affairs, was in New York with Lynch and remembers clearly the sequence of events. Lynch was due out on a flight the following evening, Saturday, from Kennedy Airport, but changed his mind. He said they would stay until the following night. No explanation was given for this, but the necessary changes were made, and they stayed until the evening flight out of New York on the Sunday. It is probable that George Colley rang him and advised that he should delay his return to arrive back on Monday morning. A press team from Dublin, which included senior journalists, had accompanied Lynch. He spoke quite freely to them of what he had initiated the previous May, saying that it was the right decision. "No-one can deny that there was this attempt to import arms", he emphasised, adding that Blaney was involved.[25]

But he also gave out a powerful message for domestic consumption, and this was splashed across the pages of the Sunday newspapers. "Lynch hits back at Haughey: Gibbons to stay," was the message across page one of the biggest mass-circulation newspaper in the country, *The Sunday Press*. Lynch would meet any challenge head-on and had every confidence in the outcome. Nor would he have Haughey or Blaney back in the Government. "He hit out at Mr Haughey for not keeping him informed on a vital matter. 'A Government must exist on complete mutual trust and confidence,' said the Taoiseach." He went on to summarise his Northern Ireland policy, though in strong terms of faith in the essential Irish ideal of republicanism. "It does not mean guns or using guns."[26]

The rival *Sunday Independent* carried a similarly strong message under the heading: "Confident Lynch cracks back: Ready for a Head on fight." Raymond Smith, who was in New York, wrote that the rift between Lynch and Haughey was "irrevocable" and that there was no question of Haughey being brought back into government. "If there is a challenge to my leadership, I am going into it with confidence and determination. I believe I must hold the situation now for the people of Ireland. To do otherwise would be wrong." The paper predicted a turnout of Fianna Fáil deputies at the airport for Lynch's arrival back the next morning. It also reported Boland as saying: "It is up to the Taoiseach to dismiss the Minister for Agriculture, and if he does not do it the new Taoiseach should. It does not matter to me who the new Taoiseach is so long as it is one of the former

---

[25] From reports in both *The Sunday Press* and the *Sunday Independent*.
[26] Michael Mills reporting from New York on the front page of *The Sunday Press*.

Ministers, Mr Haughey or Mr Blaney." But any such prospect was diminishing fast. The collective wisdom among the political commentators gathered around Lynch in New York was clearly expressed by Raymond Smith. "The feeling was that Mr Haughey had made a bad political blunder and that he would have been wiser to have preserved the silence he had shown during the past few months."[27]

George Colley also came out strongly in support of Lynch. "The Taoiseach has spoken for the Government, for the vast majority of the party, and for the vast majority of the Fianna Fáil organisation. Anyone who thinks otherwise is in for a rude awakening."

It was already clear, on the Saturday evening, that Haughey realised he had misjudged the situation and the mood of the country and of the Fianna Fáil party. Informed of Lynch's statement in New York, he said: "I have already said that my wish is to restore unity and repair the damage already done. I do not therefore wish to reply at this stage on what the Taoiseach is reported to have said."

*

Ministers in government on the previous Friday afternoon, the day of the verdict, had carried on in the normal way. No special meeting was arranged and there was no significant communication between them before the usual departure to the country of the Ministers not from Dublin. One of them was Patrick Lalor, Minister for Industry and Commerce.[28] He went ahead the next day with his usual Saturday morning constituency or "confession" as he called it.

During a discussion with one of his constituents he had a call from Dan Mullane, press officer for the Flour Millers' Association. Mullane was someone with whom he had had stormy relations in the past over the price of flour, but they had become good friends. Mullane rang to ask Lalor what he was going to do about Lynch's return to Ireland. "What do you mean – do?" Lalor responded. Mullane asked if Lalor did not see the risks involved in Lynch coming back to face a hostile reception from the press, without some kind of visible support from the Fianna Fáil party. Mullane was horrified that no special reception had been arranged; then and there on the telephone, he outlined a strategy.

Lalor agreed to travel to Dublin and meet Mullane in the house of Patrick Norton, formerly of the Labour Party but by now a Fianna Fáil senator. Before leaving his home in Abbeyleix, in the Laois-Offaly constituency, Lalor rang Pádraig Faulkner and George Colley to alert them of the risk and tell them about the advice he had been given. They agreed with the need to organise a reception

---

[27] *Sunday Independent*, 28th October 1970.
[28] Paddy Lalor came from a strong republican background, and would have been a natural supporter of Neil Blaney in the party. But he also came from a GAA background, and this made him a great admirer of Jack Lynch. He became an unwavering supporter of Lynch's policies during the troubled period 1969–1970.

for Lynch. Lalor then travelled to Dublin and Faulkner did the same. Colley joined them. Various members of the party began the process of ringing around and summoning people to be at Dublin Airport for Lynch's arrival the next morning.

When Lynch stepped down from the plane on Monday, he was greeted by members of his Government. The first to step forward, however, was the relatively unknown figure of Máirtín Ó Flathartaigh, secretary to President de Valera. As he was representing the head of state, he greeted Lynch before the others. He took Lynch's hand and bent forward to speak to him. In a few seconds he told him that de Valera sent his support and advised him to fight off any challenge to his leadership of the party.[29]

Lynch was warmly greeted by his Ministers. All of them turned out with the exception of Paddy Hillery and Seán Flanagan, who were out of the country. Lynch went inside to meet the press. That event at the airport, where he sat in front of the massed ranks of party members, was critical in resolving the crisis that had arisen following the verdict. The photographs and newsreel pictures, of the phalanx of the Fianna Fáil party supporting their leader, became a pivotal image of party solidarity and support for what he stood for, and remains emblematic of Jack Lynch's leadership.

The crisis that had flourished in highly dramatic circumstances on the afternoon of the previous Friday was all over by the Monday morning. Once again, Lynch had won. When the party met the following day Haughey's challenge collapsed. He had the support of only five members of Fianna Fáil. They included himself and Neil Blaney.

---

[29] Confidential Public Service source.

Chapter Nine

"The instruments of darkness"

– Banquo in Macbeth

"It isn't over yet."[1] Neil Blaney's words were prophetic. Jack Lynch's opponents had taken two severe beatings, none suffering more than Blaney. He was the most senior of them all. He exercised greater power within the Fianna Fáil organisation than the other dismissed Ministers. He fell from an elevated position of influence within the Government, as Minister for Agriculture. His political career never recovered. He remained on the sidelines for the rest of his life, and was regarded with suspicion and distrust by a majority of politicians of all parties, including Fianna Fáil.

Kevin Boland suffered a different fate, though no less humiliating. He also was permanently removed from any exercise of power. He started a party of his own, Aontacht Éireann, and ran candidates in the next general election, though without success. He wrote an apologia, *Up Dev*, that has become an important source book, with first-hand material on the crucial events of 1970 and, significantly, on what happened in August 1969. In an interesting judgement made by Senator Owen Sheehy Skeffington, which appeared in *The Irish Times* on 11th May 1970, Boland was described as "not overburdened with bothersome scruple" and "quite unhampered by intellectual honesty in his juggling with figures to party advantage".[2]

Skeffington wrote this mindful of the 1969 election and the earlier attempt to push through a referendum designed to change the voting system from proportional representation to the first-past-the-post system followed in the United Kingdom. In these practical and ministerial areas of responsibility there was a justifiable case for seeing Boland in a harsh light. When in power he was a tough Fianna Fáil operator, noted in his day and particularly during the campaigns to preserve Georgian Dublin for the epithet he used against the campaigners – that they were led by "belted earls". The Skeffington judgement is unfair in respect of these later events and, more broadly, of Boland's attitude to Lynch and Northern Ireland policy. On these matters, as *Up Dev* illustrates and as Boland's speeches at the time showed, he had a gritty integrity that was impressive when set beside the positions adopted at the time by Blaney and Haughey. Boland has to be

---

[1] Neil Blaney made this comment to the press after the resignation of Kevin Boland from the Fianna Fáil National Executive on Monday, 22nd June 1970.

[2] The piece in *The Irish Times* was entitled: "They'll none of them be missed...".

155

praised at least for his unsuccessful attempts, on behalf of the other defendants, to get Blaney and Haughey to be more open and truthful.

Boland's analysis of what happened is subject to question, and some of the detail he gives in the book could not have been verified by him at the time. It depended, like so much that was being alleged, on hearsay evidence. But, both in terms of what happened then and in terms of what has since come to light, it is worth giving a detailed summary of Boland's assertions of what occurred and in what sequence. He maintained that Jim Gibbons was aware of Captain James Kelly's activities throughout the period. The level of awareness is not spelled out. He claims that every member of the Government was aware of the Bailieborough meeting, and that a government decision led to two members of the police travelling to the North on the basis of intelligence provided by Captain Kelly through Gibbons. Boland's most damaging assertion is that Lynch knew "long before 20 April" of the planned importation and let it go ahead in order to "catch his colleagues, and, if possible, also John Kelly 'red-handed'".[3] This assertion was the basis for Boland's accusation of "felon-setting". In a sense it has been the nub of one particular argument about the whole Arms Crisis, including the trials and the aftermath, but it has not stood up to any serious examination. There is simply no evidence to support it.

Boland maintained that Lynch told the Government that the matter and the grounds for dismissal were "closed at a time when he was taking a personal part in further investigations to see if a charge could be brought after the importation was called off". Then, according to Boland, only after Liam Cosgrave's intervention, was the matter reopened and the two senior Ministers dismissed. "His [Lynch's] second demand for the resignations of Blaney and Haughey came immediately after Cosgrave's visit to him." In other words, Boland maintains that Cosgrave forced the issue. This was widely, and wrongly, believed at the time, and has been absorbed into the folklore surrounding the May 1970 crisis. In fact, the first demand was never withdrawn and what Lynch actually said, after having raised it at the government meeting, was that "the matter is closed *for the present*".[4] Boland also claims that Jim Gibbons and Colonel Michael Hefferon were "divorced... from the transaction" with Cosgrave's co-operation.[5] Like Neil Blaney, Kevin Boland is prophetic. At the end of his chapter on the period before the trial he writes: "This is a chronicle of sordid chicanery but it is only the unhappy 'prologue to the swelling act of the imperial theme'." The words are Macbeth's. Better to look to Banquo's lines that precede this most devious and sinister moment of human treachery and read there:

---

[3] Kevin Boland, *Up Dev* (published by the author, Dublin, 1977), p. 78.

[4] Author's emphasis.

[5] All quotations here are from *Up Dev*, above, n.3, pp. 71–78.

But 'tis strange:
And oftentimes, to win us to our harm,
The instruments of darkness tell us truths
Win us with honest trifles, to betray 's
In deepest consequence.

Lynch now faced the longer consequences of his hard and difficult struggle against conspiracy within his own Government. When he had had time to reflect, much later, he shocked himself by the realisation that, as a result of the information that came to him in April and May, he "lost all trust in his colleagues in government. How can I ever trust anybody again after what has happened?"[6]

In late October 1970 he had no time for measuring levels of trust and finding them always wanting. Following the whispered support of President de Valera came the comprehensive backing of his government colleagues. There was widely expressed public support for the Taoiseach personally, and the press reaction was also positive. But he went into the Fianna Fáil party meeting the next day, 27th October, in a sanguine but cautious mood, to measure opposition to himself. It consisted of five men, including both Blaney and Haughey. They withered subsequently and pledged themselves to support Fianna Fáil in the "no confidence" motion put down by the opposition parties for debate the next week.

An emergency meeting of the Government followed immediately after the Fianna Fáil party meeting; no chances were being taken. This seems to confirm Lynch's private conviction that he had lost trust in his colleagues. He would make sure of everything from now on, double-checking his position and ensuring that pledges of support and endorsement were acted upon. Backed by the entire Government, Lynch then gave a 1 p.m. press conference. He told journalists he was reserving his position on the critical issue of a general election and would decide only after the "no confidence" debate.

On 4th November Lynch ended his speech in the Dáil debate with a warning as hard as the tungsten steel he had shown he was made of. "I do not want any deputy to go into the lobby with me to buy time. Because I am not in the market for buying or selling time." Boland could not stomach the situation confronting him. Rather than vote against the party he had grown up in and unable to vote *for* that same party, he resigned his seat, sending a note up to the Ceann Comhairle: "It was not my intention to abstain."[7] The announcement was made at the end of the debate. There were immediate opposition calls for the writ to be moved for the by-election. Lynch did not hesitate. If others thought in terms of an imperial theme, Lynch acted out their dreams or fears with one decisive act after another. He led his party into a Dáil division and won it comfortably by 74 votes to 67.

---

[6] Michael Mills, "Lynch's line on knowledge of arms plot" in *The Irish Times*, 28th April 2001, p. 12. Mills was with Jack Lynch in New York when the verdict from the Four Courts reached him.

[7] Kevin Boland, above, n.3, p. 88.

Late that autumn Lynch became aware of a book that Séamus Brady intended to publish. Brady was the journalist who had been closely involved with Haughey and Blaney. Questions had been directed at Lynch, in particular about attempts allegedly made by Blaney to make a telephone call to his home on the night of the Bogside riots in Derry. Lynch asked Eoin Neeson, head of the Government Information Bureau, to furnish him with a chronology of the events.

Neeson responded with an outline of the events of that week. There had been a meeting between Lynch and Eddie McAteer, the Nationalist MP for Derry, held in his office in Dublin on Friday, 8th August or the following day, after which Lynch set out for holidays in Cork.[8] McAteer was reported by Neeson as being "not unduly pessimistic about the Apprentice Boys' Parade on 12th August". When Derry erupted on the Tuesday "you made immediate arrangements for a Government meeting the following morning". Lynch ordered his car and left Cork at 6 a.m. on the Wednesday morning to be present, as was Blaney, at the Cabinet meeting in the afternoon. Neeson recorded: "In fact the Government was more or less in continuous session from then on . . . It was in the early hours of the 14th, therefore, that Mr Blaney tried to contact you, and not in the night of the 12th when 'the Bogside erupted'." Furthermore, Neeson wrote: "[A]t that stage Government Policy had been decided."

The account of events set out by Eoin Neeson contradicts what Brady published in his book and what he promoted as an aspect in the book critical of Lynch. He alleged the non-availability of Lynch as the crisis erupted. "Blaney tried all night to get hold of Mr Lynch," was one of Brady's claims. This point was widely published in the media and was clearly an attempt by Brady to suggest that Lynch was indifferent to the crisis while Blaney was active in trying to bring collective government action to bear against the RUC and B Specials as the riots were going on.

Neeson's advice to Lynch was that "at all events the simple statement that Mr Blaney did not try to contact you on the night the Bogside erupted is incontrovertible". In other words, a false picture of Lynch's position was put forward in the book, either on Brady's own initiative, or, more likely, based on Blaney's claim about the call. Neeson's advice to Lynch was that he should make no response but wait and see what the book contained.

*

The truth of the situation in the autumn and winter of 1970 was that the Opposition supported Lynch against those in his party who were opposed to him. His and his Government's policy on the North was *their* policy: unity only by consent. Anything else was unthinkable. If there was a wish on the part of the Opposition to bring Lynch down – and it is very much open to argument – the dangers

---

[8] Eoin Neeson, Report to the Taoiseach, 1st December 1970. National Archives, 2001/8/ 13.

contained within a subsequent election at that time were ominous. Republicanism espoused by Blaney and Boland, with very few others supporting their position, was anathema to the vast majority of deputies.[9] When they gathered to debate the "no confidence" motion the circumstances that had driven political action and speeches on previous occasions in May had been fundamentally changed by the dismissals of the two Ministers, and were again changed by Boland's resignation. His act almost endeared him to the Opposition for all the wrong reasons. "I was the white-headed boy," he claimed, once he had made known his decision to resign his seat. Boland also observed another emerging phenomenon: bi-partisanship on Northern Ireland. It was to characterise the situation from now on, despite a continuation of the harsh criticism against Lynch. Bi-partisanship was and has remained a product of Lynch's Northern Ireland policy.

The Opposition sought to castigate Lynch for lack of judgement in keeping Blaney and Haughey in his Government when he should have got rid of them much earlier. This was a serious misunderstanding of the situation. But it was the best argument available to members of Fine Gael and Labour. It also increasingly presented itself as a means of sustaining opposition despite the growing awareness that Lynch, in offering to his party a strategy that would keep it in power, had ensured the survival of *his* administration for the full term, clearly blocking, for as long as he sought to block it, the coming to power of any other leader of the Fianna Fáil party. That circumstance was to remain until such time as he chose to resign. The importance to Fianna Fáil of Lynch being able to offer its deputies security of tenure in power transcended all other considerations. Lynch knew this, so did his opponents; so above all did the rank-and-file party members.

The extent of the damage inflicted on Ireland by Neil Blaney and Charles Haughey will never be fully explained. The more the archives deliver up supposedly revelatory material, the less it seems to tell us of the nature or extent of the conspiracy in which they had both been involved.

Files have gone missing. There are blank periods in the crowded texture of the narrative. With the trials ending in the acquittals of those charged, there was a revived interest in the Dáil in some of the issues that had been so hotly debated in the spring but were now dealt with in a calmer manner. Concern was expressed for the position of Captain James Kelly and the state of army intelligence. In one parliamentary question to the Taoiseach he was asked: "Whether he considers there should be a re-organisation of the security intelligence service embodying the amalgamation of army and policy sections".[10] He answered briefly in the negative, but the civil service arguments put to him justifying the State's position include detailed analysis of the value of the existing approach and a lengthy letter from Peter Berry himself. Events had convincingly proved the value on the

---

[9] Perhaps five other deputies, at most, would have held considered and parallel views.

[10] Parliamentary Question to the Taoiseach, 4th November 1970. See National Archives file 2001/6/551: "Illegal Importation of Arms".

ground of having two intelligence services. Lynch was also asked whether he received reports from both services. The formal answer proposed by the Department of Justice and confirmed by the Department of Defence was: "I have ensured with the Ministers concerned that information will be made known to me". Lynch crossed out this rather bland construction and replaced it with: "I receive from the Ministers concerned information of a priority nature in regard to Security matters."

The concern expressed in the Dáil for Captain James Kelly led to questions. It was pointed out by the new Minister for Defence, Jeremiah Cronin, that Kelly would be in receipt of the normal retired officer's pay, £786 per annum at the time, together with a married officer's gratuity of £1,528. There were also questions about the control of arms importation.[11]

By the end of 1970 Lynch, whose whole attitude had hardened, and whose public statements could now express his position in terms of absolute control of the Fianna Fáil organisation, surveyed as Hercules might the desolation left after his own victories.

*

Major James Chichester Clark's short period as Northern Ireland Prime Minister ended when he resigned in mid-March 1971 and was succeeded by Brian Faulkner. Edward Heath had replaced Harold Wilson as British Prime Minister, a change that was greeted with little enthusiasm in the Republic, and there was even greater apprehension when Reginald Maudling was appointed Home Secretary (the portfolio that embraced Northern Ireland). Maudling detested the North, visited it infrequently, and was unsympathetic and unwilling to learn the increasingly complicated job that was involved. Reinforced by a traditional suspicion of the links between the Conservative Party and the Unionists, the view in the Republic of Maudling, and indeed of the return of the Tories to power, was wholly, though misguidedly, negative. In due course Heath was going to emerge as a better leader of the Westminster Government, from Ireland's point of view, than his predecessor.

Lynch faced a difficult year. Before he was well into it, however, he had to face his party once again. This time he confronted them in the smoke and sweat of the party's annual conference. If he expected something akin to the Stables of Augeias to clear out, he was in a sense right. After all the internal turmoil, the challenges and counter-challenges, the party bloodletting briefly came out into the open. There were wild speeches and fisticuffs. Boland made a spirited appearance, openly challenging the platform party. Erskine Childers hid his face in his hands, with an expression of despair and loathing on it. To borrow a phrase of James Joyce's, it was the day of the "rabblement". Brief moments of excitement were expressed in the cheers supporting republicans as they stepped from the

---

[11] See National Archives file 2001/6/551: "Illegal Importation of Arms".

podium after their speeches. But then it was usually out of the doors with them, into the street, and as like as not, across to the bar on the other side of Merrion Road. The men and women of the press, whose sympathies in the main had been with Lynch, faced rough words and occasional jostling. The skills of baiting and of defence were expressed with energy from the platform as well. The soul of Fianna Fáil seemed to be almost palpable, and was wrestled with and torn apart in the process. Paddy Hillery and Jim Gibbons showed a sparkling degree of oratory in support of Jack Lynch. The stable was cleared. Lynch emerged from the event unscathed, and then gave the speech of a lifetime, designed to hold the middle ground within the party and to offer to the public, still quite excited by the access that television gave, prudent views on where Ireland stood.

The meeting was held that year for the first time in the Royal Dublin Society's premises at Ballsbridge. The hall was much larger than the Mansion House Round Room, which, since the early years of the State and even before, had been associated with Irish political meetings. The new venue, with its great space, balconies running from end to end of the hall, and its much higher roof, seemed designed specially for the drama of the event. Lynch himself had prepared very carefully for the presidential address, his speech carrying the usual cautions to the effect that it "may be amended during delivery", which indeed it was. He criticised those who perpetuated the quarrel with Britain, referring to it as "all the stronger for being a mutually valuable one without overtones of conquest. The remnants of that conquest, which is an aspect of the division of Ireland, remains the only but dangerous disaffection in what has become otherwise a unique condition between independent countries."[12] At this point he added a reference to Northern Ireland and to the futile deaths caused by terrorism. "The order cannot be wished away, the Border cannot be shot away."

In this part of the speech he confronted the recent dramatic events in the party and in the country, first proclaiming: "Fianna Fáil is a republican party". He then asserted the essential and necessary disciplines that this entailed:

> It is important that throughout the organisation as a whole no member, whether through over-enthusiasm or otherwise, will overstep his remit... As for the Parliamentary party, the primary requirement is to ensure that agreed party policy is properly presented and advocated, and that all members in their speeches and actions remain within the acceptable boundaries of policy as laid down. Should any difficulties or disputes arise, it is my task as leader to ensure that any disciplinary or corrective measures are taken. He is not worthy to be a leader who avoids or evades

---

[12] Original issued text with author's amendments taken from the speech as it was given. Though the policy content on this and other Northern Ireland speeches was worked out in consultation with Dr T.K. Whitaker at this time, the crafting of the Árd Fheis speech at the time was largely the work of Dr Martin O'Donoghue. He recalled suggesting to Lynch that the Northern Ireland material should be given at an earlier point, but Lynch, characteristically, chose to make it climactic, and did so with telling effect.

whatever problems arise and fails to face up to decisions and actions however unpalatable.

The atmosphere became steadily more tense during this part of the speech. Lynch was heckled and booed when he talked of membership of the party requiring "restraint on individual freedom of action", but then he reached a more detailed examination of differences between the individual and the party:

> Each member is free to advocate his or her views, but then must accept as party policy whatever the party decides. If the gap between the party viewpoint and their own thinking becomes too great then they are free to withdraw if they so desire.

At this point he was given a standing ovation that drowned out any expression of disagreement. He spoke of those advocating policy developments and changes:

> There are limits, freely accepted and understood, to the methods and extent of legitimate advocacy for such changes. Such limits are the necessary safeguards to avoid the tyranny whereby any group can impose its views on the majority.

For minutes on end he sustained a clear and unambiguous critique of the past disaffection, teasing out its nature and ordaining the route forward under his own leadership:

> In elaborating on our basic policy of peaceful means I believe that I have been reflecting the thinking of Fianna Fáil, and because our party is the largest and most representative one, currently forming the Government party, I believe it also reflects the views of the vast majority of our people. If I am right in this then let it be made clear now since it is important that I as leader should know what the party desires.

Though there were cries of "Union Jack!" and further heckling, the overwhelming mood was in Lynch's favour. The applause went on, punctuating each of the many references he made to the will of the party being more important than the will of the individual. Towards the end he referred to his leadership:

> I am not afraid to give an account of my stewardship over that period to any man and I totally reject any allegation – no matter where it comes from, be it from within or without – that I have ever by word or by deed reneged on the trust reposed in me by this Party or by the people as a whole in the last general election.

The applause was mounting steadily at this point, as he approached the climax of his speech. The standing ovation, which lasted for two minutes and ten seconds, was accompanied by cries of "We want Jack!"

Though the emphasis in the Árd Fheis speech was necessarily on loyalty, and on the issue of the party and its individual members, Lynch during this period developed and advanced his thinking on Northern Ireland. His speeches were worked on by Dr Whitaker. On a visit to America in the early spring of 1971 Lynch made a series of speeches in which the folksy image of the country was set aside in favour of a more adult view. But the more serious analysis of his thinking was put forward at occasions such as the Garden of Remembrance speech on 11th July 1971, where he reflected on the British agreement to Irish involvement.

Unfortunately, these attempts to grapple with the defining of Northern Ireland policy and its development through debate were punctuated by the chronology of events. There was internment without trial on 12th August 1971, which was followed the next day by Brian Faulkner's accusation that the Government in the Republic was tolerant of subversive organisations. Lynch then invited the non-Unionist members and senators at Stormont to travel south for talks. Angry exchanges with the British Prime Minister followed this move by Lynch.

In September he agreed to go to London for talks and at the end of the month he requested the chairman of the Dáil to recall members on 20th October to debate Northern Ireland issues. The process of policy-making went on. Important speeches and articles emerged, including a "Plan for Peace" that was the subject of a speech on 19th February 1972, and his lengthy contribution to *Foreign Affairs* in July 1972.[13]

*

The previous December he had continued the process of investigating what his opponents had done by setting up the Dáil Committee of Public Accounts and charging it with the investigation of the use to which the £100,000 provided for distress in Northern Ireland had been put. It was a shrewd move. The Dáil gave powers to the committee comparable to those enjoyed by the High Court. The committee could compel the attendance of witnesses and hold them in contempt of court if they failed to appear or answer questions. The work of investigation was effectively placed in the hands of the Opposition, whose members, eager to embarrass the administration, fulfilled the task with energy and skill. In reality, the committee was being used to investigate the supposed misdemeanours of the enemies within the Lynch administration. Their victory, which would have been pyrrhic anyway, was in part frustrated by a singular witness, Charles Haughey's brother, "Jock" or Pádraic. On the Wednesday before Fianna Fáil's weekend annual conference, he refused to answer questions. He was cited for contempt and sentenced to six months' imprisonment, suspended pending an appeal. The Supreme Court found in his favour on the grounds that he had been denied natural justice.

---

13 *Foreign Affairs*, Vol. 50 No. 4, July 1972, pp. 602–617 (an American journal of international politics).

His success, together with other limitations put on the committee, limited its work severely. Neither Lynch nor Desmond O'Malley were present, and Peter Berry's appearance was a limited one. He appeared carrying a gun that he placed rather obviously on the table. It was an exaggerated and slightly unbalanced mark of what he saw as his vulnerable status as a civil servant responsible for keeping the law against terrorists. He gave information but was not examined.

It was inconceivable after the Arms Trial acquittals that any further legal process would be taken against the principal figures. Yet the two opposition leaders had pressed for such an investigation, which the Government had put off until December. Timing was all. The full flood of inquiry provided an effective backdrop against which Lynch could face any residual challenge from within the Fianna Fáil organisation.

Though it did not report until the summer of 1972, the committee's findings on the money were that £41,000 had disappeared, £34,000 had been used in Belfast for "undetermined purposes", and only £29,000 could safely be said to have been used for the relief of distress. Chief Superintendent John Fleming told the committee that Haughey had met a leading member of the IRA and had promised £50,000 to the organisation. Haughey denied there had been any such meeting, in contradiction of what he had told the Government. In its report, the committee described Haughey's handling of the money as unjustified. In his evidence Captain Kelly told the committee that £32,000 had been spent on the purchase of arms in Germany.

The committee's questioning did lead to embarrassment well after Lynch had finally routed his opponents. On 21st April 1971 Gibbons told the committee that he had known from Captain Kelly on 30th April 1970 that part of the £104,000 had been used for arms. Lynch had denied this emphatically at the time. Gibbons explained that "the Taoiseach did not ask me that question".

Lynch's private misgivings about Gibbons, expressed the previous November and December in his remarks to the British ambassador, Sir John Peck, were surfacing in the evidence to the committee and would lead to more dramatic moves against Gibbons later in the year. He was the party's and the Government's weak link, and this was identified on all sides. The opposition parties recognised his vulnerability. The dissidents in the party loathed him. Lynch felt he had performed disastrously in the Arms Trial but, nevertheless, had promoted him to a senior government position as Minister for Agriculture. Lynch now had to complete the annihilation of his enemies. There were odd casualties on the way, one of them being Joe Lenehan, a backbencher who had the temerity to abstain on a dole cut vote in April and was expelled. A few days later, at the beginning of May, Kevin Boland completed the cycle of resignations by leaving Fianna Fáil and setting up his new republican party, Aontacht Éireann. He was followed into it by another backbencher, Seán Sherwin. When the new party held its inaugural meeting, the attendance included Captain James Kelly and Colonel Michael Hefferon. It was an ill-fated attempt by Kevin Boland to follow the democratic road with his republican ideals. The party came to nothing.

*

Seán Lemass, who had been ill for some time, died on 11th May 1971. Jack Lynch must have had happier times in mind when he delivered the funeral oration. He spoke warmly of the man who had led him to the honour of leadership and the darker responsibilities of power:

> The fruits of his life's work for Ireland will remain an indestructible monument to his memory and will provide for future generations of Irish men and women a most rewarding and productive source of information.

It was a strangely unheroic valedictory. Lemass had been a political visionary in a way that Lynch could never be. The challenges the two men had faced were fundamentally different. The Ireland that Lemass had handed over was now changed utterly, but not in any poetic sense. Lynch was repeatedly made aware of this. He faced private grief the following year when his father died.

Lynch was a hero in his own right. The fears that had made him diffident about the leadership, particularly when asked in interview what being leader would mean, had proved groundless. The misgivings he had felt about his capacity to fill the shoes of de Valera and Lemass had not been realised; quite the reverse. In circumstances that they had never faced and without their historic achievement as leaders of a revolutionary party that had created the independent State, Lynch had established a rock-like authority over the members of Fianna Fáil. In doing so he had transcended any supposed or actual uncertainty during the early years of his leadership. He was in control and nothing would change that.

He had achieved far more than that, however. In taking incontrovertible control over his party he had formed a bond of trust and dependency between himself and the Irish people. The cement for that bond, in many cases, was nothing short of love for the man. de Valera was revered, but as a distant, austere figure. Lemass was admired for his huge achievement. But neither of them touched the heart in the way that Jack Lynch did. He inspired affection that quickened into devotion with a remarkable number of people. One story is told of a nun in Cork who was ninety. She cried for a week after Jack Lynch was defeated in the 1973 general election. Her conscience unquiet, she went to her confessor and asked him: "Is it a sin to be in love with Jack Lynch?" The priest told her: "Not at all."

His relationship with Ireland, and the way he was seen as a person and as a politician, had transcended party politics. Party loyalty, on which the essence of democratic politics in Ireland depends, was refined into a quite different kind of loyalty where he was concerned. Several journalists, then and later, sought to undermine him. His political opponents did the same. But the contract which he had drawn up with the Irish people and the integrity with which he held to its essential principles made trivial and unimportant the continued baying of this disaffected "rabblement" that opposed him.

He achieved a different reconciliation with the people of Northern Ireland.

Those on the Nationalist side who were democrats saw with increasing clarity that the often hot-headed demand for guns had been futile and misjudged, and that Lynch's counsel to them and to his own side represented the only way in which real progress could be achieved. Those on the Unionist side, though deeply suspicious of the Republic's Government, recognised how much Lynch had done in championing a sane road to peace and containing as far as possible the growing power of terrorism.

Lynch's unique qualities, increasingly admired within Ireland, did not travel internationally. The crisis was hard to understand outside the country. Despite a distinguished group of diplomats dedicated to the task and enormous efforts made with countries sympathetic to Ireland's interests, the historical untangling of the increasingly long and complicated narrative of a people in crisis became progressively more difficult.

This agreeable man, with his avuncular manner, puffing at his pipe, ready with a friendly gesture and a word in his soft Cork accent was loved and trusted in his own country as no politician before or since. He was liked abroad and admired for his achievement, but not readily understood. In his natural way, so appealing at home, he could not face nor satisfy the international demand for rhetoric, platitude or hyperbole. It made him uncomfortable.

*

Neil Blaney, supported by the former Parliamentary Secretary from Wicklow, Paudge Brennan, continued his criticism of Lynch's Northern Ireland policy. Blaney claimed that he knew the names of twenty-five deputies and senators who had supplied arms to the North in August 1969, but named neither them nor their parties. It was an attempt, at this late stage in the conflict within Fianna Fáil, to raise the stakes. It was also an attempt to share with others the central culpability on the creation of a circle of violence in Northern Ireland for which Blaney carried a large share of responsibility. Blaney's words coincided with the worsening situation in Northern Ireland where storm clouds were gathering in anticipation of violence that August. Though British troops had steadily increased in number to a total of 11,900, acceptability of them on the streets had diminished. Riots broke out on 7th August 1971 following the shooting by troops of a van driver whose engine had backfired. Two days later three hundred IRA suspects were rounded up and interned without trial under a Special Powers Act introduced by Brian Faulkner. Twelve more people were killed in the rioting which followed this dark moment in the North's history.

The grim atmosphere of 1969, which had not been repeated in 1970, helping the Lynch Government to survive, now returned with a vengeance. It changed the character of the Government. Lynch had always held strong views on violence, now reinforced in the light of developments in Northern Ireland and the bitterness there that resulted from internment. There were also reports of threatened violence in the Republic; kidnapping, murder and armed robberies were cited in security reports. After one of these, a government press briefing indicated that detention centres were being prepared. There was also the question of invoking sections of the draconian Offences Against the State Act of 1940, which de Valera had used so effectively during the Second World War. There might even be new security legislation.

There was a credibility gap between the actual situation in the country and the reaction of the Government. Peter Berry, not slow on any real security threat, retired early from his position as Secretary of the Department of Justice, and this was seen as a silent rebuke. In a crisis, the introduction of security measures is usually immediate and not, as happened here, considered over a period of months. Yet this is what happened. It looked dilatory and precautionary, possibly motivated by the Dáil Committee of Public Accounts, possibly by the forthcoming annual conference of the Fianna Fáil party and by memories of the violent scenes of a year earlier.

The legislative changes came in May 1972 with a new Emergency Prisons Act allowing republican prisoners to be transferred from civil to military custody, and amendments to the Offences Against the State Act, bringing in the Special Criminal Court presided over by three judges without a jury. There was also a provision for the indictment of "a suspected member of an illegal organisation" on the word of a police chief superintendent.

*

Lynch had his eye on the leader of the Opposition, Liam Cosgrave, and on the prospective general election. He had time on his hands. His administration could continue until the spring of 1974, but political life had become volatile and unpredictable. The situation in Northern Ireland was deteriorating. Though Ireland's application for EEC membership was progressing well, industrial relations at home were hampered by serious strikes. The bank strike was disruptive of business life at every level, while another, in the cement industry, seriously affected the building sector.

Cosgrave was by no means a fearsome opponent, and Lynch had the measure of him. Cosgrave's political range was narrow. Its main character was that of a "law and order" leader at odds with views in his own party favouring enlightened social reform. He was an unattractive partner to a Labour Party bulging with intellectual talent; they would have found Declan Costello or Garret FitzGerald more acceptable. The onus of striking a coalition bargain rested on Labour, however, since Cosgrave was piqued about the previous failure on this front in 1969 and was reluctant to take any initiative.

Lynch's own law and order approach was a realistic response to the deterioration in the situation in Northern Ireland and the growing threat, throughout the island, represented by the IRA. It produced a change in Lynch in that he shifted towards a harder security line. At the same time, while not relinquishing his hold on the basic republicanism which had been at the heart of both de Valera's and Lemass's approach, he altered the interpretation of it. He did this in the light of the growing strength and ferocity of IRA actions and the gulf that now seemed to be growing steadily between the two parts of Ireland. One commentator at the time put it in dramatic terms:

> His present insight into the Irish mind is his most revolutionary yet. He has realised that the mass of people in the Republic have now lost not just the wish to see their island united violently but the wish to see it united at all.[14]

This experienced politician held a curiously insecure position internationally and the point was made that Lynch was formidable on his own ground but "a deceptively dim figure" in Brussels or London. "Yet most of the leaders of Europe could usefully take his course in the one indispensable of their trade: survival."[15]

Partly because of this difference over the kind of figure he cut abroad, Lynch's political initiatives had received limited response. He considered the unilateral introduction of internment in the North by Brian Faulkner under the Special Powers Act a disastrous move and called for the abolition of the "Stormont Regime". At that stage there was no question of any meeting with the Northern Ireland Prime Minister. When the Irish leaders, north and south, went to London in early September1971 to see Edward Heath, the meetings were held separately. They did, however, end in an undertaking that there should be tripartite talks. Lynch had met already with Liam Cosgrave and Brendan Corish, reconfirming the bi-partisanship that had developed in the aftermath of the Arms Crisis. But he did not have the support of the Social, Democratic and Labour Party of Northern Ireland, led by Gerry Fitt, which represented the Catholic minority. So long as internment was in force, Fitt was not prepared to back talks, and his party was not, at this stage, willing to be represented by Lynch in such inter-governmental talks.

The situation deteriorated. Refugees streamed south in the immediate aftermath of internment and in mid-August there were 4,500 of them in camps, the majority of them accommodated at Gormanston military camp in County Meath. A camp of a different sort was established at Long Kesh for the internees in the North and most of them were moved there. It later came to be called the Maze. Subsequently, another camp was opened at Magilligan in County Derry. Allegations of brutality by British troops were investigated by Sir Edmund Compton; there were 15,000 soldiers in Northern Ireland at this stage. Bomb explosions were averaging two a day and there was now no longer any question of getting through the summer months and the marching season without even further deterioration. The violence was seen by the Minister responsible as

---

[14] John Whale, "Lynch law versus the gospel of guns" in *The Sunday Times*, 3rd December 1972.
[15] *Ibid.*

endemic. Reginald Maudling delivered himself of his celebrated compromise target against the IRA, that they "would not be defeated, nor completely eliminated, but have their violence reduced to an acceptable level".

Yet for Lynch, raising his mild, tired eyes, and looking into the future, a greater desolation lay ahead. During the year that was drawing to a close there had been twenty violent deaths in Northern Ireland. In 1971 this rose to 172, and by mid-March of the following year the total since August 1969 was 262. By 1972 it had reached 467.

The sowing of dragons' teeth of change within the IRA had worked its course. The efforts of Blaney and Haughey, which had been absolutely fruitless in giving Fianna Fáil any advantage within minority communities in Northern Ireland, now contributed to a savage increase in bombings, maiming and murder in Northern Ireland.

A central figure in this campaign of violence was Seán MacStiofáin, who had been directly involved in creating the Provisional Army Council which broke with the established IRA under Cathal Goulding. He was head of the new breakaway IRA intelligence and quickly became chief of staff, directly in charge of the campaign of terrorist activities. At this time both Martin McGuinness and Gerry Adams were part of the leadership. On a single day, 21st July 1972, MacStiofáin ordered the planting of 34 bombs. Eleven died and 130 were injured.

MacStiofáin was an extremely dangerous and unstable individual.[16] Violence was an end in itself. Not having the experience or true sense of republicanism in his background, he failed to relate cause and effect to the larger objectives of the movement, which focused on the removal of the British from Irish affairs. Even within the Provisional IRA organisation, there was resistance to the brutality of MacStiofáin's tactics and even talk of assassinating him. But he achieved his own nemesis when he was arrested on 19th November 1972, charged with membership of the IRA and sentenced to six months. He embarked on a hunger and thirst strike, modified this to refusing food only, and then stopped it altogether, allegedly on the instructions of the IRA Army Council. After his release he failed to recover his position within the IRA. He had however given an interview about his activities to an RTÉ journalist, Kevin O'Kelly, which the station unwisely broadcast. It led to O'Kelly getting three months in prison for contempt of the Special Criminal Court in not giving the name of the man he had interviewed. The Government sacked the RTÉ Authority. It was judged to be in breach of section 31 of the Broadcasting Act which prohibited broadcasts of material from a terrorist source. This added to the sense of a new government hard line in the growing climate of violence.

---

[16] He was not Irish. John Edward Drayton Stephenson was born in 1928 in Essex, though both he and his mother claimed, falsely, that she came from Belfast. His parents were Cockney. He formed an Irish attachment which became obsessive and went to prison for IRA arms offences at the age of 25, moving to Dublin at the end of his sentence and becoming involved in the IRA.

*

There were substantive differences between the circumstances on the ground in Northern Ireland and the attitudes to the situation in the rest of the United Kingdom and in the Republic. It allowed for a strange and at times rambling debate to proceed. This was about options, headed on the republican side by the removal of the British and the unification of the two parts of Ireland. The options also embraced a council of Ireland, the return of Ireland to the Commonwealth, and an inter-parliamentary commission. In much of this thinking the British Labour Party leader, Harold Wilson, now in opposition, was active. He was responsible at one time for a 12-point plan for the North. It reassured the British Prime Minister, Edward Heath, that he had the same kind of bi-partisan support that Lynch now enjoyed. It also facilitated discussions, at least between the two leaders, Heath and Lynch, about the introduction of power sharing between the unequal communities in Northern Ireland.

Worse was to come. On Sunday, 30th January 1972 British paratroops opened fire on marchers in Derry and thirteen were shot dead. Lynch announced that the following Wednesday would be a day of national mourning. He withdrew the Irish ambassador from Britain. Though there was a ban in Northern Ireland on parades; 50,000 defied it and marched to a meeting on the outskirts of Newry in silent tribute to the dead. The march in Dublin was less sombre. The British Embassy in Merrion Square was burnt down. Terrible IRA retribution followed, with the Aldershot bomb that killed seven and injured more, and then the huge Abercorn explosion in Belfast that killed two but injured 136, badly mutilating many of them. The British Government ordered the transfer of security control to Westminster, which Faulkner refused to accept, and Stormont was prorogued. This necessitated giving to the North its own Secretary of State; William Whitelaw was appointed.

*

It is a measure of Jack Lynch's political skill and strength that, in the face of this security nightmare that seemed at times to be running out of control, his own position was more powerful than it had ever been. It was almost a symbolic act when, on 26th June 1972, Fianna Fáil's national executive – once the source of Neil Blaney's power and his domination of the party's structure countrywide – expelled Blaney for "conduct unbecoming a member of the organisation". Lynch undoubtedly spoke for the great majority of people in Ireland on all issues, and in 1972 he continued to steer through the country's application for membership of the European Economic Community. This involved a referendum with a five-to-one vote in favour of entry.

It was policy to draw a firm line between the two parts of Ireland. One was in safe hands, with security being strict but fair and the business of the people being protected and advanced. The other was in chaos, with Lynch's Government doing all it could to rectify this along lines that were consistent, reasonable and democratic.

In Lynch's judgement, security in the Republic needed to be rendered more strict and less fair. The sequence of security measures came to a climax with the passage through the Dáil of the Offences Against the State (Amendment) Bill in December. It was undoubtedly part of Lynch's strategy to put pressure on weaknesses within the Opposition on the central issue of the legislation, which was the power given to senior police officers to present their opinion on membership of the IRA as a justification for conviction and imprisonment. Lynch later claimed that the measure had a very significant effect on the IRA:

> It meant that for a while leading members of the organisation were safer in the North than they were in the south... I have really been perplexed by the doubts that have persisted about our determination to wipe out the IRA by all legitimate means within the rule of law.[17]

The debate was a critical one for Lynch. He had lost some support within his own party, and, with an Opposition seemingly united against a measure seen as draconian, defeat was a distinct possibility. Lynch's own firmness on security was matched by the man he had appointed to replace Micheál Ó Móráin as Minister for Justice, Desmond O'Malley. O'Malley's speech in the debate was unequivocal:

> The men of violence at whom the Bill is aimed are enemies of society. These people like to represent themselves in glowing terms as the heroes and martyrs of a holy war waged in the name of what they call patriotism. The reality is very different, very ugly and very sordid. The gospel of these people is a gospel of hatred and malice, and their only language is the language of physical force.

It was Lynch's intention to go to the country anyway. The debate, in his own words, was the prelude to the calling of the election. But opposition unity was not as clear-cut as it seemed. The Labour Party was opposed, but Fine Gael was divided. He explained later:

> I was naturally very interested in the developments. Quite obviously this would have been a propitious time for us to go to the country and offer ourselves as the alternative to a deeply divided opposition. However I didn't want to curtail the debate on the Bill and it dragged on longer than I originally assumed. It was my intention to call a general election immediately after the debate concluded but this became impossible.[18]

---

[17] Jack Lynch, "My Life and Times" in *Magill* (November 1979), p. 46.
[18] It would, in fact, have meant a poll on Christmas Eve: *Magill, ibid.*

The Fine Gael leader and some seven other deputies supported tougher security measures. Though uneven, the split was deep. The minority, despite the presence in it of the leader, bowed to majority pressure within the party and aligned with Labour. Lynch was also faced by two backbenchers who intended voting against him: the former Parliamentary Secretary and Blaney supporter Paudge Brennan, and Des Foley. But then the debate was brought to an abrupt conclusion in tragic circumstances. Two bombs were exploded in Dublin on 1st December, killing two busmen and injuring 127 other people. Fine Gael, recognising the electoral futility of voting against the measure, abstained. The Bill passed by 69 votes to 22. Brennan and Foley were expelled from Fianna Fáil.

It was said after the passing of the legislation that if there had been an election "the Opposition could have come back in a taxi." Lynch felt he could not take advantage of the widespread public outrage about the bombing. He had also decided that he wanted to complete Ireland's formal entry into the Common Market in the New Year.

*

Jack Lynch was impregnable within his own organisation and he stood head and shoulders over all other politicians of his time. He had taken the country through the crisis-torn period of August 1969 and had governed his way through the grim cat-and-mouse games of the autumn, winter and spring that followed. He had confronted the challenges during and after the Arms Trial. In its devastating aftermath, he had become increasingly tough in his attitude without losing the innate charm and appeal that seemed to protect as a halo might. He had spiritual invincibility. Opposition, in any coherent or sustained way, was impossible. He seemed to turn criticism back on those who expressed it.

He had brought the country through on his terms, and had given to Fianna Fáil its only hope of electoral survival. There had been a time when inevitable decimation and worse had faced them. By the end of 1972 the recovery had been so well organised that a victory would have been likely had the timing allowed for an early contest.

Without any great ceremony, Ireland joined the EEC on 1st January 1973, along with Denmark and the United Kingdom. Paddy Hillery became Ireland's first commissioner. It was then, in facing into the next challenge of his electoral survival, that Lynch took his opponents by surprise. He sought a dissolution of the Dáil on 5th February, the day before its reassembly after the Christmas recess. It was good timing on Lynch's part and did indeed take the opposition parties by surprise. But it was not without difficulties for Lynch.

By now Lynch had been a deputy for twenty-five years. Frank Aiken was seated beside him at the celebratory dinner the day after the election was called. Aiken intended standing again, although he was now 75, but told Lynch that he and Charles Haughey would not both be running in the election. If Haughey was selected and ratified by the National Executive, Aiken would withdraw. Moreover, he would publicly give his reason for so doing.

It was a direct challenge to Lynch's authority in the party and it threatened to bring out into the open all the damage done by the Arms Crisis. The work within the party, so painstakingly designed to resolve and consign to the past the events from 1969 to 1971, was fundamentally threatened. Suddenly, Neil Blaney's dismal prophecy, "It isn't over yet", had returned starkly to haunt Lynch. Disappointingly, it had come from a powerful and honourable father figure in Fianna Fáil, whose action, if he carried it through, could seriously damage the party's election prospects. The opposition parties, who had been relentless in their attacks on Lynch's leadership, would have a real focus for renewing them.

Immediate efforts were made to persuade Aiken to withdraw the threat to go public. Standing down, if he had to, was sad in the circumstances, but publishing the fact would humiliate Lynch at the outset of the campaign. At Lynch's request, de Valera intervened, but Aiken stood firm. The selection process went through, Haughey was ratified and Aiken withdrew his own nomination.

Aiken still intended to go public and thought he would get the support of another senior party figure, Paddy Smith, who was also standing. Smith had been a deputy since Fianna Fáil entered the Dáil and held similar views. But Smith wisely pointed out that it was too late, as the action Aiken was trying to precipitate "is at least two years too late in my view":

> This man [Charles Haughey] for better or worse has been functioning in the party ever since he made that speech after the Trial. He has voted and worked with the party and is chairman of one of its committees. At the last Árd Fheis of the party while I was in the chair he was proposed as one of our vice-presidents and he was approved with acclaim by all the delegates. I did not arrange all this but neither of us tried to stop it. He has attended party meetings; he has attended the Dáil and voted for us on all issues.[19]

Smith added that he had no brief for Haughey and was not putting his case. He was simply stating the facts. He regarded what Aiken contemplated as "a foolish course".

Aiken correctly expressed an ideal about integrity within Fianna Fáil that Haughey had seriously breached. Smith expressed the reality. Haughey had conceded to Lynch and had eaten dirt. He had obeyed party rules and sustained his position within the fold. He had voted confidence in Lynch and Gibbons, and he had parted from Blaney, Boland and the others from whom the party whip had been removed. To all outward appearances the grounds were not there for the action which Aiken sought, and which involved the party going back on what it

---

[19] The detail of this was first published by Geraldine Kennedy in *The Sunday Press*, June 1983, and summarised in my book, *What Kind of Country* (Cape, London, 1984), p. 223. A fuller version is given in Stephen Collins, *The Power Game* (O'Brien Press, Dublin, 2000), p. 96. The source is the Aiken Papers in the archives of University College Dublin.

had decided. It was not a matter for Lynch. It was a collective decision and the time for making it was long past.

Paddy Smith's contribution in pointing this out has some significance. What he identified was a failure within Fianna Fáil and not one that can be laid at the feet of the leader, though it normally is. Lynch had played his part to the best of his ability and in truly exceptional and unprecedented circumstances. He had gone on doing so for a period of three years. Haughey had conformed with what was required of him, as a loyal party member, and very few other people within the organisation had done what Aiken now belatedly attempted. Smith was entirely correct when he rejected Aiken's very belated attempt to block Haughey from any further role in the party nearly three years after his dismissal and well over two years since the Arms Trial acquittal. "You are just as guilty as I am and every other member of the party is. The time to take action or propose the taking of such action was before this history I have so crudely outlined."[20]

The rehabilitation of Haughey within the Fianna Fáil organisation, which was to run like an unbroken thread of base metal through the ore of Fianna Fáil politics for the next thirty years, was already an established fact. Each new revelation about him, in retrospect, raises the spectre of Aiken's ghost, haunting the organisation with its greatest "might-have-been". It was already too late to take the dramatic action which Aiken tried to force upon it; Jack Lynch saw clearly that it would split the party in a serious and enormously damaging way.

Aiken was not going to respond to de Valera's intervention, nor heed the logical advice coming from his old friend, the Cavan deputy Paddy Smith. Lynch was faced with a serious problem when it became clear that Aiken was going to go ahead with what he had threatened. Lynch's next move was to approach Joe Farrell, Aiken's close ally and constituency worker, who had served for twelve years in the Senate. He did not expect to succeed. Farrell, putting before his local leader a lifetime's understanding of the key issue that had made the Fianna Fáil party a great political organisation – party unity – persuaded him to withdraw any threat of going public. Aiken did withdraw his nomination and on his seventy-fifth birthday Lynch went to Dundalk and made a speech regretting the decision, made "on medical grounds". That day he endorsed both candidates who were running for the seat, Pádraig Faulkner and the man who had achieved the change, Joe Farrell.

For Lynch, it was like leading a strong team onto the field for a vital hurling game only to discover that a key player had decided to join the other side, and was telling him on the touch line. Of course he fought to dissuade Aiken and, if he failed, at least to attempt to suppress public knowledge of what had gone on. He lost Aiken and he kept Haughey. With hindsight, that moment of history might have had far-reaching effects, had Aiken followed his original course. But the conclusion reached by Stephen Collins that "the Aiken saga does not reflect any great credit on Lynch" is unfair. There was a case for Fianna Fáil to get rid

---

[20] Paddy Smith to Frank Aiken, quoted by Stephen Collins, *ibid.*, p. 96.

of Haughey in the autumn of 1970. He was the last and the most dangerous of those who had tried to subvert the organisation to their own ends. Yet he had obeyed party rules and still attracted considerable support. Smith's view is the correct one: the party should have made the move. Aiken, with the standing he had in that period, had the authority to do it then. Why he waited until early 1973 and *after* the general election had been called is the puzzle. By then his proposal was suicidal for the party. Lynch was politically correct to do everything in his power to avoid Aiken's withdrawal.

Chapter Ten

"No talk of my going as leader"

The National Coalition led by Liam Cosgrave came to power in 1973 on the basis of a 14-Point Programme for Government. It was said that much of it had been written out on the back of an envelope on the way into the talks. In fact, it had been conceived in the mind of Brendan Corish three years before, when he went to Lynch on 6th May 1970. There was a more substantial manifesto, the spirit of it stronger than the words it contained. There was a simple compulsion behind the first sentence, and it did the trick. "Fine Gael and the Labour Party have agreed to offer the electorate an alternative Government in the forthcoming General Election." In marked contrast with the 1969 general election, this meant that votes transferred. They did not transfer *from* Fianna Fáil to the parties in the proposed Coalition; quite the reverse. Fianna Fáil's vote actually went up. They transferred between Fine Gael and the Labour Party, and this proved crucial. Even so, it was a close-run contest.

The 14-Point Programme was overwhelmingly concerned with economic and social issues. Its brevity was its strength. Clearly written, without cliché and with an admirable dynamism running through it, it did indeed offer a fresh start and provided a well-reasoned foundation for trust in the essential message: the offer of an alternative Government.

Northern Ireland was given only modest coverage. The two parties committed themselves to "Peace through Justice... a peaceful solution in the North which will bring an end to bloodshed, injustice and sectarian division." Many of the other points received a more substantial outline, focusing public attention on prices, housing, rents, rates and taxes. The analysis of what the country needed, and the shift in emphasis away from Northern Ireland were less important than the personalities involved in the leadership of both parties. There were outstanding people in Fine Gael and Labour in that election and they offered a convincing potential government for the country.

Even with all the personalities, the political direction based on a sound programme, the mutual agreement to work together, and the subtle strengths of proportional representation as a voting system, Fine Gael and Labour only just made it. Jack Lynch, surprisingly enough, thought of it as his greatest electoral achievement:

Charles Haughey, right, with his
solicitor, Patrick O'Connor, at the
Four Courts for the Arms Trial,
1970. *Right:* Charles Haughey,
his arm in a sling, calling into
Government Buildings after his
dismissal, 7th May 1970.
(Courtesy of *The Irish Times*)

From top left: John Kelly, Cathal Goulding, Albert Luykx, Kevin Boland (with hat) and Brian Lenihan, Jim Gibbons, Paddy Lalor, Michael Hefferon. (Courtesy of *The Irish Times*)

ROINN AN TAOISIGH
DEPARTMENT OF THE TAOISEACH

BAILE ÁTHA CLIATH 2
DUBLIN 2

20th April 1970

Dear Mr. O'Donoghue,

I would like to have a meeting with you soon, that would last about 20-30 minutes. I would appreciate it if you rang my private Secretary, Mr O'Dowd, 675 71 Ext. 70. He will make mutually suitable arrangements

Yours Sincerely
Jack Lynch

Charles Haughey, 6th September 1969; the note Jack Lynch took time out to write to Martin O'Donoghue on 20th April 1970, the morning he was told of the attempt to import arms; Neil Blaney (with pipe) and Paudge Brennan arriving at Leinster House, Wednesday, 28th October 1970. (Courtesy of Sandol Harsch; private collection; courtesy of *The Irish Times*)

Heading into Leinster House: *from left*, Paudge Brennan, Charles Haughey and Des Foley on 5th November 1970. Paudge Brennan was later expelled for criticising Lynch's Northern Ireland policy. Des Foley later attacked Lynch's leadership and then resigned. (Courtesy of *The Irish Times*)

Jack and Máirín Lynch at the opening of the extension to the Glen Rovers Club, 1970. During the course of the Arms Crisis Lynch lost half a stone in weight. The strain shows. *Below, from left,* Captain James Kelly; Micheal Ó Moráin; Seamus Brady. (Courtesy of *The Irish Times*)

Jack Lynch at the Dublin Airport press conference on his return from New York, with Fianna Fáil ranged behind him. *In front:* Erskine Childers, Jack Lynch, Brian Lenihan, Jim Gibbons, George Colley, Gerry Collins and Joe Brennan. (Courtesy of *The Irish Times*)

Erskine Childers and Jack Lynch at the funeral of Seán Lemass, May 1971. (© RTÉ)

The President of Ireland, Patrick Hillery and the Taoiseach, Jack Lynch, sign the EEC Accession Treaty, January 1972. (Courtesy of *The Irish Times*)

From the top: Jack Lynch with his Front Bench in 1973. Brendan Corish, leader of the Labour party, with Jack and Máirín Lynch at the removal of the remains of Mr Seán Dunne T.D. at the Pro-Cathedral, Dublin, 1969; Jack Lynch and Liam Cosgrave at the funeral of former Minister Daniel Morrissey, County Dublin, 7th November 1981. (Courtesy of Maxwell Picture Agency Ltd and of *The Irish Times*)

Clockwise from top left: Jack and Máirín at Croke Park, 1966; at Thurles, centenary year, 1984; chatting to Christy Ring at the launch of the "Spirit of the Glen" club history, 1974. (Courtesy of the GAA Museum; John Sheehan Photography; *The Examiner*)

Clockwise from top left: Paddy Hillery after being nominated for the presidency by the Fianna Fáil party, November 1976. With him are deputies Kit Ahern, Jim Gibbons and Brian Lenihan; Jack Lynch at Croke Park; Jack Lynch standing among European leaders at a reception in Dublin Castle during Ireland's presidency of the European Union, November 1979. (Courtesy of Maxwell Picture Agency Ltd)

The arrival of Pope John Paul II at Dublin Airport, 1979. *Front row:* Pope John Paul II, President Patrick Hillery, Cardinal Tomás Ó Fiaich and Jack Lynch. (© RTÉ)

Mavis Arnold and the author with Jack Lynch at the funeral of the painter Maurice MacGonigal, February 1979. (Courtesy of *Irish Independent*)

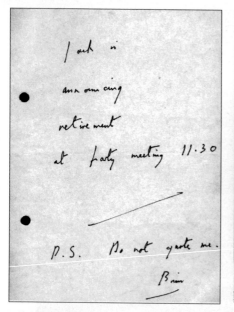

Clockwise from top left: The note sent by Brian Lenihan to the author in advance of the announcement that Jack Lynch would retire. The *PS* was intended as a joke. (From the author's collection); Jack Lynch after the 1977 general election watching the Taoiseach, Liam Cosgrave, concede defeat. (Courtesy of *The Irish Times*; photograph by Peter Thursfield); Jack Lynch returning his seal of office to President Hillery 1979. (Courtesy of *The Irish Times*)

Jack Lynch relaxes in retirement at home in Rathgar, 1992. (Courtesy of Maxwell Picture
Agency Ltd)

Jack Lynch, a Hero of our Time.

In the event we lost by a mere handful of votes. Had about 2,000 votes spread throughout key constituencies swung to us then we would have ended up with the two-seat majority instead of a two-seat minority. In the event I think that the 1973 election result was probably Fianna Fáil's greatest electoral achievement with me as leader, although the party was the loser. We increased our total first votes by almost 24,000 and pushed up our percentage vote from 45.7 in 1969 to 46.2. Never before had a political party, or combination of parties, won such a high vote and lost the election ...[1].

The fact that the main electoral talking point, then and later, was the strength of Lynch's performance, and therefore the certainty of his survival, gave a strange character to the new disposition of power. They all watched him; none more so that Cosgrave. The 14-Point Programme itself referred in its introduction to the fact that Lynch had steadily lost the substantial majority from the 1969 general election "through successive sackings and resignations from his Cabinet and expulsions from his party. It is entirely his fault that he no longer has the mandate to govern". Though this was not strictly the case, since Lynch had not lost command in the Dáil, it provided a political theme song for those in power. At the same time, it was clearly recognised that Lynch had saved the country from a very serious and pernicious crisis. He was regarded in an heroic light from then on. There was no real political advantage in pillorying Lynch for what he had done. Throughout the Cosgrave years, it never really worked. Men like Garret FitzGerald were swift to recognise that fact and to adjust their sights *away* from making Lynch their target.

Cosgrave was a strange leader for such a partnership and for such a richly varied collection of men.[2] Barely two months before the election he had come very close to being ousted from the leadership as a result of disagreements within his party over security and the Offences Against the State (Amendment) Act. His leadership was rescued by the bombs in Dublin that helped the legislation through the Dáil. This had saved Lynch from defeat, because Fine Gael abstained.

The experience had left Cosgrave bruised and distrustful of the liberal wing of his own party. He had a modest military background. He was a conservative on moral matters and a devout Roman Catholic. He had a staunch, if somewhat wooden, respect for what he saw generally as "the institutions of the State" and was not in any way in favour of reforming or changing the protections they offered. Those closest to him were essentially conservative in their outlook as well. His perceived beliefs and his manner made him seem rigid and a bit petty at times.

---

[1] Jack Lynch, "My Life and Times", *Magill* (November 1979), pp. 46 and 51.
[2] There were no women in the Government. Labour nominated five Ministers under the leadership of Brendan Corish, who took the Health and Social Welfare portfolio. Conor Cruise O'Brien went to Posts and Telegraphs. Cosgrave appointed Garret FitzGerald to Foreign Affairs.

In his period in power Cosgrave proved a good chairman, concise and deliberate, and he was a master of brevity with the redeeming quality of wit, though he made no real virtue of this. There was a lugubrious character to many of his public utterances. He would read some of his speeches in a voice like crunched gravel and with a look of boredom in his eyes. But whenever he departed from his script, he could pluck clever phrases from the air, producing a succession of witticisms from which he then retreated, often reluctantly, to the portentousness of policy. These contrasting approaches were to get him into trouble later on.

*

Initially Cosgrave's sombre and self-conscious approach proved an effective foil to the intellectual fervour and seriousness of committed social democrats and liberals like his Foreign Minister, Garret FitzGerald, who was the obvious person to succeed Cosgrave. He was also the person cast in the main role of dealing with Northern Ireland, a position for which he was well equipped. Of all the members of that coalition government, FitzGerald was probably the most understanding of the position in which Jack Lynch found himself when out of power. He had a parallel view on Northern Ireland. Owing to his background, which included Northern Ireland ancestry, FitzGerald was well able to understand the problems. The perspective gave him a sympathy for the difficulties through which Lynch had travelled and which he still faced. He admired the Fianna Fáil leader and was probably the first Irish politician to recognise just how invincible this quietly spoken Corkman had become.

Other important figures were now ranged against Lynch. Where once they had spoken from the powerless benches of the opposition side of the Dáil chamber, now they operated with the weighty support of their Departments. Moreover, they had the collective strength of a Government that soon became immersed in a busy schedule of administrative actions and legislative change. The programme of legislation, governed largely by the requirements of Ireland's membership of the EEC, proved an impressive package in the eyes of the public and became a talking point for commentators. Suddenly, Ireland had to meet equality laws, recognise the rights of women, and undertake a host of reforms affecting every aspect of life in the country. Unlike the previous Government, this busy schedule of work was not carried out under the ceaseless shadow of incipient rebellion.

In the new Government, Conor Cruise O'Brien, one of Fianna Fáil's most vocal critics, spoke out repeatedly about the differences between the two sides in Irish politics. He was also an outspoken voice on Northern Ireland and on the rump of republicanism within Fianna Fáil. Finally, and certainly not least in importance, he was a fierce opponent of Charles Haughey, and lost few opportunities for treating the disgraced backbencher (though still a member of Fianna Fáil) as Lynch's weak link.

*

Despite this, Lynch was impregnable. There was no way in which his leadership of the party would be challenged in opposition, and no-one knew it better than himself. "Because of the closeness of the 1973 election result there was no talk about my going as party leader, nor indeed did I feel myself that there was any need to consider retiring."[3]

Later, he had second thoughts. These were provoked by what became known as "The Littlejohn Affair". The Littlejohns, Keith and Kenneth, were two brothers wanted by the police in Ireland on bank robbery charges. They had fled to England before the election but had then been extradited. During the proceedings they claimed that their actions were part of an intelligence plot to provoke the Government in Dublin into the introduction of internment. The British denied the claim that the brothers had been working for the intelligence services but did admit to the Irish ambassador in London that there had been contact between the two brothers and either the intelligence services or a junior Minister.

A report on this was seen by Lynch in January, before the election, and then filed in Foreign Affairs. He forgot about it. When the Littlejohns came up for trial, there was public controversy over the intelligence aspect and Lynch denied having seen the report. His Attorney General, Colm Condon, supported him. But Garret FitzGerald checked on the Irish Embassy report and corrected Lynch. Lynch was genuinely upset. He issued a statement that went further than was needed. He said that the lapse of memory had been serious and that he felt he had to consider whether to go on as leader of the opposition. FitzGerald thought this unnecessary. Was it done for appearance? Or was it reality?

Despite press strictures, it was a minor lapse, and Lynch soon passed on from it. Publicly contemplating resignation could well have been a deliberate test of his own strength, both in public and in party terms. It certainly had the effect of rallying support for him.[4] Shortly afterwards, he had an accident in Cork:

> I had begun to give my position [as leader] some thought when I had the boat accident in which my right heel bone was broken. I was in too much pain for several weeks thereafter to give resignation or anything else much consideration and when I returned to a party meeting there was such an obvious flow of sentiment emphatically in favour of my carrying on that I committed myself to leading the party into the following general election.[5]

He looked a sorry figure at the time. Usually tall, spare and lithe, with a natural physical grace, he was on crutches for many weeks and then walked with a stick with some difficulty. The pain was obvious. The limp persisted for a long time.

---

[3] Jack Lynch, "My Life and Times", *Magill* (November 1979), p. 51.
[4] Garret FitzGerald, *All in a Life* (Gill and Macmillan, Dublin, 1991), p. 204.
[5] *Ibid.*

*

Jack Lynch was a competent rather than a good leader of Fianna Fáil in Opposition. He had been under enormous strain for a period of three years. This had been intense and unprecedented to begin with, with the crisis of August 1969 leading to events that threatened the stability of the State and could have resulted in a coup. What followed was a difficult time; costly in terms of energy and tactical resources, and exclusive of the other dimensions important to a political party leader in a democracy. It told on him. He maintained a remarkable sensitivity to the forces that threatened him while in power, and he handled them with skill and courage. But in Opposition he adopted a different view of things.

It was not in his nature to be visionary in his thinking. His judgement was superb in reacting to danger and threat, as he had shown on many occasions. He had also displayed considerable courage in confronting powerful figures in the Fianna Fáil party. But he did not have the kind of mind that could comprehend the broad range of issues presented in the National Coalition's Programme for Government, nor did he have a team in any way comparable to the team which Fine Gael and Labour put to work from their appointment in mid-March. Members of the new Government were energetic and focused. They abounded with political vision which gave a powerful sense of collective purpose to their early period in office.

Lynch, for his part, was not a man for organisational politics. Both de Valera and Lemass had recognised the vital importance of this and had presided over the party at every level; giving expressions of leadership, encouraging younger men, and operating with considerable personal authority a measure of restraint over the wilder expressions of political activism. From the time that Lynch became leader of the party and Taoiseach in 1966, he had been faced by a party organisation firmly under the grip of Neil Blaney, a man who could barely conceal his disdain for Lynch. Lynch allowed this situation to remain. Though he took a firmer hold later, he still did not find the whole business of running a political organisation congenial. It was said of de Valera and of Lemass that they never failed to preside at meetings of the National Executive of the party. Lynch, in contrast, was quite happy to hand over the chairmanship of such meetings.

Fortunately, this tied in with another more positive trait in his political character. He did not like the formal side of organisational politics, with its committees and sub-committees, its reporting functions and interminable meetings. To replace this and allow himself to relax and spend more time with Máirín, he directly recruited a small team of men who worked closely with him and tended to report to him on a one-to-one basis. One of these had been a close friend for many years and was also an able party worker. This was Eoin Ryan, who was the son of James Ryan, Lynch's predecessor in the Department of Finance. Eoin Ryan's whole life had been tied up with Fianna Fáil. He had served on the National Executive of Fianna Fáil under both de Valera and Lemass, and noted the marked difference in Lynch's approach. "They attached the utmost importance to meetings of the party's national executive, and rarely if ever missing them."[6] Ryan was involved in Lemass's constituency. Originally Dublin South, it became Dublin South Central, and there Lemass had exactly the same view. "I have a duty to the constituency and must attend meetings," Lemass told Ryan.[7]

Lynch frequently asked Ryan to act as his substitute in chairing national executive meetings. He could do this as often as four or five times a year and, although Ryan was flattered to have this key role in the party, his experience of previous leaders made him question the wisdom of it. At heart, he disapproved. It was fortuitous in quite another way, however, since it led to his much greater involvement in political matters. In due course Eoin Ryan became director of elections in the landslide 1977 general election.

Despite his lack of enthusiasm for organisational matters within the party, Lynch chose well in other appointments. In 1970, on the recommendation of Dr T.K. Whitaker, he had invited Martin O'Donoghue, who was in the Department of Economics in Trinity College, to take leave from his job and become his adviser. The day on which the Trinity College authorities agreed to the leave of absence was the day on which Lynch sacked Haughey and Blaney; it was not an auspicious start. The association worked well and O'Donoghue became both an adviser and a friend.

Lynch also appointed Séamus Brennan as general secretary of the party in 1973. He had been involved in Fianna Fáil and on its national executive since 1970, and he proved a highly effective and energetic organiser, later entering politics.[8]

*

It is perhaps of some significance in defining Lynch's approach that he took his time before restructuring his opposition team. When he announced his Front Bench at the end of July 1973 it had some surprises, including the demotion of Jim Gibbons, who was dropped from the senior responsibility of Agriculture and sent as delegate to the European Parliament, and the promotion of John Wilson, a newly elected deputy, who was given Education and the Arts.

The ebullient and gregarious Paddy Lalor was made Chief Whip. Desmond O'Malley was promoted to the major responsibility of Health, which gave him the job of leading the party's debating strategy on a difficult piece of early legislation, the Contraception Bill. This, after embarrassing and, at times, risible debate, was defeated when the head of Government, Liam Cosgrave, and his Minister for Education, Richard Burke, both voted against their own Bill.

Lynch made Michael O'Kennedy Foreign Affairs spokesman, gave Justice

---

[6] Author's interview with Eoin Ryan, June 2001.
[7] *Ibid.*
[8] He was a nominee for the Senate in 1977 and later a Dáil deputy for South County Dublin. He held various posts in subsequent administrations.

to David Andrews, Social Welfare to Pádraig Faulkner, Posts and Telegraphs to a new deputy, Ruairí Brugha, and Labour to Joe Dowling, a Dublin deputy with the voice and manner of a trade unionist agitator. Key appointments were George Colley to Finance, Joe Brennan to Industry and Commerce, and Gerry Collins to Agriculture.

The feeling engendered by the overall construction of the opposition team in the Dáil, combined with the newly recruited party officers close to him, was of Lynch's greater detachment from what was going to be a full term on the opposition benches. The political game was a long-haul process and those who had taken power were hungry for action. With the exception of Cosgrave and Corish, none of the Government Ministers had held senior office before.

It was hardly surprising that Charles Haughey received no Front Bench appointment, though the press 'wondered at it'.

*

Lynch had gone out of power, leaving behind him a legacy on Northern Ireland that was positive and welcome to the new Government. All of its members, perhaps most notably Garret FitzGerald, were ready and able to take on the task of a political initiative based on the concept of power sharing. This is what they did.

But Lynch had also left behind him the fruits of another initiative from his meeting in Downing Street with Heath at the end of November 1972. At that stage, in the wake of the arrest and imprisonment of Sean MacStiofáin and the sacking of the RTÉ Authority, Lynch put to Edward Heath the need for more protection for Northern Ireland Catholics against the casual violence from militant Protestants. He also sought British approval – if possible, expressed in the forthcoming White Paper on Northern Ireland – for a Council of Ireland.

Lynch had in mind a body where the affairs of the whole island could be raised and discussed by politicians from the North and from the Republic, and possibly from Britain as well. It would be loosely structured, but it would be permanent part of the political landscape. In theory, the request was modest. Looked at more closely, it fulfilled the all-Ireland dimension to any movement forward in Northern Ireland; Unionists, understandably, did not like the idea. This was vital to the terms of Fianna Fáil republicanism, as it had been hammered out and refined in numerous speeches. In an article which appeared at the time in *The Sunday Times*, the point was made:

> Even with the increased bargaining power given him by his new firmness at home, this was the only step which Jack Lynch chose to request towards Irish unity; and the striking thing about it is that it is an extremely small step. A Council of Ireland would in the nature of things be an ineffective body, because it would be discussing supra-national questions without supra-national authority. It would hold no promise for the future. It might

well be useful as a forum for ideas; but if any real hunger for unity existed
in the Republic, a Council could not begin to satisfy it.[9]

Nevertheless, following the changeover of power to the National Coalition,
Lynch's proposal did become part of the talks process in the autumn of 1973.
Part of the preliminaries for this was a visit to Dublin by Heath for talks with
Cosgrave. Lynch requested a meeting with Heath which, when it took place,
significantly helped towards a mood of optimism in anticipation of what was in
effect a crucial "peace conference".

The Council of Ireland was central – perhaps, in retrospect, too central – to
the Sunningdale Conference that began on 6th December 1973. As far as Cosgrave
was concerned, the outcome at home was crucial. In the aftermath of the turmoil
through which republican ideology had passed since 1969, an agreement
acceptable to the SDLP, to Lynch and to Fianna Fáil was essential. The grounds
for satisfying these parties, only one of which was represented at Sunningdale,
were common: the ending of internment, police reform and a Council of Ireland
set up before the nationalists would enter a power-sharing executive.

Though Liam Cosgrave handled the Sunningdale Conference well, supported
by a strong team, there was perhaps too little account paid to the needs of Brian
Faulkner and the Unionist Party.[10] When at the end there was a private session
of the Irish Government team and they gave a collective rating of how each
group had come out of the agreement, Faulkner was judged to have been left
significantly the worst off.

The ingredients of the deal will have a familiar ring to contemporary ears
and have proved conclusive in the sense that the British Government committed
itself to a devolution of power back to a Northern Ireland Executive and a Northern
Ireland Assembly "as soon as possible". Cosgrave's Government committed the
Republic to "no change in the status of Northern Ireland until a majority of the
people of Northern Ireland desired a change". A reciprocal undertaking on the
part of the British Government, aimed to reassure Unionists, was made confirming
Northern Ireland's status within the United Kingdom. Rather too much detail
was put into the communiqué about the role of the Council of Ireland.

The unravelling of the Sunningdale Agreement began early in the New Year.
The Ulster Unionist Council rejected it on 4th January and Brian Faulkner resigned
as party leader, leaving him as Northern Ireland's Chief Executive, though with
an administration that had begun to fall apart. The process was accelerated when
Kevin Boland, now the leader of a small and ineffectual political party not

---

[9] John Whale, "Lynch law versus the gospel of the gun." *The Sunday Times*, 3rd December
1972, Focus section, p. 17. The reason for the piece was the perceived confrontation
between the former Lynch Government and the recently arrested Seán MacStiofáin.

[10] The politicians accompanying Cosgrave were Garret FitzGerald (Foreign Affairs), Patrick
Cooney (Justice), Richie Ryan (Finance), James Tully (Local Government), Conor Cruise
O'Brien (Posts and Telegraphs, but including control of RTÉ), Brendan Corish (Labour
Party leader and Tánaiste) and the Attorney General, Declan Costello.

represented in the Dáil, took a constitutional action in the courts which forced the Irish Government to "clarify" Sunningdale. The judgement went against Boland in both the High and Supreme Courts, but not before doing serious damage to the Sunningdale Agreement and the position of the Northern Ireland Executive.

Worse was to follow. In February, Edward Heath sought a dissolution of the Westminster Parliament. He lost the election and Harold Wilson, ostensibly supportive of what had been achieved in Northern Ireland, became Prime Minister. He saw no alternative to power-sharing. But when its expression on the ground was challenged by the Ulster Workers' Council, which called a general strike, Wilson funked the challenge, as did Merlyn Rees, the new Northern Ireland Secretary of State. On 29th May the Northern Ireland Assembly was prorogued. Sunningdale was over.

The Republic stood firm in support of what had been achieved. In addition to Kevin Boland's unsuccessful case, Neil Blaney also emerged to oppose what he saw as a compromise. Fianna Fáil maintained bi-partisanship and George Colley came out on behalf of the party with a *de facto* recognition of Northern Ireland as an independent political entity.

Harold Wilson and his new Government were largely to blame in the collapse of Sunningdale. They made their position worse in the period that followed by implementing hardline security measures without new political initiatives. There is a distinctly chilly tone to the joint communiqué issued on 11th September 1974 after the Downing Street meeting between Wilson and Cosgrave. The reported discussions had been "widened" to include the EEC and "other matters". The only concession to north-south co-operation was an acknowledgement of the two leaders that:

> [needed to] take account of the special relationship which exists between the two parts of Ireland. The Irish dimension will be the subject of further consultations between the two Governments and also with elected representatives in Northern Ireland.[11]

With Heath it would have been a different story. It is a curious fact that Wilson and Cosgrave were similar in their attitudes. Wilson, through laziness, was disposed to turn his back on any fundamentally new initiatives on Northern Ireland and resorted instead to a relatively hardline security solution to the problem of the North. Liam Cosgrave, a pragmatist without a great deal of imagination, settled for security as the road to follow once the Sunningdale Agreement had collapsed.

Faulkner misjudged his own position. He was a sad figure, skilful and ambitious, but let down on all sides. Those who respected him most were his traditional opponents: the politicians from the Republic. They also knew that

---

[11] Communiqué issued by the Irish Embassy in London on behalf of the Government, 11th September 1974.

they were placing too heavy a burden on his shoulders with the Council of Ireland; though with Wilson in power the Agreement would have come down anyway.

The Dublin Government overemphasised the importance of the Council of Ireland and interpreted some aspects of Sunningdale in terms which were too favourable, Cosgrave claimed that it would lead to a united Ireland. But Jack Lynch's essential endorsement of the package, which he had initiated and which in its details conformed with the strategy he had followed since 1969, meant that the Republic came well out of the whole episode. It had a unifying effect on people generally. It educated them about the realities of Northern Ireland's political life and helped to dispel a good deal of nonsense about "unity", as well as justifying the measures required against the increasingly threatening men of violence.

*

Though never out of control, the security situation in the Republic punctuated the political narrative. A number of events seemed to endorse Liam Cosgrave's shift of emphasis towards imposing tougher law-and-order measures. The most savage of these events were the two bombings, in Dublin and Monaghan, which took place during the Ulster Workers' Council strike in May 1974. Twenty-five people were killed (two in Monaghan, the rest in Dublin) and over a hundred were injured.

Other events occurred, including the hijacking of a helicopter by the Provisional IRA which was then used in an attempt to bomb Strabane RUC station. There were prison protests by paramilitaries aimed at obtaining military terms for their detention; there were various paramilitary robberies and kidnappings. There was also the murder in March 1974 of Senator William Fox, who was travelling to see his girlfriend near the Border and may have interrupted an IRA ambush party. In August, nineteen republican prisoners escaped from Portlaoise high security prison.

Jack Lynch had been through worse. He surveyed the various individual, and largely unconnected events for the security outrages that they were. In general, they represented political bad luck rather than political misjudgement. Few of the occurrences could be laid at the door of the Government. Just as Lynch had done, Cosgrave condemned them in the strongest terms, and was justified in so doing. But they did not merit legislative action.

There was no real case to go ahead with Ireland's undertaking in the Sunningdale Agreement to introduce its Criminal Law (Jurisdiction) Bill. This legislation was designed to make terrorist offences committed in Northern Ireland subject to trial in the Republic. It was sensible as part of the wider package and broadly desirable in principle. Now, with the difficulties faced by witnesses making its implementation questionable and the rest of the Sunningdale Agreement in suspension, it seemed both bleak and unnecessarily controversial.

The Bill took a long time coming to the Dáil. It was moved first in the Senate in April 1974, where Mary Robinson gave it a detailed and severely critical treatment. She brought up the general shortcomings of the Republic's security legislation when viewed on an all-Ireland basis and raised fundamental constitutional objections. The Bill was seen as evidence of a hardening of the stand against subversives and was not, in this respect, entirely at odds with the position that Lynch had adopted during the post-Arms Trial period when violence in Northern Ireland had escalated. Both he and his Minister for Justice, Desmond O'Malley, had then seen the State undermined, Ministers' lives threatened and violence becoming endemic. Now he adopted a different approach.

*

Between the first moving of the Bill and its coming up for debate in the Dáil, a great deal had happened. In some measure, events confronted Lynch with the changing character of his leadership. It had been made patently clear to him at the time of the 1973 general election, when Frank Aiken's attempt to remove Haughey from Fianna Fáil politics failed, that Lynch faced a problem that could only grow greater.

In the period between that election and 1975 the issue of Haughey's future was far more central to Fianna Fáil's position and performance in opposition than anyone might have expected. The man himself was regularly in the news. In the spring of 1974 he had bought the island of Inishvickillane off the Dingle peninsular in County Kerry. It received a good deal of press coverage. Later the same year he made a provocative speech reminiscent of Neil Blaney in the late 1960s, reminding the public that Ireland's aspiration to unity was a central tenet of Fianna Fáil belief. The speech, made at the request of the McEllistrim family in Kerry to launch the Thomas McEllistrim Memorial Fund, was ostensibly directed at the Government on its Northern Ireland policy, although no mention was made of that Government collectively or of individual Ministers. Instead, Haughey spoke of "those upon whom the responsibility for our national affairs rests at present."[12]

It was, in fact, a coded message directed at republicans within Fianna Fáil and was one of a series of speeches that Haughey was making around the country, mainly to Fianna Fáil organisations, and was focused on the recovery of his position in the party. It was particularly pointed since McEllistrim had been the deputy who proposed Jack Lynch for the leadership of Fianna Fáil.

Haughey made a comparatively good speech on the Budget that year, contrasting with the poor quality of speeches coming from his own side. He defined the ideological differences between the National Coalition and Fianna Fáil; these were primarily based on the strategy of both the Lemass era and the period when Haughey had been Minister for Finance (from 1966 to his dismissal in 1970). Richie Ryan, he said, "will shatter the climate of encouraging capital development, built up painfully over several years."

---

[12] Michael Mills, *The Sunday Press*, 27th October 1974.

Haughey was asserting his claim for consideration in the front bench reshuffle promised by Lynch in the new year. He was helped in this process by, of all people, leading Ministers in the National Coalition. Their attacks reinforced the opposition party's overwhelming desire and its abiding duty to present itself as a united political force. Conor Cruise O'Brien was particularly virulent. During the north-east Cork by-election in November 1974 a headline in the *Irish Independent* read: "O'Brien Flays Haughey". It reported a pledge by O'Brien "that he will make it his business to see that Charles Haughey never becomes leader of Fianna Fáil."[13]

O'Brien drew a distinction between Haughey on the backbench, a position he felt Haughey should retain, and Haughey as the potential leader of the party. "I do not believe Lynch wants him back," O'Brien told Raymond Smith. "The taint of collusion with violence is not gone from Fianna Fáil... Most of those who support that party, and who have no sympathy at all with violence, have not yet fully understood the implications of the Arms Trial crisis of 1970."

Jack Lynch moved in a quite different direction. In an RTÉ broadcast on 8th December 1974, he said of Charles Haughey that their differences were over. Still, he made it clear that this required a response from Haughey himself. He also emphasised the importance of the attitude adopted by the rest of the team on the Front Bench. In other words, he was being guarded. The circumstances were made more tense by the fact that President Erskine Childers had died on 17th November, raising questions about whether Lynch would resign as Taoiseach and party leader and go to the Park. If he so wished, this would be automatic. He emphatically had no desire to be President and instead Cearbhall Ó Dálaigh, a former Chief Justice and distinguished constitutional and European lawyer, was elected unopposed. The event served to bring to the fore the largely hidden pressures on Lynch's leadership.

Lynch's resolution of his difficulties as leader was more or less complete. Bringing Haughey back to the Front Bench was part of the important placing of political pieces for the period ahead which would lead finally to the next general election. Lynch had frustrated two important Coalition objectives. The first was to have a divided Opposition; achieving this depended on vilifying Haughey to such an extent that Lynch would not have the nerve to return him to a prominent position. The second was an actual change in Fianna Fáil leadership. It was in the National Coalition's interest to bring this about, if it could, either by persuasion or by allowing Lynch the unchallenged move to the Park that others at the time thought desirable. Both now became dead issues.

On 30th January 1975 Jack Lynch reshuffled his Front Bench. Jim Gibbons was returned to his former Agriculture portfolio. Charles Haughey was brought back and given the Health portfolio. Though since condemned for what he did, mostly with the benefit of hindsight – and what a hindsight it has been in more recent years – at the time there was a clear majority of Fianna Fáil party

---

[13] *Irish Independent*, Monday, 11th November 1974, p. 1.

backbenchers and party workers around the country who supported Haughey's return to the Front Bench. There was also support from many commentators.

Politically, Lynch had restored party unity. He was himself safe from challenge and had already determined that he would lead Fianna Fáil into the next election. It was the mid-point of the Dáil and the reshuffle was vital as he prepared for the eventual general election. For the time being all was secure.

*

In September 1975 Jack Lynch made a potent contribution in the long and rancorous debate on the Criminal Law (Jurisdiction) Bill. This "last remnant of Sunningdale", introduced amid unprecedented Dáil uproar in April 1975, was not to pass into law until spring of the following year. It was emblematic of the security-conscious character of the Government and Lynch, in a subtle way, created the impression of dubious legislative relevance and questionable motive. Where had the Government's Northern Ireland policy gone to? This Bill was "the only known action" and was "a negative response" to the changed problems now requiring action. It would do nothing to help towards reconciliation and it represented the abandonment of any commitment to unity of either party in power.

The response to Lynch was lively and aggressive, particularly Conor Cruise O'Brien's speech in which he talked of "getting near the bone, and the bone is beginning to squeak. I'm getting near to what's wrong with you over there," he told Lynch. "I believe there are people over there who believe that fugitive IRA should be left alone and that is the real reason for opposition [to this measure]."

The real reason for Lynch's stance was his desire to get and hold "the middle ground" in Irish politics. Despite the major economic problems in the country, this centred on Northern Ireland. Legislation was before the Dáil designed to alter fundamentally the country's views on wealth through the introduction of tax measures. Also, there were complicated legal moves in respect of Bula Mines on the ownership of natural resources. There was, in fact, at this time an unprecedented legislative burden placed on the Dáil by the need to bring in EEC legislation as well as domestic reforms, budgetary proposals, and the complicated tax reforms. The concentration on security did seem increasingly unnecessary.

Lynch also followed an agenda that was internal to his own party. He was faced with pressures to become more hawkish over Northern Ireland, and in part these derived from his new Foreign Affairs spokesman, Michael O'Kennedy. The party, which had won two by-elections early in 1975, was faced with another in Mayo west when Henry Kenny, a popular Fine Gael deputy and junior minister, died. Midway through that by-election, on 29th October 1975, Fianna Fáil published a Northern Ireland policy document in which the party called on the British Government "to declare Britain's commitment to implement an ordered withdrawal from her involvement in the Six Counties of Northern Ireland". Lynch accepted the move under party pressure. Privately he thought the line taken might undermine the good work he had done in the debate on the Criminal Law

(Jurisdiction) Bill. He believed that the timing was inappropriate. It would be seen as electioneering, and pandering to the supposedly more republican views of Mayo west voters.

He was right. The Coalition won Mayo west convincingly. There was a retreat within Fianna Fáil from the Northern Ireland policy line based on the British "declaration of intent to withdraw". Lynch's own approach became dominant again, much to the relief of a majority of party supporters. If anything, the outcome of that by-election left him once again more firmly in control than before. He was approaching the ten-year mark in his leadership of Fianna Fáil, a longer period than Seán Lemass's leadership, and one that was more dramatic than Éamon de Valera's. Lynch had assumed their aura of invincibility without the benefit of having fought for Ireland's freedom, or of having any historic claim to public admiration. He had done it on merit.

*

In mid-1976 a crisis hit the National Coalition. The newly-appointed British Ambassador to Ireland, Christopher Ewart-Biggs, was murdered on 21st July by the IRA. A bomb was detonated in a culvert under the road leading into the embassy residence. He had only been in the country since presenting his credentials on 9th July, though he had met many politicians at a British-Irish Association conference in Oxford at the beginning of the month.

The Dáil was recalled for a special emergency sitting and Liam Cosgrave brought three measures before it: a motion declaring a new "National Emergency", a Criminal Law Bill and an Emergency Powers Bill. By so doing he set in train a series of events that would lead to acute political embarrassment and the undermining of the credibility of his administration.

The presentation of a security package was reminiscent of the autumn of 1972. Then, under Lynch's leadership, the Government had brought in the Offences Against the State (Amendment) Act, giving extensive powers to the police against the IRA. It was done in the face of supposed IRA threats to the lives of members of the Government. Jack Lynch and Desmond O'Malley had adopted what was seen as an overly stern security line, but the claims had then been reinforced by the two Dublin bombs and the Bill had passed easily into law.

On this occasion the violent act preceded the legislative moves. Horrific though the assassination had been, it did not, at least in Lynch's view, justify the draconian measures now proposed; nor was it possible to accept it as a national security emergency. Cosgrave had not consulted with Lynch before introducing the measures; nor had he told the President that the country was facing an emergency, nor what he proposed to do about it. Patrick Cooney, the Minister for Justice, called this constitutional matter an emergency with a small "e". Conor Cruise O'Brien gave the proposed measures a different explanation: that they were a form of exhortation and assurance for the people of both parts of Ireland. Cosgrave said that the legislative package was an expression of the "Government's view of the gravity of the situation".

None of this rang true.[14] It was *not* the situation as defined by Cosgrave and two of his Ministers. It was simply a terrorist strike of devastating and deadly impact, but not one which presented a threat to the State beyond what the State had been dealing with already. Jack Lynch said as much in the Dáil when the National Emergency motion was debated on 31st August 1976. He fully supported all measures needed to contain the security threats that had been present throughout Ireland for the previous six or seven years, but he rejected as unnecessarily severe the proposed suspension of constitutional safeguards. There was also something slightly odd and unnecessary about revoking an emergency that had been in place since 1939 and then re-imposing another emergency. The first had been a genuinely national response to a threat by the Axis Powers during the Second World War to Ireland's neutrality. This second occasion was prompted by a single awful act of terrorist murder.

The Emergency Powers Bill followed. It extended by seven days the period of arrest and interrogation of persons suspected of terrorist offences under the Offences Against the State Act. The Bill had been hastily drafted and it was not clear whether the seven days were to be added to the existing 48-hour period or to replace it. There were other anomalies and faults in the Criminal Law Bill. Altogether, the package was a mess and Fianna Fáil said so. In their haste to push it through the Dáil, the Government gave limited time to debate. Meanwhile, nothing happened. There was no terrorist follow-up to the murder of the British Ambassador, nor any threat to the State. The legislation, apart from its potential *electoral* merit or value was more suited to the suppression of terrorist activities in Northern Ireland and the United Kingdom than in the Republic.

Rushed through without amendment in just over two weeks, the Emergency Powers Bill, followed by the Criminal Law Bill, were then the subject of delay by President Cearbhall Ó Dálaigh, who summoned the Council of State and, after consultation, referred the Emergency Powers Bill to the Supreme Court. He signed the Criminal Law Bill. The Court found in favour of the legislation, but with important reservations endorsing the power exercised by the President in referring the Bill, and defining the extent of the emergency powers.

From Lynch's point of view, he had identified himself and his party with the exercise of constitutional restraint through the presidency and through the Supreme Court. Lynch's opposition, when the legislative package came before the Dáil, followed by the challenge by Cearbhall Ó Dálaigh on constitutional grounds, were then combined in the public mind with the judgement of the Supreme Court. It was an opposition victory of a subtle but important kind. What had, in part, started out as a political stroke rebounded seriously on the Government.

---

[14] Articles I wrote at the time were headed: "The big question: Are they playing politics?", *Irish Independent*, 1st September 1976, and "The trick that failed", *Irish Independent*, 4th September 1976.

Far worse was to come. The Minister for Defence, Paddy Donegan, a no-nonsense politician from County Louth and a heavy drinker, angered at the President's decision to refer the Bill, lost his temper at an army function in Columb's Barracks in Mullingar where he was opening an army cookhouse and dining hall. Adding additional expletives, he described Ó Dálaigh as "a thundering disgrace" for having held up the government security package by sending the Emergency Powers Bill to the Supreme Court. A local journalist reported the story. It became a national sensation and highly embarrassing. Few expected it to be more than that – but they underestimated Cearbhall Ó Dálaigh.

This former lawyer, one of the most gifted of his generation, was a stickler for constitutional law and for the dignity of official office. Over the whole period of his presidency, from the death of Erskine Childers, the Taoiseach had failed to keep him "generally informed on matters of domestic and international policy", as the Constitution requires.[16] There had been only four visits to Áras an Uachtaráin in the lifetime of the Government, only one of which had touched on policy, and only in a very general way.

Patrick Donegan, the Minister for Defence, had written more than once to the President to offer his apology. In the Dáil, Cosgrave referred to these apologies as adequate, full, sincere and unreserved. However, in part of the exchange between Ó Dálaigh and the Minister there were qualifications by Donegan about his position; these reservations provoked Ó Dálaigh into giving a long and peppery lesson to the Minister on constitutional and other points.

Ó Dálaigh was still not satisfied with the way he had been treated. He felt that neither Cosgrave nor Donegan, despite the intense argument and debate following the comments, understood any of the issues involved. Government handling of the crisis had been inadequate, but the letters of apology had all been sent before Cosgrave reported to the Dáil, so that he was fully informed of all the details. Ó Dálaigh blocked access to himself by all Ministers except the Taoiseach; Cosgrave did not go to him, nor did he dissociate the Government from the Minister's speech.

What had affected Ó Dálaigh particularly, in advance of Donegan's speech, was that Cosgrave did not inform him about the emergency into which Ireland had supposedly been plunged by the assassination of the British Ambassador. There was, therefore, a contradiction between what seemed like an off-hand introduction of special legislation and the angry reaction from the Minister for Defence over its blocking. Ó Dálaigh was also less than satisfied with the Supreme Court, making the point that it is charged under the Constitution with giving a

---

[15] Article 28.5.2°. I had predicted in an article in the *Irish Independent* written on Tuesday, 19th October 1974, for the next day's paper that Ó Dálaigh would resign. I wrote about the developing crisis during that week which ended with his resignation on the Friday evening. His final public act was to present prizes at Glengara Park School in Glenageary. I subsequently called on him the following Monday for the first of several interviews and telephone conversations from which these details are drawn.

full answer and not the temporising one that it did give. Ó Dálaigh quoted the exact requirement of the Article: "The Supreme Court… shall consider every question… and… shall pronounce…"

This all emerged publicly. A vote of censure of the Government's actions, put down by Fianna Fáil on Thursday 21st October, had been rejected by sixty-three votes to fifty-eight. But this had been achieved under false pretences. The Labour Party, already highly critical of the insult delivered by Donegan, had been misled as to the nature and extent of the apology. The two parties in Government had been given reassurances about the crisis by Ministers. These Ministers had accepted at face value Cosgrave's version of what had happened. This was now challenged materially by Ó Dálaigh's own statements. In a telling part of his own statement after his resignation, he said:

> The President has to be a person who receives a minimum amount of acceptance. When a point is reached when this is not available, the President does a service by leaving the public scene. My action was taken because I thought I could not, as things stood, continue to be President.[16]

Most strenuously of all, he defended his actions in respect of the emergency legislation. Ó Dálaigh's pronouncements, together with the way he had been treated, were seriously damaging to the National Coalition. The Emergency was further exposed and its relevance challenged. The Government was put on the defensive.

A much more alarming development took place within Fianna Fáil. Charles Haughey, again misjudging the mood in what was undoubtedly a crisis, indicated to contacts within the press that the resignation of Cearbhall Ó Dálaigh provided the opportunity for what was described as "a surprise package" to put Fianna Fáil back in power. Jack Lynch would go forward as presidential candidate to succeed Ó Dálaigh, Charles Haughey would become leader of the party, and Paddy Hillery – who was already being seen as the "agreed candidate" to succeed Ó Dálaigh instead of Lynch – would lead the Fianna Fáil group in the European Parliament.

It was a half-baked scheme, ill conceived and opportunistic. It was initially expressed by backbenchers, but Haughey himself played a part when he made a radio broadcast on Sunday, 24th October, calling upon the Fianna Fáil party "to put forward for the presidency a very strong candidate – a man with status, experience, judgement and public support". He could only have meant one person. "We must establish a Fianna Fáil President in the Park with the full support of all the people. That is the only way to repair the damage done to the presidency." There was backbencher and grassroots support for Haughey's "statesmanlike" view of what should be done. George Colley confirmed this mood in the party,

---

[16] Official statement by the President following his resignation.

192

but he wisely rejected the likelihood of Jack Lynch agreeing and was even more emphatically against the acceptability of Haughey going forward as leader.

Lynch dismissed any possibility of going for the presidency out of hand. "I have said it is my desire to lead the party into the general election. My views have not changed." Though there was some speculation as to Major Vivion de Valera, the son of Éamon de Valera, going forward, the choice in fact fell on Patrick Hillery, who was a reluctant but safe candidate.

The Coalition was in no state to fight a presidential contest. Jack Lynch made this even more emphatic after a very brief meeting of his Front Bench. He announced that the party would contest the election of a president and would be asking the people "to repudiate the attitude of the Taoiseach and the members of the Government towards the Presidency". Lynch had effectively reversed the impact of recent coalition by-election successes. The party unfortunately was still divided. This had been brought out into the open, requiring yet another demonstration by the leader of his invincibility.

It must have been getting a bit tedious to have that threat expressed through rumblings of pointed yet inept dissatisfaction. Those loyal to Jack Lynch were dismissive of the concept of Charles Haughey taking over as leader at any time, but especially not as the Dáil term moved towards its conclusion with an election virtually certain the following year.

*

Troubled by the economy and committed ideologically to a widely unpopular piece of legislation designed to tax wealth, the National Coalition surged forward into yet another damaging legislative undertaking when Justin Keating introduced a Bill on mineral rights. The details of the Bill were complicated by the existence of a secret agreement, by the emotive issue of land ownership, and by arguments over who owned the minerals beneath the surface. There was also a constitutional dimension to these arguments.

The legislative move, which in hindsight might have been better left until after a general election, coincided with a broadly based recovery programme within Fianna Fáil designed to prepare the party for the general election. As part of this, more focused energies were deployed in the Dáil. The effort was led by George Colley and Desmond O'Malley. Others who proved effective were Vivion de Valera, Tom Fitzpatrick, Ruairí Brugha and Sylvester Barrett. They performed aggressively on the economy, on the taxation legislation, and on Bula.[17]

The National Coalition remained confident but, under their increasingly startled eyes, the Opposition that had not performed particularly well during the

---

[17] Bula was the name of the company that had been set up to take over land and mineral rights at Nevinstown, where Europe's largest zinc ore body, of some 21.6 million tons, lay.

previous four years began to make a serious impact. Whether or not Cosgrave read this as a warning to move swiftly towards a general election, he ignored advice from Garret FitzGerald to wait, and geared himself and his party for a June campaign.

CHAPTER ELEVEN

The National Affinity for Jack Lynch

The 1977 general election was called for 16th June, a Thursday. This was unusual since campaigns normally concluded with a Wednesday poll. Someone had overlooked the presence of the Whit Bank Holiday in what was legally the shortest possible period for the campaign and the time between dissolution and polling day had to be extended. For those who read signs and portents, this initial miscount of the days available suggested that not all had been prepared with the scrupulous care an election needs. However, other indicators predominated.

A former military man, Liam Cosgrave bore the impressive ancestry of his father having been the country's leader during the 1920s and up to 1932. Dedicated to the preservation of law and order, Cosgrave led his most gifted team of Ministers from the two ideologically different parties, Fine Gael and the Labour Party, to a successful conclusion of their period in office. Holding the two parties together was one of his more signal achievements, and was in marked contrast with the two previous coalitions under the leadership of John A. Costello.

When Liam Costello went to Áras an Uachtaráin at 9.15 a.m. on the evening of Wednesday, 25th May, to request formally the dissolution of the Twentieth Dáil, he did so with punctilious brevity and confidence in the campaign that lay ahead. He was twenty minutes with President Hillery while the instrument for dissolution was signed. When he emerged, it was to say that the two parties under his leadership would fight the campaign as a national coalition. This alone gave him a certain air of omniscience from the outset.

For all his Government's shortcomings in the previous four years, there was in this small, precise man a steely set of qualities which was not to be disparaged. The achievement was all the greater in that the members of the Government he had successfully held together were rich in intellectual talent, diverse and outspoken in opinion, and enormously capable in presenting their political views. Garret FitzGerald, Patrick Cooney, Peter Barry, Mark Clinton and Richie Ryan were leading figures within Fine Gael; the Labour Party had powerful voices in Conor Cruise O'Brien, Justin Keating, Michael O'Leary and Jim Tully.

For Jack Lynch, the prospect was daunting. His task would not be easy. He could in no way match the same united front that was presented by his adversaries. Beneath the surface, his own party was irrevocably divided. No matter what kind of united front it put up for the election, the divisions would remain there as a handicap. His Front Bench did not provide him with the same qualities of argument and debate. The two leading figures, Charles Haughey and George Colley, were so obviously waiting to take over and so much in rivalry that their use as leading election protagonists was unwise.

Though all of those against whom Lynch was pitted had been battered in the legislative battles of the Twentieth Dáil, they were still an effective fighting team. Lynch was in no doubt that defeating the rich and varied talent against which he had committed his and his party's energies for close on five years was going to require a different strategy and different strengths.

Ironically, on that first day a shadow from the past was thrown across Lynch's path from an unlikely source: a courtroom in Hamburg. A residual case arising out of the Arms Crisis appeared there before German judges. The coalition Government was seeking to recover money which, according to the court reports, had been paid by Captain James Kelly to the German arms dealer, Otto Schleuter. Schleuter was contesting the Irish Government's demand for the return of £20,000. Though the case in Hamburg was adjourned until after the June 16 polling day, it foreshadowed one of the more uncomfortable prospective election issues, that of the Fianna Fáil party's Arms Crisis skeletons. Holding together, presenting a united front, demonstrating solidarity over policies and past achievements: these would be common ground for both sides in the forthcoming battle.

As if to give substance to this, the last day of the Dáil's work saw Desmond O'Malley, Charles Haughey, George Colley and Vivion de Valera all debating aggressively on the final pieces of legislation which had been guillotined in order to make way for the election campaign.

A British all-party parliamentary delegation was on a visit to Leinster House on the day of the dissolution. It included Ian Gow, later to be assassinated by the IRA, Michael Mates and Kevin McNamara. When they had finished signing the visitors' book, it was full up, with signatures going over onto the inside back cover. The autographs stretched back to 1961 and included, among others, that of Muhammad Ali, who had written: "The man who has no imagination stands on the earth. He has no wings. He cannot fly. Peace!" One of those with feet firmly planted was Stevie Coughlan, a controversial Labour deputy. He had written beside the message: "Introduced by Stevie Coughlan."

*

Vivion de Valera, a Dáil deputy since 1945, was now head of the family and forceful in representing the family's ownership of the controlling interest in *The Irish Press* newspaper. It was at that time a significant force in journalism, with an outstanding political correspondent in Michael Mills. Its role would be considerable in the election campaign.

As chief executive of the paper, de Valera played an active part in its editorial direction. Not surprisingly, in its main editorial on the morning after the dissolution, it poured scorn on the "undistinguished" Twentieth Dáil with its "squalid" end. The Barnum and Bailey apophthegm on politics – "You can fool some of the people…" – was invoked, as were criticisms of unemployment, high taxation, the high crime rate, a weak economy, and a talented ministry pulling every which way. Shrewdly, Vivion de Valera also identified the central issue of the election. This lay in the contrast between what was described in the editorial as the "rational and persuasive" style of oratory adopted by Jack Lynch and what was seen as the intemperate and abusive approach of Liam Cosgrave.

Liam Cosgrave's capacity for sharp and intemperate language had been given additional focus as a result of his extraordinary outburst at his party's annual conference in the Mansion House just the weekend before. The curious Jekyll and Hyde approach which Cosgrave had as a politician manifested itself in his speeches. When talking from a script he was effective, but somewhat dull. When he departed from his script he could be witty, inventive, eccentric and vigorous. This often happened with Árd Fheis speeches, the most famous example being that of 1972, when he referred to liberals within the party who had attacked him as "mongrel foxes". They would be unearthed, he went on, "and then I will let the rank and file of the party, the pack, tear them apart".

The 1977 Árd Fheis speech had been much worse than the mongrel foxes speech because it had attacked real and imagined enemies of the party and enemies of law and order. He had also attacked the author of this book, singling him out for a celebrated sobriquet, that of a "Blow-In." *The Irish Press* referred to this speech at some length.

But there was something much more substantial hanging over Jack Lynch. In electoral terms the real nub of what he faced, at the beginning of that crucial 1977 election, was the electoral map. To conform with the Constitution and electoral law in respect of the ratio between voters and seats in the Dáil, the constituency boundaries had been redrawn and the number of seats revised.

In his first, page-one article on the campaign for *The Irish Press*, Michael Mills assessed the circumstances that had been created by the Minister for Local Government, Jim Tully, in the electoral legislation. In Mills's opinion, what was perhaps unjustly condemned as a gerrymander (nicknamed a "Tullymander"), namely the revision of seats suggested, was bad news for Fianna Fáil. On his reckoning, and on the basis of the 1973 vote, the party could lose four seats in the country, and two or more in Dublin.

What Tully had done was in strict conformity with the constitutional requirements for the ratio between voters and representatives, but, cleverly, he had altered the sizes of constituencies. He had done this in favour of the two parties in power acting together and transferring their votes. An obvious example was in the strategy adopted towards a number of Dublin constituencies. The Minister had flexibility within the large concentration of population to create a number of three-seat constituencies. If the votes for Fine Gael and Labour were sustained, the parties in power would take two seats out of three. Given that the National Coalition partners were fighting the election together on their record, an even better transfer result might reasonably be expected. By introducing a number of three-seaters and five-seaters where the population allowed this Jim Tully had, in the process, made it more difficult for Fianna Fáil to win.

Jack Lynch was the pivot of political action. In stark terms, his leadership was on the line in the general election. In the previous Dáil he had contemplated retirement, but went on into the 1977 election for the sake of the party and because the only leadership choice was the old choice – present in Fianna Fáil since Lemass's departure in 1966 – between George Colley and Charles Haughey. Lynch favoured a younger man. His choice at the time would have been Desmond O'Malley, but a further period in power, which would give the younger candidate experience and the chance to develop a power-base, was necessary.

Broadly speaking, the general election outcome, from the very beginning, depended on Jack Lynch's personal stature. All eyes were on his capacity to fight effectively throughout the gruelling three-week period. He had to maximise the Fianna Fáil vote in every part of the country so as to turn on its head the overall constituency circumstances loaded against him and Fianna Fáil by Jim Tully.

The announcement of election programmes followed immediately on the dissolution. I had suggested to the editor of the *Irish Independent* that I would write an "Election Diary" throughout the campaign, and the first one dealt with the Fianna Fáil manifesto. I found both the document and the performance of the party's Front Bench spokesmen – there were no women – "uneven". More important by far was the perception I had of Jack Lynch as an "isolated leader at the outset of the toughest campaign of his political career, and one on which that career now depends". He seemed on that occasion detached from the triple ranks of Fianna Fáil's undoubtedly powerful team of experienced and determined politicians, who were ranged behind him for the launch of the document.

> They did not seem entirely with him. The fault is neither theirs nor his. Time has isolated Jack Lynch. The burden of leadership has set him apart. Eleven years, during which he has repeatedly been forced to open the eyes of Fianna Fáil to the reality of a changing Ireland, have taken a steady toll on the relationship between himself and those closest to him. And now the realisation within the party that its biggest single asset at the moment lies in the person of Jack Lynch has added a further dimension between himself and the rest. Though many are fiercely loyal to him, as well as being effective in their own right as Front Bench spokesmen, the battle on which Jack Lynch embarked, with the launching of the election manifesto, is largely a battle which he will fight on his own.[1]

---

[1] *Irish Independent*, Friday, 27th May 1977. This "Election Diary" appeared daily throughout the campaign, usually on page one or the back page. That isolation, and the way he filled the political space around him, marked the whole campaign and gave to his performance its heroic stature.

To Jack Lynch, the sporting comparison evoked by those inescapable preliminaries of any election, including the manifesto presentation, would have seemed like the stepping out of two hurling teams prior to a game: it was a ritual, a display of wares, not seriously material to the game itself. Fianna Fáil has often been blamed for "buying" the 1977 general election; notable among the commitments used in evidence is the abolition of rates, which had been proposed by Fianna Fáil before the previous election and dismissed as eve-of-poll insanity at the time. Yet the Coalition proposed the same thing in its 1977 programme: the abolition of the rates. They combined it with an uncosted programme of objectives, outlined in general terms, and containing plans for the establishment of a controversial National Development Corporation, which seemed to be in the programme more to satisfy the Labour Party than to present a new dynamo for economic progress.

The reality was that the two coalition parties were standing on their record. The 1973 Fourteen-Point Programme for Government, which had been hastily grafted together when Jack Lynch had dissolved the Dáil in February of that year, had served the partners reasonably well. Garret FitzGerald, the Foreign Minister, reckoned that they had delivered 85 per cent of their promises and this position, shared with carefully presented detail by other Ministers and by Liam Cosgrave himself, represented a compelling agenda for the days of campaigning which lay ahead.

The four years from 1973 to 1977 had been difficult. Though the country was moving towards a recovery, the oil crisis, high inflation and widespread unemployment earlier in the period had left their mark and made the Cosgrave-led team of Ministers vulnerable to attack. Jack Lynch initiated this on the first Saturday at the opening Fianna Fáil election campaign for the city of Dublin, held in the Metropolitan Hall in Lower Abbey Street. He challenged Liam Cosgrave to meet him and debate the issues on television. It was an innovative move; no such exchange between political leaders had taken place during any previous general election, though it would later become commonplace. Lynch knew he had the edge over Cosgrave, who was a far less relaxed man and prone to excitement in his off-the-cuff remarks. Cosgrave turned down the challenge.

The opening rally for Dublin, attended by all the candidates for the city constituencies, was an impressive occasion for Fianna Fáil. Jack Lynch was far better prepared for the election than anyone had anticipated. The party had accurately anticipated the date on which Cosgrave would call the election and had planned for it. No-one is clear on the reasons for the choice, though it did fit in with Fianna Fáil's own assessment of the best use of surprise. Unfortunately for the National Coalition, Cosgrave appeared to have shocked his own side more than the opposition. Whatever the reasoning, Jack Lynch and his party came out fighting on a platform that was detailed and effective.

Well before the election, Lynch had approved the establishment of two separate committees. The first was responsible for policy and involved members of the front bench. The key figures were George Colley and Desmond O'Malley, with other spokesmen called in for their expertise. The second committee was organisational and effectively took control of managing the election. It was headed by Eoin Ryan. He was a senator with a lifetime involvement in Fianna Fáil. Like his father, James Ryan, he had become a father figure of the party. This second committee included the Fianna Fáil team of Martin O'Donoghue, Esmonde Smith, Séamus Brennan and Michael Yeats. Yeats had an important role, acting as liaison with Jack Lynch.

Well before the election, Eoin Ryan had realised that the party's usual public relations arrangements, which had in the past been handled exclusively by the firm of O'Kennedy Brindley, would be insufficient for the forthcoming campaign. Two other agencies were taken on for specific projects. Peter Owen was to handle all issues relating to women, and Des O'Meara and Partners had responsibility for Youth Affairs. This was all part of the party's decision to launch on the electorate further "secret weapons" by targeting the youth vote and the women's vote.

At least 330,000 new voters were on the register. This was in part the result of the reduction in the voting age from twenty-one to eighteen. The vast majority of these new voters were under twenty-five years of age, and their support was clearly significant. Additionally, the 1970s had already seen a good deal of work aimed at bringing women more directly into the political process. This was addressed by Fianna Fáil with a countrywide distribution of T-shirts to women and girls bearing the slogan, "Bring Back Jack!" The young Mary Harney campaigned on this front. Without making a psychological or moral meal of it, Jack Lynch was inherently sympathetic to the participation of women in public life.

Liam Cosgrave, in contrast, was not. A more serious issue affecting women was the controversial and unresolved matter of contraception. Without telling colleagues, Liam Cosgrave had himself voted against his own administration's legislation, which had been designed to legislate for the availability of contraceptive devices. He had helped to bring about the Bill's defeat. He had also indicated that no change to this situation was envisaged by the coalition partners.

Mistakenly, as it was to turn out, the Taoiseach, Liam Cosgrave, failed to bring a woman into his own team in Dun Laoghaire. A powerful worker within the Women's Political Association there, Monica Barnes, was attempting to get the nomination. Instead, two poor vote-getters, both men, in the Fine Gael establishment were chosen to fight with Cosgrave. Another woman candidate with a good record in the women's movement was Nuala Fennell. She was later to become a Fine Gael member and then a Minister under Garret FitzGerald, but in 1977 she entered the election as an independent. Jack Lynch, on the other hand, brought in six women candidates in key constituencies.

*

Fianna Fáil had prepared for the election with great care. A year before, under George Colley's chairmanship, the election committee concerned with policy had been set up and had met on a weekly basis, preparing the manifesto and election strategy generally. On Colley's recommendation, Eoin Ryan was appointed director of elections.

From the first day, posters, car stickers and other election literature were ready for immediate distribution. Advertisements for the press, radio and television had been vetted, changed and refined. Séamus Brennan, at twenty-nine remarkably young to be the party's general secretary, had seen how important the youth vote was likely to be now with the voting age reduced. He was responsible for the emphasis in the election programme on attracting young voters.

The party maintained a regular private polling of the electorate and found that support, well before the election, was running very steadily at over fifty per cent. It stayed at that level. The organisation committee responded carefully to its findings. When these showed a fall in support on a single issue, such as health or agriculture, the party machine issued compensating speeches, advertisements or statements. Eoin Ryan recalls the remarkable effect this had. Within three or four days of such action, support for the party on the issue would be restored. Jack Lynch himself stayed clear of the detailed work of preparation. His programme was simple and straightforward – virtually a non-stop tour of the country, managed separately by Eoin Kenny. This started on the day following the launch of the party's election manifesto. Thereafter, it was Jack Lynch's normal practice to keep in contact by phone, though not necessarily on a daily basis. He would discuss his own programme with Ryan or other members of the organisation committee and be briefed on the overall situation. His main task was simply to get on with meeting people and address the many public meetings on his schedule. He brought a natural charm to this task from the outset. There was nothing artificial in his warmth of manner. At the same time, it was combined with a sense of purpose and a political direction. Every town in Ireland wanted him to visit and Lynch was tireless in trying to meet that demand.

He barnstormed his way around County Kildare on the day following the manifesto launch. This county was a marginal constituency where Fianna Fáil badly needed to win two seats.[2] It was the first stop in a gruelling, 3,000-mile schedule of campaign visits that had been announced to the press and he demonstrated, in carefully prepared brief speeches on campaign issues, that Jack Lynch's personal approach went beyond the usual "pressing the flesh" form of campaigning. Pushing a woman's baby carriage across the main street of Kildare town under the admiring eye of the Labour Party candidate in Dublin, Dr John O'Connell, Lynch demonstrated the apotheosis of normal campaigning into a form of political magic. It expressed his great experience of three elections as party leader. One of the most important lessons for survival on the campaign trail was also one of the simplest: how to shake hands. Anyone who shook Jack

---

2 Charlie McCreevy won a second seat in Kildare at the expense of Fine Gael, who lost their representation in the constituency. Paddy Power took the first seat, and Joe Bermingham of Labour the third.

Lynch's hand never forgot the hard, powerful grip and the ridge of muscle that ran along the top edge of the palm and forefinger. A legacy of sport as much as of political handshaking, his grip was a memorable experience that totally belied the soft smile and the warm expression of greeting given in his Cork accent. But even Jack Lynch admitted that his arms became sore after the thousands of handshakes, together with the back-slaps and the jostling from enthusiastic crowds. "It is important that you grasp the other person high up on the hand first and take the outside grip. Otherwise you could have the arm pumped off you."

*

At the end of that first week, Conor Cruise O'Brien, who had been one of the more controversial Ministers in the administration, launched a strong attack on Charles Haughey, saying that he was "a dangerous force" and that there was still "a lot of mystery about him". Haughey's return to the Fianna Fáil Front Bench two years earlier and the possibility of his serving in a Fianna Fáil Government, if the party won the election, would represent a threat to Northern Ireland. O'Brien rated the policies of Fianna Fáil on the North and those of the Provisional IRA as much the same. These views were published in *The Times*, broadcast on BBC and then carried by RTÉ, and provoked a swift rebuttal by Haughey.

Haughey was clearly a weak link in the Fianna Fáil election programme. He had been denied the key position of director of elections, which had gone to Eoin Ryan, but there was no doubting the fact that his Northern Ireland republican militancy and questions about his remarkable wealth would be repeated during the campaign.

At the end of the first week Jack Lynch was in Kerry. The large county contained two three-seat constituencies, in each of which Fianna Fáil was targeting two seats. The election had been fought in fine weather up to that point. The Friday was warm and sunny, the county crowded with tourists, and Lynch enjoyed a festive circuit of the Ring of Kerry, stopping at Cahirciveen, Waterville, Sneem, Kenmare and Killorglin. He concluded the day with rallies in Killarney and Tralee. Stephen O'Byrnes, reporting for *The Irish Press*, said of the Killarney meeting:

> Cruise O'Brien bashing was certainly the order of the evening and his name certainly replaced Mr Cosgrave's infamous 'blow-ins' remark as the suitable warming up cry for the hustings in South Kerry.

One of the Fianna Fáil Kerry south candidates, Timothy "Chubb" O'Connor, "said that Dr Cruise O'Brien was anti-Irish and pro-British and another speaker from the platform described the Minister for Posts and Telegraphs as a 'West Briton'."[3]

---

[3] *The Irish Press*, Saturday, 4th June 1977, p. 4.

Jack Lynch carefully avoided making any criticism of what was already a controversial and bitter theme in the campaign, and concentrated on positive aspects, committing himself, when in Government, to the creation of jobs for the county. What Conor Cruise O'Brien had attempted to do was to use the suspect past behaviour of Charles Haughey, and especially his attempt to import arms illegally, in order to suggest that Fianna Fáil would not be trustworthy on national security. He had also attacked Haughey's unexplained wealth, suggesting by his criticism that financial corruption was inextricably part of the Fianna Fáil culture. They were in power for what they could get. Charles Haughey was a leading contender to take over from Jack Lynch in due course. It was a prophetic judgement, subsequently vindicated in startling and explicit terms by the McCracken and Moriarty tribunals at the end of the century. But that was a lifetime away.

The electorate in 1977, although it had good reason to see the logic of Conor Cruise O'Brien's arguments, valued at the same time Lynch's leadership as a safeguard against such an occurrence. Many people shared O'Brien's fears of a takeover within Fianna Fáil by those who sought to use the party to gain wealth for themselves. They feared also that there were people within the party who might seek to use it to assist militant republican objectives in Northern Ireland. Yet it was precisely for these reasons that Fianna Fáil supporters, as well as uncertain voters who had lost confidence in the Coalition, favoured Jack Lynch. He was beyond challenge within his own organisation. He stood head and shoulders above everyone in the Fianna Fáil party.

*

Sunday 5th June was really the mid-point in the campaign, and commentators were expressing surprise at how weak the National Coalition had been so far. Joseph O'Malley, in *The Sunday Independent*, wrote of them having "a disastrous start", being badly organised and badly co-ordinated. He gave examples of how they were "more surprised and less ready for the electoral battle than Fianna Fáil". The manifesto was hastily drafted, did not add up, was in other respects inaccurate, and the electoral strategy had become one of defensive arguments with the thrust of action dictated by Fianna Fáil.[4] The same view was held by Chris Glennon, political correspondent of the *Irish Independent*, and by Michael Mills, who held the same job in *The Irish Press*. Writing the following day, both referred to the gap closing between the two sides.

Then Liam Cosgrave developed laryngitis and withdrew from active campaigning. He was to remain out of the picture for three or four days, prompting adverse comment about his determination for the fight. His speeches were delivered by his son. Conor Cruise O'Brien attacked journalists for predicting a

---

[4] Joseph O'Malley, "Election Special", *The Sunday Independent*, 5th June 1977.

swing towards Fianna Fáil in the campaign. Mills responded to this with an article in *The Irish Press* suggesting that Fianna Fáil, both in urban and rural constituencies, was experiencing growing support in its canvass. The party had undoubtedly a higher public profile, with a countrywide poster campaign, much bigger and more successful electoral rallies, and a relentless tour through the west of Ireland by the party leader, who was warmly received everywhere. Jack Lynch kept entirely clear of the controversial exchanges initiated by Conor Cruise O'Brien's attacks on Charles Haughey and, by implication, on the integrity of Fianna Fáil.

In the final few days of the campaign, the main focus became Dublin, where the struggle involved forty-three seats, a little over a quarter of the total. Fianna Fáil had conducted a successful canvass in the city and the Coalition had responded with a housing-and-jobs package, and the promise of several new hospitals. This was effectively turned against them. Two days later Jack Lynch responded at a press conference on the final Saturday in the campaign:

> Last Thursday's so-called unveiling of a plan for Dublin showed, in my view, that the Coalition had conceded defeat and were playing in panic their only remaining option, a cheap cosmetic cover-up to be backed by one of the most panic-stricken, last-minute publicity efforts ever seen in a General Election.[5]

It was a bullish, fighting final statement as the country entered the climax of the campaign. Michael Mills's front page article that morning in *The Irish Press* gave details of an opinion poll carried out on behalf of the Coalition showing Fianna Fáil and the government parties neck-and-neck. The National Coalition still enjoyed the potential advantage of the re-drawing of the constituencies, particularly the creation of the new three-seaters. It was clear indeed, in these closing stages, that the two sides were running neck and neck; Fianna Fáil having the longer neck.

*

Fianna Fáil suffered an electoral embarrassment during that final week. James Gallagher, a former Dáil deputy in Sligo-Leitrim and a candidate trying to regain a second and marginal seat for the party, publicly promised to work for the abolition of the Offences Against the State Act. This was the main piece of security legislation and the cornerstone of the Coalition's package brought in after the assassination of the British ambassador, Christopher Ewart-Biggs by the IRA. Its repeal had been part of the election platform of Neil Blaney, expelled from Fianna Fáil at Jack Lynch's insistence in 1971 and now running as an independent.

---

[5] Author's Archive.

It was a sensitive issue. Fianna Fáil had successfully kept the campaign clear of the related matters of national security and Northern Ireland. Not a line in the press conference statement on the Saturday, 11th June referred to either. Now Lynch was forced to condemn publicly this candidate and to reiterate party support for a form of legislation first introduced by Fianna Fáil and still regarded as essential in the fight against subversion.

Garret FitzGerald chose the occasion to warn voters that within six months Charles Haughey could well be leader of Fianna Fáil and Taoiseach. Conor Cruise O'Brien renewed his attacks on Fianna Fáil's record on Northern Ireland, condemning the central plank of policy, namely a British withdrawal. Joseph O'Malley, writing in *The Sunday Independent*, described the Gallagher affair as "a blunder that could be fatal for Fianna Fáil".

Yet the reality was extraordinary and could best be characterised by a witticism that at this late stage was repeated in a column by Vincent Browne: "The election caught the Government by surprise."[6] The significant advantage of being able to choose the date for dissolution and of preparing for it with policies, legislative and administrative decisions, and all the tactical and strategic provisions that a general election demands, had been squandered. The two parties in Government had entered the campaign riding on their record and on the supposed copper-fastening of the constituencies in their favour by the Jim Tully legislation. There had been no provision for any contingency, however modest or mediocre.

What then met them was a campaign by Fianna Fáil that was quite unprecedented both for its brilliance in delivery and the detail that had been put into it. Their manifesto took the Government entirely by surprise. On top of all this, the performance on the hustings by Jack Lynch was nearly flawless. No coalition politician could match him. His country-wide tour had gone without a hitch, and he was still moving from place to place displaying an easy, relaxed charm and a good deal of humour. In Tipperary, Cork's great rival in Lynch's own sporting days, he was photographed hitting a ball with a hurling stick that had been presented to him.

He also had more serious things to say. In Limerick, on the night of Monday 13th June with just two campaigning days left, Lynch appealed to his audience for three seats and said that, if he got them, he would let the local representative, Des O'Malley, take over as party leader. He predicted a Fianna Fáil victory and a majority of 6 seats. He went on the offensive again, accusing the Coalition of using security to divert public attention from the real issues of unemployment, inflation and taxation. If there was any justification for security doubts about Fianna Fáil, the same applied to the Coalition. Lynch did not go into detail, but Desmond O'Malley, who had been Justice Minister in the wake of the Arms Crisis and was noted for his firm stand on the State's security, named deputies

---

6 Quoted by Vincent Browne, *The Sunday Independent*, 12th June 1977.

such as Stephen Coughlan and David Thornley, who had shown public support for the Provisional IRA.

The Ministers in the National Coalition held a final election press conference in the Shelbourne Hotel on the Tuesday. It was headed by the Taoiseach. Brendan Corish, the Labour leader, and both Garret FitzGerald and Conor Cruise O'Brien, largely responsible for making security a contentious issue during the final week, had things to say about the relative positions of the two sides in the election. Cruise O'Brien admitted Labour had been wrong to oppose the Offences Against the State legislation and expressed his own regret.

It was a lacklustre occasion. Cosgrave predicted "a comfortable majority" but no one knew whether to believe him. The problem was that the campaign had gone in favour of Jack Lynch and Fianna Fáil, but the constituencies were still seen as presenting problems in the way of achieving an overall Dáil majority. This uncertainty was widely reflected in the final pre-election pieces by political commentators. Although some of them had spent some time on the ground with Jack Lynch during his campaigning, they had for the most part been based in Dublin and not fully aware of the universal high regard with which the Fianna Fáil leader had been greeted wherever he went. The reality, at that final press conference, was that virtually no one really believed that Lynch could win. The "Tullymander" generally and the three-seaters in Dublin were seen still as favouring the return of the two parties in power.

It was meant to be a euphoric affair. Members of the press were met with wine and smoked salmon. I offered one colleague an evens bet of five pounds that Fianna Fáil would win more seats than the National Coalition. Rather patronisingly, the wager was accepted. A senior figure in Fine Gael, hearing of it, offered to take more money from me. He was particularly amused at the idea I expressed that Fianna Fáil might take second seats in Kildare and in Tipperary north. In the afternoon I laid out ten pounds in a branch of Terry Rogers at four-to-one that Fianna Fáil would win more seats than the two coalition parties: such were the odds against Lynch.

*

The Coalition had favoured the broad-based approach of putting forward the majority of its electoral team at the end of the campaign; the Fianna Fáil focus was on Jack Lynch himself. Stephen O'Byrnes, who had followed Lynch throughout the general election campaign, wrote at the end:

> One is impressed above all with the enormous personal popularity of the man. Perhaps it is due to the absence of multi-channel television from most of the western half of the country, but the turnouts and the sheer adulation of the crowds ... were quite flabbergasting. And the sheer excitement of the turnouts on the Corpus Christi Holy Day last Thursday in North Clare, at places like Corofin and Ennistymon and Ardrahan in South Galway seemed from an age which one would have thought was long

gone. There were the traditional musicians and dancers. Everywhere the greetings were in Irish, hurleys were waved, there were wild shouts and the odd bonfire blazing along the road.[7]

O'Byrnes made the point that Jack Lynch's campaign speeches had avoided attacking the Coalition and concentrated simply on the main features of the Fianna Fáil manifesto, what they meant and how much they would cost. Remarkably, said O'Byrnes, he would follow several local speakers and, though he would often speak for thirty minutes, he would hold his audience silent and attentive to what he was telling them. He controlled the excitement and seemed to be able to choose from the party's programme precisely those things that would have the right appeal. For the market town, agricultural issues and the need to repeal taxation on the co-operatives were put forward. For the larger urban centres, the emphasis was on jobs, prices and a future for young people. In the Border counties, the Fianna Fáil party's goal of reunification was still such, but was to be achieved by peaceful means.

Lynch had been determined throughout to win. That capacity in him to be tough, uncompromising and extremely competitive, identified by his team mate, Con Murphy, on the hurling field thirty five years before, and summarised in one phrase – "I never really saw him beaten" – was fully expressed in that 1977 general election performance. He had become invincible. Yet there was in his whole approach a gentleness and sensitivity expressed in the capacity O'Byrnes recorded: "He would often stop the motorcade at crossroads or in small villages to shake hands and exchange words with the small groups out in the fine weather."[8]

> And when all the campaigning and vote-wooing is over, the abiding memory will be of the affinity that so many people in every corner of the country feel for Jack Lynch – and not just the more impetuous that rush forward at every gathering. There were the ordinary, even shy people, who came out and waited quietly to shake the man's hand and wish him well.[9]

The result was a landslide victory for Fianna Fáil. The party won 84 seats. The combined coalition parties took 60, which included that of the outgoing Ceann Comhairle, Seán Treacy of Labour. Four seats were won by independent deputies. The marginals went to Fianna Fáil and the Dublin three-seaters also went mainly two-to-one in its favour. It was unprecedented, the greatest majority ever won in the State's history, and a surprise to the whole population. Three senior Ministers in the outgoing administration, Conor Cruise O'Brien, Justin Keating and Patrick Cooney, lost their seats.

Liam Cosgrave conceded defeat at 9.15 p.m. on the Friday night, well before the count was over. The front page of *The Irish Times* on the following morning

---

[7] Stephen O'Byrnes, *The Irish Press*, Thursday 16th June 1977, p. 1.
[8] *Ibid.*
[9] Stephen O'Byrnes, *The Irish Press*, Thursday, 16 June 1977.

carried a photograph of a relaxed Jack Lynch, pipe in mouth, watching the Cosgrave announcement on television. Some time after midnight on Saturday, Lynch made an announcement that the undertakings given by Fianna Fáil would be implemented as promised and that the essential decisions by the Coalition would be honoured. The programme for jobs and prices would follow without delay. Garret FitzGerald expressed confidence that Jack Lynch's approach on Northern Ireland would be consistent with what the Coalition had done.

There was total surprise in Britain at the election outcome. The British press had confidently predicted otherwise. Westminster had misgivings, despite the record of co-operation when Lynch had last been in power. What worried British Ministers was the changed Fianna Fáil policy on Northern Ireland. In opposition, the party had called for a British declaration of intent to withdraw. There was no possibility of Lynch sustaining this approach in Government. But misgivings there were. A shadow, of small proportions but persistent, hung over the future.

CHAPTER TWELVE

"Steadfast and loyal support"

– Jack Lynch's resignation statement

Jack Lynch returned to power totally in command of his party and of the country. He had spent four years and three months in opposition. He was elected Taoiseach when the Twenty-First Dáil assembled, on 5th July 1977, by 82 votes to 61. He appointed George Colley as Tánaiste and made him Minister for Finance and the Public Service. It placed Colley in the main line of succession. Charles Haughey, who was next in seniority among Ministers, was given Health and Social Welfare. It represented a large area of responsibility and included, in the short term, the issue of the legalising of contraception which had been mishandled by the National Coalition and then abandoned.

Brian Lenihan went to Fisheries, something of a demotion in light of portfolios he had held in earlier administrations (embracing Education, Justice, Transport and Power and Foreign Affairs). Pádraig Faulkner, a close and trusted, if underrated, colleague of Lynch's, was appointed to Tourism and Transport as well as Posts and Telegraphs. James Gibbons was restored to a major Department, that of Agriculture. Another highly important and central responsibility, for Industry, Commerce and Energy, was given to Desmond O'Malley. In personal terms he was closer to Lynch than any other member of the Government.

Gerard Collins had first joined the Government under Lynch at the time of the dismissal of Blaney and Haughey, and had served as Minister for Posts and Telegraphs. He was now appointed to the Department of Justice. Michael O'Kennedy, who had served briefly during the final four months of the outgoing Lynch Government of 1973, was made Minister for Foreign Affairs.

The remaining five members of the Government had no previous ministerial experience. Sylvester Barrett had been a deputy since 1968 and was given the Department of the Environment. Gene Fitzgerald, first elected at a by-election in Cork in 1972, was made Minister for Labour. Denis Gallagher, first elected in 1973, was Minister for the Gaeltacht; and John Wilson, also first elected in 1973, became Minister for Education. Finally, Martin O'Donoghue was not only appointed to the Government on his first day as a deputy, but was given a new ministry, that of Economic Planning and Development. Anthony J. Hederman was made Attorney General and there were seven Parliamentary Secretaries whose status was raised to that of Minister of State through legislation introduced in November of that year.

Lynch's eleven nominees to the Senate included three who had worked on the organisational committee for the 1977 general election. These were Séamus Brennan, Michael Yeats and Noel Mulcahy. Lynch nominated three women to the Senate, Mary Harney, who had been a Fianna Fáil candidate in the election, Lady Valerie Goulding and Eileen Cassidy.

In preparing his list of nominees, Jack Lynch decided to offer a Senate seat to Dr T.K. Whitaker. He reached him in the west of Ireland by telephone. Whitaker, at first, said that he could not accept. He felt that his role as a public servant precluded his taking the Fianna Fáil whip in the Senate. Lynch said it was not his intention to have him there in the party interest. He wanted him as an independent Senator, free to speak his mind on any issue and not tied in any way to voting for the party. On this undertaking, Whitaker agreed to the appointment. There was one other independent Senator, Gordon Lambert, a businessman and art collector.

Whitaker was grateful for the terms of his appointment – the first nomination of a public servant to the Senate – since he found himself crossing swords with the new administration on more than one issue. Though he had been responsible for suggesting Martin O'Donoghue as economic adviser to Jack Lynch in 1970, he did not approve of the economic strategy that had been promised in the general election and was now in process of being implemented. It was, he thought, illusory and dangerous to attempt to reach full employment in a few years on the back of heavy foreign borrowing.

Nor did Whitaker approve of the new Department of Economic Planning and Development to be headed by O'Donoghue. A lifetime in the Department of Finance, where he had been largely responsible for economic planning and fiscal strategy, had left him cool about fundamentally reorganising those functions which had proved their worth over several decades. He made his views clear when the Senate debated the necessary legislation for setting up the new Department. He did so without any reflection on the personal abilities of those involved, describing both George Colley and Martin O'Donoghue as assets in any Government.

Essentially, what Whitaker wanted to see was a Department of Finance confirmed and strengthened in its developmental responsibilities. What he actually did see before him was a plan that had been constructed as part of an electoral strategy, without the benefit of the views of the Department of Finance and without sufficient regard to economic fundamentals.

In face of a universal electoral largesse of extensive proportions, financed largely out of foreign borrowing, the new Senator put forward some sober observations about the real conditions of economic development. A comprehensive set of policies needed to be consistent with the available resources, to be integrated in a fair and balanced way, and to be so arranged that they would cover an appreciable period of time. This Whitaker put at four to five years. Most importantly, they should be proposed in a format that allowed for consultation with the major economic and social interests.

What had happened was the reverse of this. The election had been won on a platform of promises that were controversial during the campaign and became more so as the serious business of government was undertaken. There was something quite pointed in Whitaker's Senate speech when he welcomed Martin O'Donoghue's undertaking about involving the social and economic interests:

> I was glad to hear the Minister say tonight that that sort of consultation is intended. This would mean that, in advance of the final settlement of a plan and its presentation to the Dáil, objectives of social and economic policy would be considered under the compulsion of necessary choice between alternatives. Since scarcity still obtains, this choice between alternatives is imperative.[1]

He warned that if this was not the case, the proposed plan "might merely express wishful thinking and irreconcilable desires and a lack of consensus would in any event tear it apart". There was, he said, a significant difference between a plan and a pre-election manifesto.

Whitaker tried in his Senate contribution on that occasion to be both positive and realistic. He spoke as though the circumstances of what was being proposed were open to the kinds of amendments that he viewed as essential. He gave good advice in pointing out that there was a limit on what governments could, or should, try to do. "There are limitations to government action in the economic and social fields. Indeed, it could be said that governments tend at times to assume management responsibilities beyond their capacity." In the present situation there was the added handicap of power resting with the Department of Finance, while advice could come only from the Department of Economic Planning and Development. He described George Colley as the "performer on the field of play" while Martin O'Donoghue was giving advice and encouragement from the sidelines.

The whole speech, though cast in positive terms, and including a wish that the new structure would not fail, was a well reasoned and comprehensive criticism of what the Government had done. It did no damage to the personal friendship between Whitaker and Lynch but it did emphasise the difficulties that had been created by the election programme.

Martin O'Donoghue responded to the implied criticism of the way things had been done by preparing an economic White Paper, *National Development 1977–1980*. This was published in January 1978. It was followed by another economic White Paper, *National Development 1979–1981*; this was published in January 1979. There were encouraging signs of economic co-operation in the commitment by the Irish Congress of Trade Unions to a wages agreement, and this helped to bring to an end two long-running strikes, those of Aer Lingus and of Post Office workers in May 1978.

Whitaker's words were also reflected in the characters and political strengths of the two new leaders who emerged out of the ruins of the defeated coalition parties. Liam Cosgrave had abruptly resigned as leader of Fine Gael on the

---

[1] Speech by T.K. Whitaker to the Senate, 23rd November 1977. The speech is printed, virtually in full, in T.K. Whitaker, *Interests* (I.P.A., Dublin, 1983), pp. 169–175.

Thursday after the election. He was only 57. The meeting to choose a successor was fixed for Friday, 1st July, and though Peter Barry attracted some party support, in the end the choice of Garret FitzGerald was agreed without any vote. FitzGerald was a leader of towering intellect and great integrity, and he had the distinct advantage, in the immediate political circumstances, of being an able economist.

Brendan Corish had resigned as leader of the Labour Party the previous Sunday, and the election to replace him occurred on the same day. Frank Cluskey, a rugged, no-nonsense, working-class Dublin man with a background in trade unionism, was elected to lead Labour. He had a caustic manner, a rare turn of wit, and dogged persistence as a parliamentarian.

Together, Cluskey and FitzGerald represented precisely the economic and social penetration and the judgement needed to confront the new Government. They measured accurately the gap between the vast promises that had been made by Jack Lynch and his team, and set to work to criticise and oppose. Both men not infrequently acknowledged that the task, which should have been comparatively easy in objective terms, was made much more difficult by the immense popularity of Jack Lynch. On economic issues, which of course became central in the light of the election manifesto promises, the confrontation was between them and Lynch's lieutenants. They turned their attention to others, notably George Colley, Martin O'Donoghue and Desmond O'Malley. Lynch, with his own position so strong, presided at times like some relaxed giant over the numerical supremacy that made their task so difficult.

Northern Ireland was in a state of military constraint; its bitter existence punctuated by outrages such as the La Mon Hotel bomb in February 1978 in which sixteen people were killed. Political initiative was at a low ebb. The British Prime Minister, Jim Callaghan, and the Secretary of State, Roy Mason, were facing an election in which the main policy emphasis was on security. This was also the underlying principle for Margaret Thatcher at the time. Jack Lynch, not an initiator, found himself in the unusual position of being informed of views and attitudes about the North by the opposition leader, Garret FitzGerald, who said of the period:

> Throughout these years from 1977 to 1979 I kept in close touch with Jack Lynch on Northern Ireland affairs. While there were, inevitably, some differences in emphasis between our approaches, we were much closer in our views than he was to the 'rhetorical republicans' in his own party, some of whom had forced on him in 1975 a shift towards the 'British withdrawal' theme from which he was clearly most anxious to pull back. I knew that so long as he was in charge any information I passed on as a result of my contacts in Northern Ireland or with British politicians would be used for constructive purposes, and accordingly I kept the Department of Foreign Affairs, and, where appropriate, Jack himself, fully informed of anything I learnt on these matters.[2]

---

[2] Garret FitzGerald, *All in a Life: an Autobiography* (Gill and Macmillan, Dublin, 1991), p. 331.

Politically, it was an extraordinary relationship, involving genuine friendship with genuine admiration. As well as Northern Ireland, Garret FitzGerald, who was indefatigable on every issue, gave helpful advice to Lynch on Europe and on Ireland's diplomatic representation in the United States. He persuaded Lynch to appoint Seán Donlon to be ambassador in Washington. Donlon, who had been with Lynch on the visit to New York when the verdict in the Arms Trial came through, was a formidable figure. He joined Michael Lillis in the Washington embassy. Lillis had developed excellent contacts on Capitol Hill, and the two men formed a powerful team.

Jack Lynch imbued in FitzGerald, as he did in so many other politicians, an admiration for his reliability and his judgement. His leadership, both in power and in opposition, had been uncompromisingly for the country's benefit. He had disciplined his own party with rigour and courage. He had confronted the problem of Northern Ireland and the difficulties of working with four different British administrations and even more Northern Ireland Secretaries of State. The policy that he had fashioned was one of consensus. He sought it in the North. He sought it with and within the United Kingdom. Most important of all, he had achieved it among the main Irish political parties.

Without the help of history he had become as much a father figure to the Irish nation as Éamon de Valera. Without it being apparent at all, he seemed to have become invincible. He was similarly perceived by the media. Yet that unassailability, so powerful a weapon on behalf of the members of the party he led, was now to be undermined. Deliberately, conspiratorially, the enemies within regrouped and plotted Lynch's departure and replacement. The country was now to witness the steady undermining of his position. His decline during his final period in power represents a sad, even tragic, conclusion to a wonderful career. It was inspired by a disloyalty that cost the party dearly.

*

Jack Lynch had given hostages to fortune in the party's policies and its electoral promises. He had created difficulties within his own party by the size of the majority. Deputies had been elected in the most unlikely circumstances. The election of two out of three deputies in a three-seater constituency, where normal expectation would be for one Fianna Fáil victory out of three, made for hungry political mouths. The same was true in the five-seat constituencies, Carlow Kilkenny, Cavan-Monaghan, Cork City, Mid-Cork and Laois Offaly. There were even three four-seat constituencies where Fianna Fáil took three seats. Unsavoury jealousies between deputies who were ostensibly working together developed. There also emerged a group of deputies within Fianna Fáil who became susceptible to the argument that the party would need a new and dynamic leader if the vulnerable seats were to be made safe.

There was a persuasive background, however, to their flawed thesis. The economy began steadily to unravel. Wage awards exceeded the levels set by

Government. On its own 1978 could be judged a good year. At the end of it, Jack Lynch claimed in the closing Dáil adjournment debate, "when the House rises at the conclusion of this debate, it will do so at the end of one of the most successful periods on record for the Irish economy."

It might have been a timely moment for Jack Lynch to resign. Instead, he decided to complete the next year, which included in the second half the presidency of the European Community. It was to be an *annus horribilis*.

*

Early in March 1979 Lynch came home to Cork for the weekend, as usual a great relief. He often said, coming over Watergrass Hill, the sense of being back home swept over him. The difficulties of that year were already developing and Lynch was under pressure from industrial unrest – the first national postal strike had begun two weeks before – and from the agricultural sector where a 2 per cent levy had been imposed by George Colley. This was provoking mass protests from farmers. The car came down into the city and took the usual route along the quays beside the River Lee. John Kelleher had sold newspapers on the streets of Cork all his life. He spotted the Taoiseach's official car, as he usually did, and, with *The Cork Evening Echo* in his hand, knocked on the window. "I've bad news, Mr Lynch," he said. Lynch, resigned to political problems, replied "What's happening now?" "Christy Ring is dead." "That can't be," said Jack Lynch, falling back in his seat overcome by shock. John Kelleher noticed the face drained of blood, the yellow streaks under the eyes. He had given him the paper through the car window. The driver pulled away. Jack Lynch still held the 10p coin that he had forgotten to hand over.

The Government had to stand firm against the postal workers and did so. In the end the stance was justified and the unions climbed down. Nevertheless, the political damage was considerable, undermining confidence in what should have been a trouble-free period of economic progress. Wage restraint was the key to this. If it was to work, then some kind of parallel restraint by the farming community was required. But the farmers took grave exception to Colley's levy; as a result urban and rural discontent set the stage for the European elections in June.

Fianna Fáil did badly. Their share of the vote dropped from the 50.63 per cent that had given them the victory in the 1977 general election to 34.68 per cent. The party took only five of the fifteen seats. That granite-faced shadow over Jack Lynch's past, Neil Blaney, running as an independent, won a seat in Europe. The pattern of disaffection and disillusionment was also reflected in the local elections.

The party understandably held a post-mortem into the extraordinary about-face on the part of the electorate. Having enjoyed their sweep back into power just two years earlier, they were now faced, or so it seemed, with a potential wipe-out. Not surprisingly, the impact within Fianna Fáil caused members of the

214

party to focus on the leadership issue. Five men met on the night of that parliamentary party meeting. They were all on the back benches. Albert Reynolds, Tom McEllistrim, whose father had proposed Jack Lynch as leader of Fianna Fáil in 1966, Jackie Fahey, Seán Doherty and Mark Killilea came to be known as "The Gang of Five"; they began on that night to organise a change of leadership.

Their strategy was secretive and subtle. In the first instance, they decided to organise a "caucus meeting", different in character from the rather formal, staid and strictly controlled parliamentary party meetings. It was inevitable that any meeting of a group of Fianna Fáil deputies would become known to the party more generally; with this in mind, the intention was that the group would discuss issues of policy and the general direction of the party into the 1980s. It would *not* focus on the leadership question.[3]

The meeting on Tuesday, 3rd July 1979 was lively and well-attended, in marked contrast with the usual party gatherings. It did indeed deal with economic and social policy issues and with agriculture. There was an attempt by Paddy Power to raise the question of the leadership of the party but Jackie Fahey, who was chairing the meeting, ruled such discussion out. The group did debate more marginally on a question relating to the leadership: the question of Northern Ireland. The Republic, at the time, was seen widely as contributing more to British security requirements in the North than to any more positive initiatives, and there was some expression of the party's loss of its "republican image". The concerns of the debate were voiced with control and in general terms only. No overt challenge to Lynch was evident.

From that caucus meeting the architects of change read a mood in the party of unrest and potential disaffection. Though the debate had concentrated on policy issues, the underlying interest focused on the leadership. A dutiful succession allowing Jack Lynch to leave "in his own time" would not satisfy the concern of many deputies, who wanted to get on with the business of preparing for the next election under the man who would lead them into it. This mood was exacerbated by Lynch's own reaction to the caucus meeting. He expressed anger that it had taken place and unsuccessfully demanded at the next parliamentary party meeting the names of those who had attended.

> He was met by 'a wall of silence.' That factor, almost as much as the fact that the meeting took place, was an indication of the extent to which the Taoiseach had lost the support of the backbenchers even then.[4]

The caucus dissolved; it was clear there could be no repetition. But the Gang of Five worked on. Charles Haughey's own position was to remain neutral. He

---

[3] The members of "the Gang of Five" were all subsequently given appointments in Charles Haughey's first administration, Albert Reynolds as a member of the Government, the other four as junior ministers.

[4] *Magill* (January 1980), p. 34. "The Making of a Taoiseach" by Vincent Browne is the best account of the plotting against Jack Lynch, and the sequence of events during 1979.

increasingly presented himself as the new man who would bring radical and dynamic leadership, but he took no central part in the strategies of disaffection that punctuated that increasingly grim year.

The revolt itself was not untimely. The Dáil was two years into its term. If a new leader was to achieve the kind of status and the degree of momentum that would maintain Fianna Fáil in power for a new Dáil term, and moreover allow him to fill the shoes of a truly remarkable incumbent, then further delay seemed to many to be ill-judged. Yet delay, and a certain mood of self-protection, seized on those close to Lynch. George Colley acted the part of the favoured successor, though it is arguable that Jack Lynch would have preferred Desmond O'Malley as the next leader of Fianna Fáil.

Martin O'Donoghue was closest of all, as adviser, and did indeed keep Lynch informed about the mood within the party. The overall effect of these attitudes and positions being adopted was divisive. Haughey's close associates had created an atmosphere of uncertainty. Lynch's close supporters had responded with behaviour that indicated they were slightly under siege. The natural isolation of governments did the rest.

In August, Lord Mountbatten was murdered in Sligo. Lynch was on holiday in Portugal. He had indicated, before leaving, that he would return in the event of a crisis. Despite Mountbatten's position, as a member of the British royal family, the killing was not a crisis. The Earl had repeatedly ignored security advice not to visit his home at Classiebawn Castle on the west coast. However, to the public mind, faced with the shock of the carnage in the aftermath of the bombing of the Earl's boat at Mullaghmore, and then the pageantry of the funeral in London, which Lynch did attend, his coolness seemed misplaced and ill-judged. His enemies in the party covertly used it to infer a slackness on republicanism and a poor grasp of the implications of this violent act for the stalemate on Northern Ireland generally. Those of a quite different point of view thought Lynch was being less than positive about Anglo-Irish relations.

A month later Jack Lynch came under attack from an unlikely source and one that caused him some resentment. Síle de Valera, granddaughter of the party's founder, made a speech in Fermoy that implied the loss of Éamon de Valera's republican ideals within Fianna Fáil. With de Valera dead, and a clear claim to personal familiarity with his views and opinions, her words carried a degree of weight in excess of her political experience or known views. What she said was too vague to be contradicted, but it created confusion, and Jack Lynch over-reacted. He summoned her, went through the text of the speech with her, and told her he would prefer her to withdraw it but that he did not wish to censor what she wished to say. The matter came to the Dáil and further emphasised Fianna Fáil divisions.

It is not known how much Charles Haughey knew of the events of July to September, how much he was involved in the planning of them, nor how much of a conspiracy it all constituted. But immense care was taken with the plotting during the second half of 1979 and the intensity of energies concentrated by the

Gang of Five on efforts to remove Lynch as leader. The issue of how much Charles Haughey knew is a matter of judgement about his character. The plain fact about Haughey, then and later, was that he sought to know *everything*, and very little was voiced, threatened or done affecting him that he did not swiftly hear about from his group of followers.

The plotting followed a pre-arranged programme. After the caucus meeting, individual deputies from the Gang of Five identified and questioned members of the party, sounding out the degree of dissatisfaction of each and trying to identify where the emphasis lay, whether it was on leadership or policy issues. More specifically, was the support there for Charles Haughey? There was obviously no future for Haughey supporters among the conspirators if they achieved Jack Lynch's resignation only to see him replaced by George Colley.

Lynch did himself a disservice by coming to an agreement on security with Margaret Thatcher, the British Prime Minister. The Conservative Party victory in the British general election of May 1979 had been followed by security catastrophes, the death of Lord Mountbatten coinciding with the Warrenpoint slaughter of British soldiers by the IRA. After the funeral of Mountbatten in London, Lynch had held talks with Thatcher where the emphasis had understandably been on security co-operation. Out of this there emerged a proposal for an air corridor on the Border that would facilitate the British security forces in pursuit of terrorists. Objectively, and certainly in today's terms, this was unexceptional. But in the conspiratorial views of those seeking to undermine Lynch, it was presented as some kind of humiliating concession by the Irish Government.

The Gang of Five set to work to use the issue against Jack Lynch within the Fianna Fáil party. Tom McEllistrim tabled a motion in late October against the proposed air corridor. Lynch received it and sent it quite properly to the relevant Ministers: Collins (Justice), O'Kennedy (Foreign Affairs) and Molloy (Defence). The contents of the motion were leaked to the press. At the subsequent parliamentary party meeting, Lynch assured members that sovereignty was not being infringed and the rebels backed off. They were not ready for any kind of showdown and would certainly have lost on such an issue.

The party mood became more truculent, however, when Lynch went off to America on 7th November, leaving George Colley in charge. While in Washington he gave some details of the security arrangements made between himself and Margaret Thatcher, indicating slight alterations in air control regulations on Border and other over-flights. What he said seemed to be in conflict with his assertion to the Fianna Fáil party that sovereignty was not involved. This was challenged by a backbencher, William Loughnane. Colley, backed by the Government with two dissenting voices, Martin O'Donoghue and Charles Haughey, moved against Loughnane, seeking his expulsion. The party objected. A crisis developed and the party meeting held to resolve the matter dragged on and on. Eventually, a compromise statement emerged and the criticism of Jack Lynch by a very marginal backbencher was withdrawn.

Jack Lynch departed for the United States on polling day in the two by-elections in Cork city and Cork north east. He went as President of the European Community and was accompanied by William Shannon, the United States Ambassador to Dublin, and his wife Elizabeth. She recalls the terrible shock of the Cork by-election results in which both seats went to Fine Gael. "His face drained. He was pale and shaken. He told us he could not believe that his own beloved Cork could do this to him. It affected him deeply." He intimated that as far as he was concerned it was the end of his leadership. Lynch had canvassed personally in the contests, seeking from them an endorsement of himself and a revival of his flagging fortunes. He returned to Ireland bitterly disappointed, feeling that his own beloved Cork, for whose people he had done so much and in whose eyes he had once stood as a hero, had betrayed him. More than any other of the setbacks of 1979, these two by-election defeats convinced him that his time as leader of the Fianna Fáil party, might as well be terminated without further delay.

A similar sense of this personal dismay concentrated the minds of all commentators, and produced a flurry of speculative articles and programmes. Set against Lynch, neither of the two main contenders for the leadership, George Colley and Charles Haughey, seemed adequate. I wrote of the succession shortly after Lynch's return:

> In absolute terms George Colley is short on creativity. Charles Haughey is short on civility and maybe integrity as well. Led by either, Fianna Fáil would lose the next election... There are too many question marks over Charles Haughey. He stalks the corridors of Leinster House, the silken predications of control and power emanating from his person. Yet nobody knows the nature of his republicanism and how it would manifest itself in terms of policy on Northern Ireland. Nobody knows what the economic recipes would be... He has created an illusion. And it is this – that, once the mantle of power falls upon his shoulders, he will then get it all together. But at what price?[5]

Whatever the misgivings, and they were fairly extensive and deep-seated, Jack Lynch had nevertheless decided on the departure date of January 1980. This was after the end of the Irish presidency of the European Community, and seemed a fitting occasion for his resignation. It was the news from Cork, combined with reports given to him by Martin O'Donoghue of the discontent in the party, that caused Lynch to bring forward the decision to early December 1979. It was also

---

[5] Bruce Arnold, *Irish Independent*, Saturday, 17th November, 1979. Haughey contacted the paper immediately on the appearance of the article through his solicitors and threatened legal action unless the references to his integrity were publicly withdrawn. I declined to stand over such a withdrawal and the newspaper's Editor, Aidan Pender, supported this position. No legal action was taken, but, through an intermediary, Dr John O'Connell, a luncheon was arranged to "discuss" my views, with O'Connell hosting it.

partly owing to claims by George Colley that his prospects for succeeding were good.

Lynch had been subjected to an orchestrated period of "spin-doctoring" by his opponents within the party. They had acted conspiratorially. He had no liking for such actions in politics at all. When it was pointed out to him that the perceptions of what the Government had been doing were not getting across and that his press arrangements were not working, he responded by saying that it was his practice not to attempt to promote or explain himself.[6] This had always been the case and he would not change it. He preferred his actions to be seen for what they were, without gloss. In his remarks, the matter was not related to how the press were handled, but to what impact his actions had on the public, and also how his party reacted.

He referred specifically to the situation that had arisen in the early period of his leadership, when Donogh O'Malley, Brian Lenihan and Charles Haughey had been particularly close. They had often entertained, together or separately, the *Irish Times* columnist John Healy, who wrote a personalised political piece in the paper each Saturday signed "Backbencher", as well as contributing a Dáil "sketch". "I had to put a stop to that, and I don't think John Healy has ever forgiven me," Lynch told me. He was clearly aware of what had gone on and was quite relaxed about it.

He felt that his approach meant that he was subject to certain handicaps. But it was the way he operated and he could not easily depart from it. He felt that there were faults in the system, but that they were actually caused by conflict between the so-called "promoters" and the ordinary members of his staff whose business was the dissemination of *information*. He had doubts about the reliability of bringing in people who had party loyalties. They could become fickle. He told me not to worry about the next day's event. He had decided what he was going to do and everything would be all right. I wrote privately at the time:

> He was relaxed, easy, confident... He felt free to give me 45 minutes of his time though his desk was covered with papers, and only towards the end – possibly because of the news broadcast – did he become impatient.[7]

The following morning the Dáil met at 10.30 a.m. and Brian Lenihan took the initial business of the House. I was in the Press Gallery and the Minister sent up a note with an usher which read. "Jack is announcing retirement at party meeting 11.30. P.S. Do not quote me. Brian". The last phrase was clearly a joke.

---

6   Interview with Jack Lynch, 4th December 1979. I went to see him on the evening before he resigned on the instigation of the Independent Senator, Gordon Lambert, who was also distressed at the circumstances which seemed to be surrounding Lynch.

7   Author's contemporary journal entry. I mentioned on the occasion Jack Lynch's own article in the November issue of *Magill*. "It was started in 1978," he said. "It has grown and snowballed ever since."

At the appointed time, in the party rooms, Jack Lynch opened the meeting with a statement of some considerable length making clear his position. It was that he had decided, after the 1977 election, to resign in January 1980. This "would leave about two years to the ensuing General Election during which period my successor could establish himself as leader". He referred to the fact that he had signalled a reshuffle earlier in the year (one in which his own departure was included) and then mentioned the Cork by-elections:

> These, with other associated events, created some uncertainty among members of the party, but I was especially concerned that doubts about my intentions as to my continued leadership of the Government were creating uncertainty among the public and this was not good for our country.

He outlined his own career. He was in his sixty-third year and had spent half of his life in active politics: nine as Taoiseach, thirteen as leader of Fianna Fáil the rest in various government appointments. He continued:

> It is obvious to me that the time has come when someone with a new approach and fresh thinking should take over the leadership of the Government, a leader who will carry on the traditions established by the founders and successive leaders of Fianna Fáil.

He concluded with words that he knew were ironic:

> I thank all of you, Party members, who have given me such steadfast and loyal support over all these years. I assure you I appreciate it sincerely. I want to thank the Fianna Fáil organisation at all levels throughout the country for their adherence to the ideals and policies of Fianna Fáil and all the people who have reposed trust in me. And finally, my thanks to the Cork Fianna Fáil members, workers and supporters and to all the people of Cork who have helped and encouraged me in many difficult moments during my thirty-two years as their Dáil representative.[8]

*

Jack Lynch's departure was immediately overshadowed by the battle for succession. All eyes were on the two main contenders: Charles Haughey and George Colley. At a relatively early stage, a third candidate, Desmond O'Malley, announced his withdrawal, throwing his support behind Colley. Intense canvassing went on in Leinster House throughout Wednesday and Thursday. The party meeting was scheduled for the following day. The rooms and corridors were filled with heated argument and debate. Journalists and commentators from radio

---

[8] Printed text issued after the meeting. From the author's personal archive.

and television crowded the Dáil in search of stories and speculated on the outcome of the vote. The logic of our position invited a host of predictions.

The article I wrote for the next day's *Irish Independent* was filed early enough for me to turn my attention to the leadership struggles during what was left of the evening. It was mainly a valedictory on the departing leader.

> At his press conference yesterday afternoon the Taoiseach, Mr Jack Lynch, named four possible contenders for the leadership of the Fianna Fáil party. He referred at another point to there being five men within the Government 'whose shoulders were broad enough and whose minds were good enough' to take on the task. The four named contenders were the Tánaiste, George Colley, Charles Haughey, Desmond O'Malley and Michael O'Kennedy. The possible fifth would be Brian Lenihan.
>
> More is at stake than office, preferment, or an easy pathway to a seat in the Dáil at the next election. Mr Lynch mentioned physical strength, mental ability and integrity as qualities essential to the person taking his place. He firmly resisted any indication of where his own preference lay, and will vote on Friday as an ordinary party member.
>
> But his presence and stature, and the qualities of courage and sure judgement which have characterised his own leadership through one of the most difficult and dangerous periods in the history of the State will weigh heavily on the minds of his party colleagues. The standards which he established, and to which he has held with a graceful and determined skill, have been the best of all in political life: country first, party second, self a poor and honest third.
>
> He will wish upon Fianna Fáil the same priorities in his successor. And if the party seeks to survive, and gain for itself the respect and support of the country, it will demand the same sense of what is right in the man it now has to choose.
>
> On basic appeal it is universally accepted that neither man of the two candidates, Colley and Haughey, competes with Jack Lynch. Charles Haughey is seen as the more skilful, with a highly developed sense of public relations; George Colley is seen as the more dogged, relying on natural rather than created perceptions.[9]

Jack Lynch did not attempt to pre-empt the situation. He did not choose a favourable time for the man he supported. He declared no preference. He quietly gave the party out of his own charge and initiated a democratic process by which it chose a successor.

I managed to sustain a brief journal of the events of those three days. Among other activities, I engaged in doing sums with Vincent Browne over the names and inclinations of Fianna Fáil deputies. A picture began to emerge by Wednesday evening, marginally favouring Haughey. What I had also done in my *Independent* piece was an analysis of a list of Fianna Fáil deputies, dividing them into five

---

[9] Bruce Arnold, *Irish Independent*, 6th December, 1979.

categories. Two were obvious enough; these were the deputies claimed by one or other side, and not disputed. This accounted for forty-five deputies: twenty-one favouring Haughey, twenty-four favouring Colley. Two more categories were more difficult, but it seemed necessary to list off those claimed by each side, but disputed by the other side. A fifth category was of those who wavered in the middle, uncertain which way to go. I ended the note about the day with the words: "The situation is grave."

It was a judgement fed by almost two decades of political journalism. From entering *The Irish Times* as a sub-editor in the autumn of 1961, I had been observing and writing about all of these politicians and had formed clear views about them. These had been expressed all over again during the previous six weeks, as the realisation dawned on all of those covering political life that Jack Lynch was departing and that the new leader of the Fianna Fáil Party could well be Charles Haughey. I never did approve of the idea of him as leader and this coloured my judgement during those three tense and crowded days.

Thursday, 6th December was a long day of discussion and debate. Overhanging it was the imperative of filing an article in anticipation of the party meeting the next morning that would decide between George Colley and Charles Haughey. Throughout the day I met and compared notes with Vincent Browne and other journalists. I lunched with Ger Connolly and Tom Meaney, whom I had listed as firm supporters of Charles Haughey, and with Michael Smith, whom I had equally firmly, though wrongly, put down as a Colley supporter.

Shortly afterwards I met Charles Haughey in the corridor and he told me he had 53 supporters. "My more conservative backers," he added, "suggest 49." He was very agreeable and I asked him for the list. He undertook to give it to me later that afternoon. In the end I wrote a piece for the next day's paper listing a series of questions on the issue of leadership which Fianna Fáil deputies should ask themselves.

I went to supper in Leinster House with Vincent Browne and Gordon Colleary. We had a long discussion over a mixed grill and Vincent Browne criticised me for being unjournalistic. He felt that I should be more impartial. I told him that judgements had to be made. How could I write otherwise? As we were debating this matter I received a phone call from Haughey's secretary inviting me up to his office.

Haughey marked off on my list the supporters of whom he was sure. The total was forty-five. Then, late in the evening, on his way out of Leinster House, Ray MacSherry stopped beside me and announced: "I will be proposing Haughey for leader tomorrow." I went back in to have a drink with Martin O'Donoghue, Jim Gibbons and Willie Kenneally. A mood of inevitability pervaded the room. Jim Gibbons quoted Shakespeare and drew on a pad. Willie Kenneally talked about Mussolini.

Charles Haughey's final prediction had been almost right. He won the contest by forty-four votes to George Colley's thirty-eight. At the press conference that followed, he announced: "Two wonderful things have already happened to me...".

These were that George Colley had pledged the "total and fullest co-operation in my new task, and I have been assured by Jack Lynch that all his vast reservoirs and experience as Taoiseach will be totally at my disposal in my new position."[10]

Lynch gave no such undertaking. Colley made no such pledge. Haughey had begun with an exaggerated and false presentation of his position. It was to continue on these lines and grow worse. Colley, in his response to this misrepresentation of himself, distinguished between loyalty to the party and loyalty to the man, and made his position clear by a public statement in view of the possibility that Haughey's words might lead people to think otherwise. Deception, incipient in much that had gone before, was an inferred part of the new leadership.

On the Saturday before Christmas that year I called on Jack Lynch at his home. The Guards at the gate simply did not know how to handle my presence there; it suggested that not many private individuals called. Lynch was polite and friendly, asking me in. Máirín greeted me almost like an old friend. Whiskey was poured out; she drank sherry. We had a discussion in general terms about the press reaction to George Colley's decision to go public about his qualified support for the leadership. I asked Lynch if he thought George Colley had been right.

He replied: 'On balance, yes.' He felt that the truth needed to be stated and that the context was right. He mentioned Martin O'Donoghue and expressed his own very real feelings of concern about his future. His own view of Colley, which he also gave me, was interesting. When they had been first thrown together, at the time of Colley's first appointment as Parliamentary Secretary in 1964, his attitude to the younger man had been one of admiration. "At that time the difference in age between us was very marked. One notices ten years most at the 30–40 stage." His view was that Colley had been consistently underrated and Haughey consistently overrated.

Within Fianna Fáil, tributes to the departing leader were lukewarm. An inquiry was made of the party's new Chief Whip, Seán Moore, some time later, as to whether a presentation had been decided upon and what had happened about it, since no action followed. He could not remember whether or not there had been any formal presentation. When he checked on this, he discovered that nothing had been done. It seemed that Jack Lynch had been allowed to slip away from his involvement in the party, ignored by the short and ungenerous memories of the human moths that flutter round the candles of power.

But that was not the story. In fact, Jack Lynch had written a letter to Charles Haughey telling him that he had already informed a party official that he did not want any kind of presentation. In his concluding paragraph, he was firm: "As well as it being my own desire in this regard, I am satisfied that it would be entirely inappropriate for the party to make such a presentation in the circumstances."[11]

Charles Haughey was elected Taoiseach the following Tuesday, 11th

---

[10] His speech at the press conference, attended by the author.
[11] The letter was shown to me by George Colley, who, as Tánaiste, received a copy.

December. He appointed his Government, dropping from it Jim Gibbons and Martin O'Donoghue, among others. Albert Reynolds was the only member of the Gang of Five to be given a government position, but the other four were all given junior ministries in due course.

Jack Lynch remained a backbencher, but retired at the next election, in 1981, which Haughey lost. Haughey went on floundering through his twelve-year period of leadership, losing elections, leading Fianna Fáil into an unprecedented coalition, and eventually being forced out of office in disgraceful circumstances. Worse was to follow. Revelations about his financial dealings emerged to haunt and humiliate him.

After his departure from power, Lynch gave no interviews. He kept very few papers, most of them of marginal significance, and for the next twenty years until his death, he withdrew into a private life that was contented and relaxed. His resolve not to open the Pandora's Box, which would have involved reliving his dramatic past, was maintained for the rest of his life.

The Death of a Hero

Jack Lynch died on Wednesday, 20th October 1999 in a Dublin hospital. He was 82. He had been ill for some time, having suffered a stroke six years earlier. This caused growing blindness which prevented him from enjoying the sporting events that had been an important recreation. As a result he had become a more remote figure, visited by a small circle of friends and cared for by his wife, Máirín. They had no children, and continued to live at 21 Garville Avenue, Rathgar the house where they had been for much of their life together in Dublin. To the country the death came as a surprise, reviving and provoking memories that had many warm and human aspects connected with his sporting exploits and his contribution to political life. Controversy and crisis were there as well, but distant in time; a generation unaware of the detail had grown up since his departure from active politics. To many people, Jack Lynch had already become a figure in political history.

Yet the tributes paid to him had a special quality of affection and admiration. Clearly, from all that was said and written, the country experienced an immediate, instinctive sense of grief. It was evident from innumerable reactions and tributes that Jack Lynch was loved in a way enjoyed by no other politician in Ireland before or since.

At the time of his death, the recognition of what Jack Lynch had done and what he had represented in Irish public life was remarkable for the consistency and character of the praise. For the short period of those late, sad October days the whole country dwelt lovingly on his peerless nature. People added up and savoured his charismatic appeal, his vicissitudes in times of political stress, his ability to define a country's way forward out of crisis, his easy manner with people, his personal dignity and the simplicity of his private life.

The tributes that marked him out came perhaps most notably from those who had been directly opposed to him in political life, or had dealt with him as adversary. Liam Cosgrave, who defeated Jack Lynch in the 1973 general election and was then in turn defeated by him in the 1977 landslide election which brought Lynch back to power, expressed a universally held truth when he said, "Jack Lynch was a gentleman". Garret FitzGerald, who succeeded Cosgrave and then opposed Lynch during the difficult two years after the 1977 victory, made the telling observation: "He was impossible to oppose." He went on:

His modesty and self-deprecation belied a remarkable political skill. He

225

> was indeed a public servant in the truest sense, and served the Irish people
> especially well by his skilful handling of the arms crisis in May 1970.

Both Cosgrave and FitzGerald seemed to speak of the era as well as the man, and of how different politics had become.

Edward Heath, leader of the Conservative Party and British Prime Minister in the aftermath of the Arms Crisis, said of Jack Lynch:

> He showed great statesmanship and courage in becoming the first premier
> of the Republic to acknowledge that peace in Northern Ireland could only
> come about through consent. Although it was his successor, Liam Cosgrave,
> who helped set the final seal on the Sunningdale power-sharing agreement
> in December 1973, Jack Lynch fully earned his share of the credit for
> helping to create what is still the only cross-community executive to have
> been established in the province.

The President of Ireland, Mary McAleese, though of a different generation, echoed the essential sentiments about an integrated personality: "He was a gentleman, a complete gentleman, in absolutely everything he did, in every aspect of his life, in everything he touched." His former close colleague in government, who became European Commissioner and then President of Ireland, Paddy Hillery, said of Jack Lynch: "Something emanated from him that made you feel good about him and good about yourself if you were near him."

One of those in Northern Ireland paying tribute to Lynch on his death was the Alliance Party Chief Whip, David Ford. He described Jack Lynch as "one of those in Fianna Fáil who first recognised the need to move away from the traditional position and towards a better understanding with people in Northern Ireland." Ford was here expressing a key contribution made by Jack Lynch, displayed a level of understanding that is to be traced back to Seán Lemass, who broke new ground in visiting Northern Ireland in 1965.

To an extent, the public servant who helped Lynch most in the formulation of this Northern Ireland policy on which so much depended in the critical years from 1969, was Ken Whitaker, who served under Lynch when he was Minister for Finance in 1965 and 1966. They became friends. In his tribute, the day after Jack Lynch's death, Whitaker wrote:

> Jack's whole nature induced loyalty and affection. Softness of speech and
> manner, consideration for others, readiness to listen, absence of pomp, a
> sense of humour, were elements of a most attractive personality which
> combined modesty and unpretentiousness with good judgement and a
> deep sense of responsibility and firmness of purpose. I never heard him
> in a rage or heard him say anything disparaging or hurtful about others.
> The country – and his party – were fortunate that he was Taoiseach at the
> time of the Arms Crisis. Decisive action was then taken and the widespread
> loyalty he enjoyed avoided a real risk of internal division and even of civil
> disorder.

The event of his death was received with the greatest difficulty of all by his former party, Fianna Fáil. The appropriate things were said by his successors, the three leaders of the party during the twenty years since his resignation. They praised him, they honoured him, they assembled to pay their respects, and they participated in the state funeral. But the man who gave the funeral oration was not a member of Fianna Fáil. It was Desmond O'Malley, former leader of the Progressive Democrats, a party that had been created as a result of conflict within Fianna Fáil following immediately after Lynch's resignation. Though O'Malley's speech concentrated on the great qualities of the man under whom he had served in Government, there was both an implicit and an explicit judgement on a past thick with controversy and denial.

All those of Jack Lynch's successors as leaders of Fianna Fáil had things to say about him in tribute, in the days following his death. Some of it did not quite ring true. Charles Haughey, who had schemed against him almost throughout their association as active politicians, was not widely believed when he talked of working "closely together in friendship" with Lynch; even his presence at St Finbarr's Cathedral in Cork on 23rd October was considered both insensitive and inappropriate.

Albert Reynolds remembered Jack Lynch:

> [as] a very caring, thoughtful leader that we could all look up to. A man who was gentle in many ways but at the same time, when toughness was needed, toughness was always forthcoming. He was the same on the sports field. He will always be admired, revered and remembered in Cork for his achievements on the sports field. He was a Corkman through and through.

As a tribute from someone who had been actively part of Fianna Fáil for more than twenty years, it was slightly detached and impersonal. Albert Reynolds's direct knowledge belonged to the short period between the time when he had first entered the Dáil as part of the 1977 landslide and Lynch's own resignation two and a half years later. The circumstances of that time undeniably reflect little credit on the party.

Like Albert Reynolds, Bertie Ahern spoke of the historical figure. As Taoiseach at the time of Lynch's death, and as the current and sixth leader of Fianna Fáil, he had a double duty to perform. There was the state funeral in Cork, and there was some kind of reconciliation needed between the party and the man. It was clear to anyone reading the inner language of the event that no real relationship had been sustained between Jack Lynch and the political party to which he had belonged.

Here was a man who claimed the immediate and overwhelming attention of the Irish people at his death. Moreover, he claimed it in terms which in more than one attempt to apostrophise him had invoked the name of Daniel O'Connell as the only comparable political example of popularity. Yet his own party did not quite know how to handle the event, how to remember him, what to say or do. They were collectively faced with a gap, both in time and in understanding.

From the moment of Jack Lynch's resignation, twenty years before, at the end of 1979, the party he had led did not know what to do about him. Charles Haughey's immediate reaction had been to expunge Jack Lynch and all he stood for from the record. There were no tributes, no references, no sense of any continuum from one leader to the next, with the character, membership and policy of the organisation sustained and deepened in the process. Jack Lynch was deliberately painted out of the picture. Jack Lynch, still of course a Dáil deputy, made no appearance at the party's *Árd Fheis* early the following year, 1980, and attended no public party event of any significance, then or later. He retreated from party politics, seemingly with relief. That situation prevailed, and was deliberate.

Jack Lynch had cast a lengthy shadow over his own time in politics and this could not be altered or denied. It lay over Fianna Fáil just as it lay over the country. But it had become the matter of history, to which it was consigned with almost indecent haste. Understandably, with the new leader in place, new views prevailed. These were hugely reinforced, and perhaps understandably so, by the sense of rivalry and conflict which stretched back through the previous two decades, in respect of the relationship between Charles Haughey and Jack Lynch. This was inescapably in the minds of people, at the time of Lynch's death, in part because of the reaction of Haughey himself.

At that earlier time, twenty years before, Jack Lynch simply slipped away and wasn't there anymore. People have to live with the consequences of their actions. Political parties have to do the same. On the afternoon of the service at the Church of St Paul of the Cross, at Mount Argus, a member of the Government who had been loyal to Jack Lynch at the time came up to me to remind me of the parting of the ways between Jack Lynch and Fianna Fáil, and did so in words of deep regret and emotion. I did not need to be reminded. I had written about it then, with astonishment and foreboding, and those feelings remained with me and have guided me ever since in my judgement of the political life and of politicians generally.

In reaching back over his life I have been mindful that it began before the existence of the State. It embraced remarkable sporting achievements. It carried him to the highest political office in the land. It sustained him through crisis and gave us a distinguished example of statesmanship on many significant occasions. In it he exercised courage and political skill that shine like beacons for succeeding generations.

*

He went through changes of perception in his life, perhaps the greatest of all being his loss of trust in those around him which he expressed to Michael Mills in the rhetorical question: "How can I ever trust anybody again after what has happened?" He learned, through uniquely unprecedented circumstances, that law is a containment of human actions, not of feelings. He discovered the impossibility of legislating for loyalty. No legal frame can be created for singleness of heart, for honesty, or for integrity.

Jack Lynch, after many vicissitudes, saw his task as leader to be that of correcting and of disciplining those who followed him. Yet in order to do so he required the democratic mandate of the party itself. If there were difficulties, if there were disputes, if any member of the party decided to overstep agreed policy – either through enthusiasm or because of disagreement – then the leader failed if he did not act. The membership of the party demanded this of him.

He genuinely believed that the party could collectively define itself. It could decide where it was going, what it believed, and what it would not tolerate. He saw that it was then his task as leader to formulate and process the definitions. He was prepared to follow this interpretation of the nature and purpose of political life. He never deviated from that view. He never dealt with it other than honestly. He never sought to coerce or threaten those over whom he exercised power, or those who commented and judged upon his and his party's performance.

There are no hidden matters in his life. There is resolute and absolute singleness of purpose in respect of the human essentials of truth and integrity in both personal and professional motivation.

He never feared the account which he was called on to make to democracy's ultimate guardians: the people. He used the biblical term, stewardship, in one of the truly great speeches of his political career, the presidential address to Fianna Fáil at the 1971 Árd Fheis. That stewardship was a lifelong commitment. It transcended the individual occasions of his political life. It reinforced him immeasurably when faced with crisis. It was a reassuring and constant resource to him during the periods in power and the single and distinguished tenure as party leader on the opposition benches in the Dáil.

He put his hand to an invisible contract with the Irish people when the coin, tossed in 1948 by Máirín, fell in his favour. He debated that contract in terms of the small and precarious demands of constituents brought to the attention of his helper in Cork, the shoemaker Séamus O'Brien in the backroom of his cobbler's shop in Shandon. He doubted some of the clauses in what he had agreed and what they would come to mean in his life, but he never amended or altered their design and purpose. As junior party officer in Opposition after the 1948 general election, as junior Minister and then as member of the Government, he was marked out by Éamon de Valera and by Seán Lemass for the supreme role of leader. Instinct as well as approval and even admiration seem to have guided their hands and their hearts as, indeed, it guided the mind and heart of Jack Lynch.

He was destiny's child, and we did not recognise the fact. He was shaped by his times to fulfil a job on behalf of Ireland. That job involved remarkable and complex qualities.

The people of Ireland saw instinctively the great qualities that were in him.

They saw his strength, his determination, his clear judgement and his undoubted courage. To a very great extent indeed, as I have tried to show, he was shaped by his early sporting experiences and by his outstanding success as a sportsman. He thought of his favourite sport, hurling, as more than a game. To him it was a way of life, with physical, mental and cultural dimensions that for him were of a very positive kind. "The true hurler is a man of dignity, proud of his heritage, skilful, well-disciplined and a sportsman . . . [the game of hurling] is an expression of all that is vigorous and skilful, artistic and exciting in our nature."

Politics was different. He brought to that art or craft or way of life dignity, pride, skill and discipline. But he met attitudes, shortcomings and defects for which he did not have the same kind of praise or admiration that he extended towards great sport and great sportsmen . When his own party became less sure of the value of his leadership with many of its members turning their back on him, he was wounded and shocked. To their shame, they doubted his abilities, his strength of purpose, his sticking power. And in the end they were the sufferers, not he. He resigned himself to the shifting ground of political loyalty and simply went on with the fulfilment of his own contract with the people of Ireland.

He was buried in October 1999 in St Finbarr's cemetery in Cork. More than a year later, in the first half of 2001, a gravestone was erected. It carries the simple epitaph: "Happy is the man who finds wisdom."

Honours won on Field of Play

Championship and League Victories (1929–1950)

1929: North Parish Under-16 Football Championship.

1930: North Parish Under-16 Hurling Championship, City Division, Minor Football Championship.

1931: North Parish Under-16 Hurling Championship.

1932: Cork County Minor Football Championship.

1933: Cork County Minor Football Championship. Cork County Minor Hurling Championship.

1934: Cork County Senior Hurling Championship. Cork County Minor Hurling Championship (Captain). Harty Cup Colleges Senior Hurling Championships.

1935: Cork County, Senior Hurling Championship. Harty Cup Colleges Senior Hurling Championship. Munster Colleges Senior Football Championship. Inter-Provincial Colleges Senior Hurling Championship. City Division Minor Hurling Championship (Captain). City Division Minor Football Championship.

1936: Cork County, Senior Hurling Championship. Harty Cup Colleges Senior Hurling Championship (Captain). Munster Colleges Senior Football Championship. Inter-Provincial Colleges Senior Hurling Championship (Captain). Cork County Schools and College 120-yards Hurdles Championship (16.6 seconds).

1937: Cork County Senior Hurling Championship. Cork County Intermediate Football Championship.

1938: Cork County Senior Hurling Championship. Cork County Senior Football Championship. Inter-Provincial Railway Cup Hurling Championship.

1939: Cork County Senior Hurling Championship (Captain). Munster Senior Hurling Championship (Captain). National Hurling League (Captain). Inter-Provincial Railway Cup Hurling Championship.

1940: Cork County Senior Hurling Championship (Captain). National Hurling League (Captain). Inter-Provincial Railway Cup Hurling.

1941: All-Ireland Senior Hurling Championship. Cork County Senior Hurling Championship. Cork County Senior Football Championship.

1942: All-Ireland Senior Hurling Championship (Captain). Inter-Provincial Railway Cup Hurling Championship. Munster Senior Hurling Championship (Captain).

1943: All-Ireland Senior Hurling Championship. Inter-Provincial Railway Cup Hurling Championship (Captain). Munster Senior Hurling Championship. Munster Senior Football Championship.

1944: All-Ireland, Senior Hurling Championship. Inter-Provincial Railway Cup Hurling Championship. Munster Senior Hurling Championship. Dublin Senior Football Championship.

1945: Munster Senior Football Championship. All-Ireland, Senior Football Championship.

1946: Munster Senior Hurling Championship. All-Ireland, Senior Hurling Championship.

1947: Munster Senior Hurling Championship. Kelleher Shield Senior Football League (Captain).

1948: Cork County Senior Hurling Championship. National Hurling League.

1949: Cork County Senior Hurling Championship. Inter-Provincial Railway Hurling Cup Championship.

1950: Cork County Senior Hurling Championship.

Awards

Team of the Millennium.

Team of the Century (1984).

Texaco Hall of Fame (1984).

Hurling Captain of the Forties.

Cork Millennium Team.

Bank of Ireland All-Time Hurling Award (1981).

Jury's Hall of Fame (1983).

Championship and League Runners-Up Medals (1930–1951)

1930: Cork County, Minor Football Championship

1932: Cork County, Minor Hurling Championship

1933: Munster, Minor Hurling Championship

1934: Munster, Minor Hurling Championship (Captain). Munster Minor Football Championship. Cork County Intermediate Football Championship.

1935: Munster Minor Hurling Championship (Captain). Munster Minor Football Championship. Cork County Minor Hurling Championship (Captain). Cork County Minor Football Championship.

1939: All-Ireland Senior Hurling Championship (Captain)

1940: Munster Senior Hurling Championship (Captain)

1941: Munster Senior Hurling Championship. Inter-Provincial Railway Cup Hurling championship.

1946: Cork County Senior Hurling championship.

1947: All-Ireland, Senior Hurling Championship. Munster Senior Football Championship. Cork County Senior Football Championship (Captain).

1948: Munster Senior Hurling Championship.

1949: National Hurling League.

1950: Munster Senior Hurling Championship.

1951: Cork County Senior Football Championship.

Jack Lynch played in 79 championship and league finals from 1929, at 12 years of age until he retired at 34 in 1951 (playing only one game in that last year). On that occasion, St Nicks had qualified for the Cork Senior Football Championship final and as they had a depleted team, due to injuries and suspensions, they asked him to play. He agreed to do so, and despite his lack of training and fitness, contributed greatly to the team's performance.[1]

---

[1] I am indebted to Liam Ó Tuama for this record, taken from *Where He Sported And Played*, pp. 200–202.

Bibliographical Material

PERSONAL ARCHIVE

From October 1961, when I began work as a journalist in Ireland writing leaders for *The Irish Times*, I kept careful documentation, including journals, newspaper cuttings, speeches and press statements, and these have been a primary source in writing this book. I had meetings with Jack Lynch, in and out of office. I also met with most of his contemporaries among Irish politicians of all parties.

Because of the nature of the crisis which formed the central political challenge of his career, the events of his life have remained of abiding interest to historians, politicians, journalists and the general public. Having worked on the stories then, and having continued to write about him and the impact of the events on later political history, I continued to add to my own archive for thirty years. This material has been central to the writing of this book.

Other contemporary sources:
Newspapers and magazines. These are identified and credited in the text. Special mention should be made of the articles in *Magill* magazine (November 1979, May, June, July 1980).

PUBLISHED MATERIAL

Directories, Political and Biographical
Boylan, Henry: *A Dictionary of Irish Biography* (Gill & Macmillan, Dublin) 1978.
Browne, Vincent: *The Magill Book of Irish Politics* (Magill Publications Ltd., Dublin) 1981.
Nealon, Ted: *Ireland: A Parliamentary Directory 1973-1974* (Institute of Public Administration, Dublin) 1974.
Nealon, Ted: *Guide to the 21st Dáil and Seanad* (Platform Press, Dublin) 1977.
Who's Who What's What and Where in Ireland (Geoffrey Chapman, Dublin and London) 1973.

Books and Pamphlets:

Anonymous, *Fianna Fáil – The IRA Connection*, pamphlet, no place, no date.

Arnold, Bruce: *Haughey: His Life and Unlucky Deeds* (HarperCollins, London) 1993.

Arnold, Bruce: *What Kind of Country* (Jonathan Cape, London) 1984.

Bishop, Patrick and Mallie, Éamonn: *The Provisional IRA* (Heinemann, London) 1987.

Boland, Kevin: *The Rise and Decline of Fianna Fáil* (Mercier Press, Cork) 1982.

Boland, Kevin: *Up Dev!* (Published by the author, Dublin) 1977.

Browne, Terence: *A Social and Cultural History 1922-1985* (HarperCollins, Fontana Press, London) 1981.

Collins, Stephen: *The Cosgrave Legacy* (Blackwater Press, Dublin) 1996.

Collins, Stephen: *The Haughey File* (O'Brien Press, Dublin) 1992.

Collins, Stephen: *The Power Game: Fianna Fáil since Lemass* (O'Brien Press, Dublin) 2000.

Coogan, Tim Pat: *The Troubles* (Arrow Books, London) 1996.

Downey, James: *Lenihan His Life and Loyalties* (New Ireland Books, Dublin) 1998.

Farrell, Brian: *Seán Lemass*. (Gill & Macmillan, Dublin) 1983.

FitzGerald, Garret: *All In a Life: An Autobiography*. (Gill & Macmillan, Dublin) 1991.

Horgan, John: *Seán Lemass: The Enigmatic Patriot* (Gill & Macmillan, Dublin) 1999.

Joyce, Joe and Murtagh, Peter: *The Boss* (Poolbeg, Dublin) 1983.

Kelly, James: *The Thimble Riggers* (Published by the author, Dublin) 1999.

Kenny, Shane: *Go Dance On Somebody Else's Grave* (Kildanore Press, Dublin) 1990.

Keogh, Dermot: *Twentieth-Century Ireland: Nation and State* (Gill & Macmillan, Dublin) 1994.

Lee, J.J.: *Ireland 1912-1985: Politics and Society* (Cambridge University Press, Cambridge) 1989.

Mansergh, Martin: (Editor) *The Spirit of the Nation: The Speeches of Charles J Haughey* (Mercier Press, Dublin) 1986.

Maye, Brian *Fine Gael 1923-1987* (Blackwater Press, Dublin) 1993.

McCarthy, John F: (Editor) *Planning Ireland's Future, The Legacy of TK Whitaker* (Glendale, Dublin) 1990.

O'Brien, Conor Cruise: *States of Ireland* (Hutchinson, London) 1972.

O'Brien, Justin. *The Arms Trial* (Gill and Macmillan, Dublin) 2000.

O'Ceallaigh, Seamus and Sean Murphy: *The Mackey Story* (GAA Publications, Limerick) 1982.

O'Connor, Seán: *A Troubled Sky, Reflections on the Irish Educational Scene 1957-1968* (Fallon Publications, Dublin) 1983.

O'Mahony, T.P.: *Jack Lynch: A Biography* (Blackwater Press, Dublin) 1991.

Ó'Tuama, Liam: *Where He Sported And Played: Jack Lynch, a Sporting Celebration* (Blackwater Press, Dublin) 2000.

Savage, Robert: *Seán Lemass* (Historical Association of Ireland, Dublin) 1999.

Walsh, Dick: *Des O'Malley: A Political Profile* (Brandon, Dingle) 1986.

Walsh, Dick: *The Party: Inside Fianna Fáil* (Gill & Macmillan, Dublin) 1986.

Whitaker, T. K.: *Interests.* (Institute of Public Administration, Dublin) 1983.

Index